DATE DUE

NOV - 5 1994	OCT 2 2000
DEC - 8 1994	[DEC - 5 2003]
APR - 6 1995	
OCT 1 9 1995	
DEC 1 8 1995	
FEB 1 0 1996	
APR 1 6 1996	
NOV 2 1 1996	
DEC - 4 1996	
DEC 19 1996	
MAR 1 9 1997	
MAR 3 1 1997	
FEB - 9 1999	
JUL - 8 1999	
OCT 1 2 1999	
FEB 1 1 2000	

Combat Stress Reaction
The Enduring Toll of War

The Plenum Series on Stress and Coping

Series Editor:
Donald Meichenbaum, *University of Waterloo, Waterloo, Ontario, Canada*

Current Volumes in the Series:

A CLINICAL GUIDE TO THE TREATMENT OF THE
HUMAN STRESS RESPONSE
George S. Everly, Jr.

COMBAT STRESS REACTION
The Enduring Toll of War
Zahava Solomon

HUMAN ADAPTATION TO EXTREME STRESS
From the Holocaust to Vietnam
Edited by John P. Wilson, Zev Harel, and Boaz Kahana

INFERTILITY
Perspectives from Stress and Coping Research
Edited by Annette L. Stanton and Christine Dunkel–Schetter

INTERNATIONAL HANDBOOK OF TRAUMATIC STRESS SYNDROMES
Edited by John P. Wilson and Beverley Raphael

POST-TRAUMATIC STRESS DISORDER
A Clinician's Guide
Kirtland C. Peterson, Maurice F. Prout, and Robert A. Schwarz

THE SOCIAL CONTEXT OF COPING
Edited by John Eckenrode

STRESS BETWEEN WORK AND FAMILY
Edited by John Eckenrode and Susan Gore

THE UNNOTICED MAJORITY IN PSYCHIATRIC INPATIENT CARE
Charles A. Kiesler and Celeste G. Simpkins

WOMEN, WORK, AND HEALTH
Stress and Opportunities
Edited by Marianne Frankenhaeuser, Ulf Lundberg, and Margaret Chesney

---

A Continuation Plan is available for this series. A continuation order will bring delivery of each new volume immediately upon publication. Volumes are billed only upon actual shipment. For further information, please contact the publisher.

Combat Stress Reaction
The Enduring Toll of War

Zahava Solomon

Israeli Defense Forces Medical Corps
and Tel Aviv University
Tel Aviv, Israel

PLENUM PRESS • NEW YORK AND LONDON

Library of Congress Cataloging-in-Publication Data

Solomon, Zahava.
    Combat stress reaction : the enduring toll of war / Zahava
Solomon.
        p.   cm. -- (The Plenum series on stress and coping)
    Includes bibliographical references and index.
    ISBN 0-306-44279-5
    1. War neuroses. 2. Post-traumatic stress disorder. 3. Veterans-
-Mental health. 4. War--Psychological aspects.   I. Title.
II. Series.
    [DNLM: 1. Stress Disorders, Post-Traumatic. 2. Adaptation,
Psychological. 3. War. 4. Veterans--psychology.   WM 170 S689c
1993]
RC550.S64 1993
616.85'212--dc20
DNLM/DLC
for Library of Congress   93-22991
                                                                    CIP

ISBN 0-306-44279-5

© 1993 Plenum Press, New York
A Division of Plenum Publishing Corporation
233 Spring Street, New York, N.Y. 10013

Printed in the United States of America

To the memory of my father, Moshe HaElion,
who has left me his love of books and
his sensitivity to the suffering of people

Preface

Like all Israelis of my generation, I have always lived in the shadow of war. By age 32, I had experienced four wars: as a 6-year-old child during the 1956 Sinai campaign, as a teenager with friends at the front during the Six-Day War in 1967, as a university student with a husband fighting in the Golan Heights during the 1973 Yom Kippur War, and then as a mother of two small children during the Lebanon war in 1982, by which time I was an officer in the mental health department of the Israeli Defense Forces (IDF) medical corps. My life, like the lives of all Israelis, has been indelibly marked by this interminable battling and by the forced awareness of humanity's capacity for cruelty. Our society has lost many of its sons to war, and many others have been wounded.

Those who are killed or injured in war are highly esteemed in Israel. It is understood that they sacrificed their lives so that we could live ours. In the words of a famous Hebrew poem, they are the "silver platter" on which we were granted our own sovereign state. There is one group of war casualties, however, that is viewed with skepticism and ambivalence, both in Israel and elsewhere. I first came across these casualties during the 1982 Lebanon war, when I was serving as the head of the research section in the mental health department. In this war, 23% of all casualties were diagnosed as suffering from combat stress reaction (CSR), better known as "battle shock." Over the following years, the total number of those affected more than doubled, as veterans with delayed reactions, or those who had put off seeking help, applied to our clinics for treatment.

Although combat stress reactions are inevitable in war—and wars are commonplace enough for us—a great deal remains to be understood about these reactions. During the Lebanon war, my colleagues and I in the IDF mental health department found ourselves confronted with numerous crucial unanswered questions: What are the scope, nature, and duration of combat stress reactions? What happens to CSR casualties after war? Does war leave stress residues among those who did not sustain stress reactions in combat? Which soldiers are predisposed to break down in combat, and which cope with the stress of war without emotional impairment? Does the exposure of many Israeli men to more than one war strengthen them or wear them down psychologically? What factors aid or inhibit recovery from CSR? How is the course of the disorder affected by continual exposure to military stimuli, as is the norm in Israel? My colleagues and I thought that answers to these questions not only would satisfy our own academic curiosity but, more important, would provide a better foundation for prevention and treatment.

In light of the importance of these questions and the paucity of answers, my colleagues and I at the research branch of the IDF mental health department conducted a long series of studies that began during the Lebanon war in 1982 and continue to this day. This book is based on the findings of these studies and on hundreds of clinical interviews with casualties.

The first chapter presents a personal account of life in the shadow of war. The second chapter takes the reader "behind the scenes" and describes how the study was conceived, developed, and conducted. The third and fourth chapters describe and examine acute CSR, using both research findings and the personal stories of casualties, which demonstrate the gradual disintegration of psychological defenses. Chapters 5 through 9 ask, does the war end when the shooting stops? These chapters present longitudinal follow-up of CSR casualties and a control group of matched combat veterans who emerged from the war unscathed. The research answers the question in the negative; many of the soldiers who incurred stress reactions during the war continue to suffer from deep and debilitating posttraumatic stress residues that are manifested in psychiatric disorders, somatic complaints, and dysfunction in social relations.

Chapter 10 asks, why don't they recover? With the assistance of extensive clinical material, the combined impact of three major factors is explored: (a) the "imprint of vulnerability," (b) the impediment of shame at having failed in a most highly valued masculine role, and (c) the salience of war in Israel.

Chapters 11 and 12 present a series of studies that examine the effects of recurrent participation in war. They explore whether recurrent exposure to war strengthens or weakens soldiers, and what happens to CSR casualties who are reexposed to war. Chapter 13 looks at a particular group of psychiatric casualties: those in whom the onset of symptoms is delayed or who put off applying for treatment. Comparisons are made between the delayed onsets of symptoms following the Lebanon and Vietnam wars.

Chapter 14 demonstrates the transmission of traumatic stress from one generation to another. It presents research findings showing that parents' traumatic experiences during the Holocaust may cross the biological barrier and create vulnerability to war stress in their soldier offspring.

As was the case with Vietnam veterans, a significant proportion of the Lebanon war veterans in our study were found to be suffering from undiagnosed and untreated posttraumatic stress disorder (PTSD). Chapter 15 looks into the question of why these veterans don't seek treatment. Finally, Chapter 16 examines the complex attitudes of society—both overt and covert—toward psychiatric casualties of war. Diagnosis, treatment, and research of posttraumatic disorders are discussed in light of the universal human difficulty in acknowledging and accepting the cruelty and violence that people can inflict upon one another.

Acknowledgments

The preparation of this book and the work on the studies on which it is based took place over approximately 10 years with the help of friends and colleagues in the mental health department of the IDF medical corps. These studies could not have been carried out without the support and encouragement of the surgeon generals: Brigadier Generals Eran Dolev and Moshe Revach, and Professor Yehuda Danon. I am also grateful to the heads of the mental health department over the years: Colonel Ron Levy, who believed in me and helped to transform an illusive idea into reality; and his successors, Colonels Moshe Kotler and Avi Bleich. I also gratefully acknowledge the financial support of the Federman Foundation and the Israeli Ministry of Defense (Entebbe Fund and Mafat).

My colleagues on the research team contributed professional expertise and creativity: Professor Joseph Schwarzwald, Professor Matisyohu Weisenberg, Dr. Rami Benbenishty, and Professor Mario Mikulincer. Each in his own special way has enriched this work over the years. For their effort and dedication in carrying out the study, I am grateful also to Ora Aroch, Batya Fried, and Gaby Levy. Each helped at various points over the years, whether in scheduling subjects, administering questionnaires, or conducting and analyzing interviews. A special thanks also to my two colleagues, Dr. Toby Mostisher and Mark Waysman, who helped in rewriting and editing the various versions of the manuscript. They spared no effort over many hours and made a unique contribution to the presentation of this research. For this I am grateful to them both.

Finally, I would like to thank my husband, Reuven, for his unwavering and unconditional support from the start. Under circumstances that were not always easy, he encouraged me to complete these studies on combat stress and to write this book.

Contents

1

In the Shadow of War

Life in Israel is life in the shadow of war. Our population is small, our ties are close, and our wars affect everyone—not only the men who fight them. I grew up in a family whose orientation was not military. My father was the only man in the family, and he had two daughters. Neither my husband nor his father or two brothers chose a military career. Yet despite all this, I have vivid memories of five wars.

THE SINAI CAMPAIGN

In the Sinai campaign of 1956, I was 6 years old and in the first grade. I remember my mother trying to hide her fear as she explained that she was stripping the windows with tape so that they wouldn't break, and covering the shutters with black paper so that the light wouldn't seep out of the cracks. I remember her listening nervously to the hourly broadcasts and anxiously awaiting my father's return.

THE SIX-DAY WAR

The years passed. In June 1967, when I was in the 11th grade, the Six-Day War broke out. The days before this short war were long and hard. The 3 weeks before the outbreak of the war, known in Israel as the "waiting period," were full of uncertainty and anxiety. The Arab nations

1

moved their armies up to our borders. Israel was then a tiny country, and its narrow waistline ended just a few miles from my parents' home in Kfar Shmaryahou, north of Tel Aviv. The fear that the Arabs would cut us in two was a real fear for our continued existence. The Voice of Cairo, broadcasting in Hebrew, was conducting a scare campaign against us. The threat of Arab extremists to throw us into the sea seemed very real; we feared for our very existence. We went on with our lives—to school in the morning, to the youth club/organization in the afternoon—but something was different. People were moving closer to one another. Old quarrels were forgotten, and all the day-to-day trivia dwarfed, in the face of this collective existential anxiety.

I remember one afternoon at choir practice. I looked at the other children, including those I didn't like, and thought, "The war won't make any distinctions, not between the pretty and ugly, or between the kind and cruel." To overcome our anxiety, we became more friendly and helped each other.

In the town where I grew up, which has gradually become a suburb of Tel Aviv, there were still a number of farmers at the time. Most of them were drafted. The town was emptied of men. Most of the farm work was usually done by Arab women, but now they wouldn't come to the Jewish town. Would all their work be for nought? Would the unharvested produce rot? The town's youths were called upon to help. One of the neighbors organized the transportation, and all of us from well-to-do homes went out to help. For a moment there was a feeling of exultation.

One morning at 7:50, while we were on our way to school, there was a blast of sirens. No, it wasn't another test. It was the real thing. The bus driver turned the radio on, and we all heard that war had broken out. At school, we were taken down to the shelters. We were very crowded and very frightened, but we organized group singing and tried to keep each other's spirits up.

There were no classes that day, and we were sent home. Buses were infrequent. I was waiting at the bus stop, and a man who was on his way to Netanya in the north offered some of us a ride. On the way, he told us bits and pieces of rumors; the situation was unclear. I got out at the main road and walked the 20 minutes to my house. I could see the busy movement of planes and helicopters in the clear, blue June sky. Fear: Were they our planes or the enemy's? I ran home as fast as I could.

My mother served lunch and turned on the radio. She and my little sister were listening to Chaim Herzog—today the president of Israel, then a military interpreter and, in practice, the national pacifier. He was speaking in a quiet but self-assured voice, telling us that although the enemy was superior in numbers, we had the upper hand. We wanted to believe him, but it was not easy. My mother had spent her adolescence in Auschwitz. In Israel she had already been through the war of independence, with my father on the southern front, and later on, the Sinai campaign. She clasped her hands together and whispered quietly, as if to herself, "Till when? How many more wars do I have to go through in my lifetime?"

My father returned a while later. As an older man, he wasn't drafted even to the civil guard. He was glad not to have been called up, but more than that, he was embarrassed; he offered the neighbors help with whatever masculine work he could do. In our small town, no one had a shelter. Following the instructions of the volunteer security patrol, we all went out to our yards and dug trenches. We took out blankets, and at night the neighbors would sit around and discuss the situation. They fed each other with rumors. Mainly, though, the feeling of togetherness—not very common in our daily lives—helped to cast out fear.

At night, we heard the sound of explosions. As the sirens went off, we went down to the improvised shelter in the trench behind the house. Flames blazed in the distance, and in the dark our fear led us to believe they were nearby. They came from Kalkilya, an Arab town that was being shelled. Planes flew overhead, creating sonic booms. I was afraid, trembling. My younger sister laughed at me. My parents tried to calm me down, but I sensed that they, too, were afraid.

I had two friends in the army, Jacob and David, who were just a couple of years older than myself. They were somewhere fighting the war. Where were they? What was happening to them? Later, we went home and slept in our own beds. The passing time brought news; one quotation from a newspaper read, "Our Planes Destroyed the Arab Air Forces on the Ground." Gradually, our fear subsided. In the course of the week, we learned also of the wounded. None of our relatives or close friends were injured or killed, but still the feeling of sadness, of mourning, tinged our victory. It was as though even those who were not close to us were close.

The euphoria of the 6-day victory made Israeli society giddy. People made victory albums glorifying our heroism and achievements. Some spoke in apocalyptic terms: liberation of the Temple Mount; the Western Wall, so sacred to the Jews, in our hands. Rabbi Goren, the chief military rabbi, entered Jerusalem sounding a ram's horn, like a messianic act from the days of the fathers. There was a glorification of the army, of the victors. Generals became celebrities and took part in glittering public events. We were a victorious nation.

THE YOM KIPPUR WAR

With the outbreak of the Yom Kippur War in October 1973, the feeling of euphoria evaporated in seconds. By this time, I'd been married for a year to Reuven, whom I had met when we were both in the army doing our compulsory military service. We were both students and lived in a small apartment in the university dormitories. On that day, which was a Saturday, we were resting. Suddenly, a siren screamed through the quiet sanctity of Yom Kippur. I clutched my checkered quilt and sat up. Reuven pulled me toward him and said, "Don't be silly. It must be a mistake."

Army vehicles and civilian cars began to move along the roads. On Yom Kippur, the entire country is usually still for 24 hours. No one works, and there is no TV or radio. No one drives. No one dares violate the holiness of the day. The lively traffic was a sure sign of something amiss.

One of our neighbors was called up. He packed a knapsack. His wife was away, and he asked me to send her his warm regards. I felt a tremor run through my spine. Reuven, my husband, rushed downstairs to call his parents from the pay phone; he hadn't informed the army of his new address. His father told him that he hadn't yet been called up. Reuven was very upset. He phoned his parents again and decided to go collect the military equipment he had stored at their house. Although he doesn't have a high or especially important position in the reserves, Reuven resembled many Israeli men who hate war but rush to the front when it breaks out. He wouldn't miss the war.

In the evening, Golda Meir and Moshe Dayan appeared on television. I was sitting with the other women whose husbands had left for their bases, a few men who had not yet been called up—some of them trying to explain why not—and the Arab students, all men. A lot of Arabs were living in the dormitories. In fact, our next-door neighbors were Arabs. There was tension in the air, though no one talked. We were all anxiously glued to the TV screen. We watched Golda and Dayan as they informed us of the catastrophe. Even on the black-and-white set, we could detect how defeated and disillusioned our casualties looked. We became more disquieted. Mofid, an Arab student in my husband's class, came over to me quietly and said, "If you need anything when Reuven isn't here, I'll be glad to help."

My mother-in-law called. She thought it would be a good idea if I came to stay at her house. I thanked her for the invitation and spent the night talking with her. This was the beginning of 8 months as the wife of a soldier. During the first days of the war, I waited for news from Reuven. Since we didn't have a telephone in our room in the dorms, I decided to stay with his parents. His father, who had been seriously wounded in the 1948 war of independence (and who could have gotten a discharge), volunteered for duty and worked in an army vehicle warehouse. Because we hadn't heard from Reuven, who was on the Syrian front, for more than a week, and because we were all worried, he decided that it wasn't such a good idea to sit at home, waiting for the phone to ring. He got into his car and went up to the Golan Heights to look for Reuven and his other son, or, as he said, "my children." Naturally, he came back empty-handed.

After a while, I returned to the dorms and resumed my studies. I was also working then at two jobs: one in a rehabilitation center for the physically disabled, and the other as a guidance counselor for the youth organization in which I had been a member and then a leader as an adolescent. At age 23, I was the only "old lady" there. The men had all been drafted. We did volunteer work, mainly aiding old people in the community and in various old-age homes in the area. Our work included shopping, carting, and the like. The number of adolescents who came to us as volunteers looking for a way to contribute was astounding. It was as though the nation was undergoing a wartime metamorphosis. Cars stopped to give lifts not only to soldiers, as was customary, but to everyone. In peacetime, people are concerned that the upholstery of their cars might tear or get dirty, or that their doors will be slammed. In wartime, all of these things are pushed aside. We become a truly wonderful people. All our energy is poured into love and caring for others, and in our hearts there is an ongoing prayer for the people we know and love, and for everyone else, too. During war, we are all connected, and the Hebrew cliché, "All of Israel are brothers," is filled with meaning.

At night, I would return to the dorms exhausted, crawl into bed, and begin my nightmares. They were variations on a single theme: The sound of heavy boots against the pavement, slowly approaching my house—soldiers who had come to tell me of Reuven's death. I would wake up three or four times a night, covered in a cold sweat. I would try to calm down by taking cold showers. The dream repeated itself almost every night. In the meantime, classes resumed at the university. This was my first year of long-awaited graduate studies. Now, as I worried about my husband in the war, it all seemed so unimportant. From time to time, Reuven would send short postcards: "Everything's fine. Don't worry. Take care of yourself." They were splattered with mud and less than reassuring. They brought out my greatest fears.

After 2 or 3 weeks of fighting, Reuven called from the guest house at kibbutz Ayelet Hashachar. They were on furlough. I immediately wanted to come visit with his parents. "No," said Reuven, in a tired, impatient voice. "Relatives aren't allowed to visit." It sounded strange to me. How could they be so cruel? He was going back to the Syrian front, and the Syrians were a cruel enemy. After such difficult battles, why wouldn't they let us visit? Only years later, when I was working in the department of mental health, did I understand that a direct transition from the front to home can weaken resistance. The first days away from the front are thought to be a time of high risk for the emergence of psychological reactions to the stress of battle.

The weeks passed. I got back into my routine: study, work in the rehabilitation center, work in the youth organization. At the university, I was not only studying social work but also attending lectures in accounting and economics, Reuven's majors. I was trying to help him avoid losing the year by going to his lectures and taking notes. The classes were half-empty, filled mostly with women and Arab students. Mofid, the Arab who had offered to help me in Reuven's absence, suggested that I photocopy his notes. I was very grateful for his generosity. In his offer, there was a great deal that illustrated the complexity of our relations with the Arabs. I never felt any hatred, only anger that we had been set to fight each other. It all seemed so meaningless and purposeless.

Reuven finally came home on leave. He called from the Golani intersection in the north; his parents, his younger brother, and I went to pick him up. Instead of my usually energetic husband, I was greeted by a tired young man: physically and emotionally exhausted, introverted, taciturn, uninterested in the family, and decidedly disinclined to share his thoughts and feelings. He spent most of the vacation at his parents' house, sleeping. When he finally opened his eyes, he watched television, and I wondered if he was really following the action or simply staring at the screen.

The days passed in tense expectation—actually, not days but months. Reuven was on the Syrian front for 8 dangerous months of reserve duty. In the following leaves, once every 2 or 3 weeks, he remained closed. He wanted to go to the movies. He asked about his friends but didn't actually want to get together with them. I felt very rejected. It was as though he were looking through me. He didn't need me. I pressured him to talk, and he became even more withdrawn.

A close friend of ours was serving on the same front, in a similar unit of the same regiment. This single friend spent most of his vacations with me and told me what he knew about what Reuven was going through, about the wounded and dead, about myths that were shattered because the war caught us unprepared—with our pants down, it was said. The support units were not functioning properly. Sometimes ammunition didn't arrive. The supply of food was irregular. There were instances where Israeli soldiers stopped ammunition or supply trucks, threatening them with their weapons, and took equipment intended for other units, simply because they had no alternative. The feeling that the Israeli Defense Force (IDF) took care of us melted away.

Another deep myth was that of the medics, glorified after the Six-Day War in Yehoram Gaon's popular "Ballad of the Medic." The song describes how the medic is always ready and always helps the wounded, even at risk to his own life. In this war, Yitzhak, our friend, told me about his and Reuven's units: "Guys were wounded. We called for a medic. No one came." Years after the war, when Reuven opened up, he told that once when someone was wounded and the shells were exploding, they called for the medic. He was hiding in a trench and wouldn't emerge. Reuven ran over in a blind rage, oblivious to the shells, grabbed the medic by his shirt, and dragged him, with a generous dose of blows, over to the wounded man. Yitzhak spoke about his experiences. Reuven didn't.

Other than his withdrawal, there were two outstanding changes in Reuven, both of which passed in time. One was that his body temperature dropped markedly. Reuven, who had always been hot, huddled up in himself, and his body was cold. His body temperature rose only several months after he returned home. The second thing was his nightmares. Reuven talked in his sleep, jumbled words about planes circling above him, and tossed and turned in bed. These nightmares lasted many years. He had them even when we left Israel for a while to study in the United States. Over the years, they gradually became weaker and less frequent. Yet on the surface, Reuven came through the war without any emotional injury.

The first semester at the university ended with a paper for a course on psychopathology. We were asked to write about the emotional reactions of soldiers in combat. This was the first time that I read the pioneering works of American psychiatrists, such as Kardiner (1947) and Grinker and Spiegel (1945), who had studied psychological reactions to the stress of battle during World War II. What they wrote seemed very far from me, but in some ways also very near. I received an "A" for my paper, but I made no connection between what I wrote and what Reuven went through. It would be quite a number of years before I'd find myself deeply involved in the subject and, at that later time, connect or understand things that were previously remote and incomprehensible.

The war was over, but not before the names of the casualties were published. Yashke, a good friend of ours from the youth movement who had married just 6 weeks before the war, fell on the Golan Heights while in a jeep, single-handedly trying to fight off Syrian tanks. Yashke began to appear in my dreams, always with some moral message. In my dreams, he was an old man, completely bald; in reality he died at 23, with a thick head of hair. But in my dreams, his face was friendly, and he talked like a tribal chief bequeathing a spiritual heritage.

The husband of a classmate of mine was killed while crossing the Suez Canal. She was in the last month of her first pregnancy, and she learned of her husband's death after her son's birth. After the boy's *brit mila* (the ritual circumcision ceremony), the young widow and her son went to live with her parents.

The handicapped veterans began to arrive at the rehabilitation center where I worked. The hardest ones to look at were those with head injuries. They seemed to have recovered from their physical injuries, but in fact they weren't the same men they had been when they left for war. We heard about battle shock; rumor had it that there was a lot.

At this time, one of my courses was taught by Dr. Victor Florian, who, as a quadriplegic, did not go to war. He had a tape of a therapy session with a battle-shock patient who had been tranquilized with pentothal. Before he started the tape, he warned us that it might be tough listening, and that anyone who felt he or she didn't have the stomach for it could leave the room. No one moved. The room was silent, and everyone strained to listen to the very poor recording. Even we, professionals, knew very little about the subject.

The war ended, and gradually life returned to normal. In the dorms, I heard loud screams coming from the room of the young man who had asked me to send regards to his wife before going off. There were lots of arguments, even blows. They were both successful psychologists studying for advanced degrees. The neighbors said that their relationship, which was good before the war, had become impossible. He had trouble controlling his aggression and would beat her. The unavoidable happened; they divorced.

Two Arab students lived in the apartment opposite Reuven and me. Both of them were studying literature. One was blind, and he liked very much to listen to classical music. I often invited him to listen to our record player, since they didn't have one in their room. He talked openly about various things in his life, but he would tense whenever he heard footsteps. He often asked, "Are you sure it's all right with your husband that I visit?" I would laugh and assure him, "Of course!" I always thought that it was because he came from a traditional Arab village and thought it inappropriate to be alone with a woman. Only years later did a friend tell me that there were rumors among the Arab students in the dorms that Reuven, who had been in the army for so many months, was in army intelligence. They were afraid of him, and the less they had to do with him, the better.

A few years later, Reuven and I went to the United States so that I could pursue my studies in psychiatric epidemiology. The war was in the past, except for when it came up in Reuven's dreams. Our two children were born in Pittsburgh. Then we returned to Israel; the best employment offer that I got was from the army. Battle shock was still remote emotionally. Then, 6 months later, the Lebanon war broke out. This time I spent the war as an officer in the mental health department.

2

Sisters in Sorrow

When the Lebanon war broke out on June 6, 1982, I had been with the IDF mental health department for about half a year. This department is part of the headquarters of the army's surgeon general and is responsible for the provision and supervision of mental health services to all army personnel. It employs psychiatrists, psychologists, and social workers who work on bases and in clinics all over the country. The headquarters where I was located, on the Tel Hashomer base outside Tel Aviv, also houses the IDF central mental health clinic, one of whose units is an outpatient clinic specializing in the treatment of combat-related mental disorders.

I had been taken on to head the newly formed research unit. For the first 3 months, the entire unit consisted only of myself. After this, I was joined by three more soldiers. I worked in an isolated cabin, dating back to the days of the British mandate, and was told to proceed. Neither the subject nor the research aims were defined. I was looking for a direction, and I spent most of my time reading up on military psychiatry, mainly on psychological breakdown in combat—known today as *combat stress reaction* (or CSR), the term coined by Mullins and Glass (1973). My feeling was of floundering in splendid isolation, not really needed or wanted.

The outbreak of the war only strengthened the feeling that no one knew what to do with us. Now I was joined by sisters in sorrow, highly experienced mental health officers who could have made a real contribution but, because they were women, were not allowed to serve beyond the borders. They were frustrated, like myself. The war was not far away. To wear a uniform in wartime and to feel that you are not needed is very unpleasant.

The men in the department were organized to treat CSR casualties in special treatment stations at the front and along the border. In this war, as in all wars, soldiers were exposed to the terrible sight of death and destruction, and there was a very real threat to their own bodies and lives. Yet these are the conditions under which soldiers must function for long periods of time, often with insufficient food, drink, and sleep. Their physical and mental resistance is thus substantially lowered, and many, if not all, naturally feel some degree of anxiety. The experience of psychiatrists in many wars all over the world has shown that under these conditions, a small percentage of soldiers will inevitably experience anxiety so great, and so overwhelming, that they will cease to function as combatants. Their behavior becomes quite extreme and strange, and they may endanger both themselves and others. The treatment of these casualties is the primary function of all mental health professionals during wartime.

ESTABLISHING THE PSYCHIATRIC
WAR CASUALTY DATABASE

In the Lebanon war, the treatment of CSR casualties was documented right from the beginning. The therapists started a file for each casualty. In some cases, they had official forms on which to report the diagnosis, treatment, and course of the disorder; in others, they wrote on pieces of scrap paper.

Considering the medical corps' need for clear and comprehensive information as to psychiatric casualties, I suggested to the women mental health officers that we collect and organize all the data that were accumulated on them. The suggestion was accepted enthusiastically. At first, the women would come to my isolated cabin and work with me, collecting the data in a primitive way on huge handwritten tables spread over stapled-together sheets of paper. Eventually, one of the women offered us the use of her office in the new building to which the rest of the mental health department had moved.

At this stage of the work, we recorded the number of casualties, examined the clinical features for common patterns, and looked at data on predisposition and types of treatment interventions. Our records were purely descriptive. The information reached us mainly through mental health officers who came from the field for updates and brought lists of the casualties.

Some of the treatment stations within Israeli territory were staffed by women, and visitors were permitted. As each of these treatment units was about to close down, we would travel up north and request their files. Thus, people gradually learned of our work, and when the other stations—to which we did not have access—ceased operating, their files were also transferred to us.

Once we were permanently settled in the office to which we had first come as squatters, we began to set up a casualty file. We brought together the information on every patient from all the treatment stations he had been to; some soldiers had been in up to seven separate facilities. This was the foundation for our data base. In essence, almost every person who reached the IDF mental health department on account of emotional problems related to the Lebanon war was registered with us and had a file opened.

In the following years, we expanded our files to include data from the IDF data base. The IDF routinely collects data on every soldier from the moment he receives his first predraft call at age 16½ until he is released from reserve duty at age 55. These data, which were available to us, are updated in the course of the individual's military service.

The files that were in the possession of the mental health department—that is, in my office, at first on the floor and eventually in appropriate cabinets—were taken by the various therapists before each treatment session and returned afterwards with updated information on the therapy. This is how our files were developed.

CONDITIONS THAT ENABLED THE LONGITUDINAL STUDY

To the best of my knowledge, this was the first time in military history that a data base of this sort had been established. The work was made possible in large part by a constellation of features unique to Israel: the relatively small area and population of the country; the small size and reserve nature of its army; the provision of free military mental health services throughout the country; and the availability of frequently updated, centralized computer records of information relating to every soldier's military service. Together, these features greatly facilitated locating veterans, enlisting their cooperation, and following them up over time—tasks that were obviously preliminary to the longitudinal empirical research we undertook with large, representative samples of both healthy and injured soldiers. These essential preliminaries may be daunting obstacles to empirical research in a larger country, such as the United States, with a more mobile and dispersed population. In Israel, the overall disadvantages of the country's small size and large military needs were the features that made our study possible.

Another essential feature was the cooperation of many of the therapists and other staff of the mental health department. At the time, however, we did not have our own computer, and all the work of creating the data base had to be done manually. The gathering, sorting, and transcribing of data was tedious and hard; drudgery that none of us who did it had done or would be willing to do in peacetime. But in Israel during war, there is always a special atmosphere of support, concern, and togetherness. I myself often left the office at 3:00 P.M., drove three-quarters of an hour home to fetch my 3- and 4-year-old kids from nursery and spend some time with them, and then returned to the office later in the evening to continue with the labor.

About 2 months after the war had begun, a formal cease-fire was signed, bringing the period of the active warfare to an end. A central unit for the treatment of combat reactions was established in the central mental health clinic. The filing system became more organized. We developed an index. The files, which formerly had been in numerical order in piles on the floor, were placed in cabinets. And we, who read with diligence and sorrow every shred of information in the files, began to plan the research. I was no longer wondering what type of research needed to be done in the mental health department. I knew that the subject would be combat reactions.

PLANNING THE STUDY

At this stage of the research, in 1982, the relevant available literature was largely American. I had behind me the general literature on stress, which I had read for my doctoral work on the nuclear accident at Three Mile Island, and literature on combat reactions in World War II. The literature on Vietnam, which was only just starting to appear at that time, was not yet available here. Nor, aside from summaries and abstracts of American sources, was there much Hebrew literature on the subject. In my naïveté, I was surprised to learn that the treatment approach adopted by the IDF was based on very little empirical research and on a great many clinical impressions, few of them original, mostly stemming from the experience of American military psychiatrists in two world wars.

What mainly concerned me at that time were questions such as these: What are the typical clinical pictures of CSR? What are the relative prevalences of various symptoms? Do the various manifestations of combat stress represent the same disorder? Are our treatment methods effective? Which soldiers are at highest risk for stress reactions? What factors foster or retard recovery from combat stress reactions? They struck me as the cardinal questions not only on account of their scientific value but also, and perhaps mainly, because of their practical application. I felt it incumbent upon me to join in helping the CSR casualties, and I thought that perhaps a better understanding of the above issues could improve the services they were given.

Shortly after the cease-fire, we embarked on an odyssey of planning the research, which lasted almost a year. Up through the summer of 1983, we kept ourselves busy defining the research aims, establishing criteria for and selecting the sample, choosing and constructing the research instruments, and forming and training the research team. Quite a number of people were thus added to the project: a full-time research assistant, a part-time statistician, and two consultants (Joseph Schwarzwald and Matisyohu Weisenberg, well-known psychology professors who did 1 day a week of reserve duty with the mental health department).

For many months, I would spend the first 5 days of the work week reading, looking for research instruments, and organizing my thoughts. On the sixth day, the consultants would come to assist and advise on the final stages of formulating the research. In addition to giving me the benefit of their extensive knowledge and know-how, they also rescued me from the isolation that a researcher without support may feel, especially in a clinical setting where she is looked upon somewhat askance by people who perceive her as neither working nor contributing in the way that they know.

SUBJECTS

In the winter of 1983, we began to select the sample. Although the war in Lebanon was officially over, many of our troops were still in Lebanon at that time and were still exposed to fighting. We decided to summon all the casualties who had come for treatment in an IDF mental health facility up through February 1983.

The criteria for inclusion in this group were: (a) participation in frontline battles during the Lebanon war; (b) a referral for psychiatric intervention made either by the soldier's battalion surgeon or an IDF mental health clinic; (c) a diagnosis of CSR made by IDF clinicians trained and experienced in the diagnosis of combat-related reactions; (d) no indication in the clinician's report of serious physical injury; and (e) no indication in the clinician's report of other combat-related disorders, such as brief reactive psychosis or factitious disorders. The research staff determined eligibility by using records of clinicians' diagnoses made on the battlefield and in mental health clinics. When information on the presence or absence of combat stress reaction and other inclusion criteria could not be obtained from the clinicians' reports, the soldier was dropped from the sample.

The CSR group was composed of 382 soldiers who participated in this study and represented 82% of those chosen from the original sample. Data retrieved from official military records indicate that the soldiers who participated in this study did not significantly differ from dropouts in their sociodemographic and military background, premilitary adjustment, or intelligence.

In order to answer our research questions, we also selected control subjects for comparison, as is customary in scientific research of this kind. There were, in fact, two control groups, each chosen with the help of the IDF computer.

The first control group consisted of soldiers who fought in the same units as the CSR casualties. For every CSR soldier, we decided to select a partner who had fought in the same unit but who had not been identified as an emotional casualty. This enabled us to examine the unique features of the CSR casualties and at the same time to control for variables that were common to all combatants, irrespective of whether they sustained a CSR. The fact that soldiers in both these groups had fought in the same battles implies, for example, that they were exposed to a similar amount and type of objective stress during the war.

In order to ensure that the partners would be as similar as possible, the control partner had to be the same age and to have the same military rank and assignment as the study soldier. In cases where several soldiers in a unit met these criteria, we chose the one who lived in the most similar type of neighborhood. Since assignment to military duties in the IDF is not random but based on the soldiers' personal and sociodemographic features, we were not surprised that the matching was optimal. Of those chosen, 334 subjects took part in the study, representing approximately 93% of the sample chosen for the first control group.

The second control group consisted of soldiers who were combat ready but did not actively participate in battle. Subjects in this group were comparable in every other respect to the subjects of the other two groups. The fact that these soldiers were not sent into battle was attributable to pure logistic considerations, unrelated to personal factors or psychiatric vulnerability. This group was included in order to enable an examination of the effects of combat common to *all* combatants, whether or not they had been officially diagnosed as suffering from CSR, by comparing them with soldiers from similar backgrounds who, for purely technical or administrative reasons, were not sent to the front. Although these subjects had not been exposed directly to combat, they had been alerted for active battle participation. Eighty-eight subjects participated in this second control group, representing approximately 95% of those chosen.

The majority of our subjects (62%) were born in Israel, and approximately two-thirds were married. About three-quarters of the subjects ranged in age from 18 to 33; two-thirds were reserve soldiers, and the rest were draftees doing their 3 years of mandatory military service. The study groups did not differ significantly in any sociodemographic or military variable (for full details on the sample, see Appendix A).

MEASURES

With regard to the research tools, most of them were instruments that were constructed and tested by well-known researchers in various fields of psychology. Not all had been translated, adapted, or standardized for use in Israel, however, and in a few cases we did not find appropriate instruments and had to construct our own. Once the questionnaires were prepared, we had to conduct pretests. We looked for a cooperative unit with combat experience and decided on an armored battalion in the Golan Heights. Week after week, we would drive up to the Golan and hand out the questionnaires. We checked the precision of the Hebrew version, how well the soldiers understood the questions, and how long they took to answer. On the basis of our findings there, we put together a large battery of self-report questionnaires that took an average of 1½ hours to complete. (These research instruments will be presented in the relevant sections of the book.)

PROCEDURE

Once the population had been defined and the questionnaires formulated and printed, the time had come to request permission from the army to proceed with the study. The project was presented to Dr. Ron Levy, founder and (at that time) head of the mental health department. He immediately realized the potential value of the study and gave us his strong support. He helped us to "sell" the project and gain official approval within the army. Later on, we received the blessing of the surgeon general, Dr. Moshe Revach.

At the advice of Dr. Levy, we decided to deepen our data collection by means of clinical interviews. Social workers, clinical psychologists, and psychiatrists in the department were assigned to conduct the interviews, and a semistructured interview format was prepared. Now we were ready to get under way.

Since the study was being conducted by the IDF, and because its findings would first of all serve the army, it was decided that the most efficient procedure would be to summon all the subjects for a day of reserve duty in the mental health department.

Call-up orders were sent out. To each summons, a personal letter was appended explaining that the medical corps periodically conducted surveys to assess the impact of major events such as war on the health and well-being of its regular, reserve, and career soldiers. The letter explained that the recipient was being summoned for a day of reserve duty during which he would fill out a series of questionnaires and take part in an interview. In order not to arouse unnecessary anxiety, the letters were signed "Medical Corps Research Team," and the subjects were invited not to the mental health department but to nearby buildings.

The first subjects were scheduled for the summer of 1983. We were all very excited. I had several sleepless nights. Technically, carrying out research in which the army requires the subjects to show up sounds like the easiest thing in the world. But all sorts of worries ran through my mind: Will the soldiers we summoned actually appear? How will they react to filling out questionnaires and being interviewed? How will they feel about answering penetrating questions about their personal and family lives?

I was very wary of the famed Sabra (native Israeli) abrasiveness and worried about getting barbed, hostile responses. My trepidations were fed also by my own inner doubts. What right did I have to drag these men, many of them psychiatric casualties, to Tel Aviv from every corner of Israel? What pain might the questioning cause them? Could forcing them to remember war experiences bring on reactivation of their trauma? What was the justification for all this? To obtain information? To satisfy our own intellectual curiosity? After all, would our data reveal something new? Something useful? And if it did, would our findings be accepted in a department run by clinicians, not all of whom liked or even understood research? Would recommendations based on these findings be implemented? Or perhaps the saying that one of our consultants often repeated—"My mind is made up; don't confuse me with the facts"—would apply here too. Our data and conclusions would be shoved into some drawer and forgotten.

I am glad to say that my fears soon dissipated. The subjects did arrive, and most of them were pleasantly surprised by what awaited them. They were met by an assistant, a civilian employee of the IDF. She registered them, collected their reserve duty summons, and offered them drinks and light refreshments; certainly an unusual welcome to military reserves.

After that, the subjects were referred to 1 of the 10 rooms (in the same cabins where I had begun my work with the army) where they were to fill out the questionnaires. Every room had two examiners. These were either psychology and social work students or research assistants who were soldiers doing their 2 or 3 years of compulsory military service. All of them had received special training for the job. Their task was to help the subjects, to explain questions or items that they did not understand, and to make sure that the questionnaires were filled out in their entirety.

As each room filled up, I would come in and introduce myself by my full name and position. I explained that the purpose of the study was to learn about the impact of events such as war on the health of soldiers, and that the medical corps conducted such periodic surveys. I also assured them that all the data would remain in the research unit, and that no information would be transferred to their medical files or in any way affect their military placement or assignments.

Finally, I asked for their cooperation. I explained that participation was not compulsory, and that no measures would be taken against anyone who refused to sign the consent form. At the same time, I emphasized the importance of the research in helping us provide better care for soldiers. I also let them know that I would be glad to help with any personal problems they had, and that when the questionnaires were completed, I would be willing to meet privately in my office with anyone who so desired.

Attendance at the first session was around 60% of the subjects. Since we could not accept such a percentage, we checked all the addresses and sent out a second round of summons. The final attendance was 82% of the CSR casualties and 93% of the controls.

The vast bulk of the men who arrived agreed to participate readily. The few who objected were either vaguely suspicious ("How did you choose me?") or were concerned with the confidentiality of their answers. I talked personally with each of these veterans. I was able to reassure most of them that the tests would have no impact on their military profile (the numerical rating designating their physical and mental fitness for army service) or assignment. And in the end, almost all of them went into the rooms and filled out the questionnaires.

There was a small number of exceptional cases. Three soldiers arrived drunk for the early-morning intake and were sent home. One soldier in his mid-30s arrived looking extremely confused and disoriented and had a hard time answering such simple questions as "What is your name?" It was clear that there was no point in his filling out questionnaires or being interviewed. From the summons he held in his hand, we were able to identify him and check his medical file; it revealed that he had been a doctoral student before the war and was in a difficult emotional state and in treatment. With a great deal of heartache, we hurried to release him and sent him home, too.

INTERVIEWS

When the subjects completed filling out the questionnaires, some of them (about 40%, who had been chosen at random) were told that they would be interviewed by an officer from the mental health department. A few of them reacted with suspicion and anger; they asked questions like "Why me?" and "What will they ask me?" But in the end, all those who were chosen agreed to participate in the interviews, and when they were finished, some came to thank us for the interest the army was taking in them.

The clinicians were told that they could ask the questions in any order so long as they covered all the areas mentioned in the format. They were instructed to summarize the interviews in maximum detail, verbatim where possible—as is the practice in clinical work—and also to rate the interviewees on a questionnaire that was developed especially for the purpose and inquired about the emotional and functional status of the interviewee.

In practice, the interviews were not uniform. Some clinicians were enthusiastic and put their best efforts into the work, conducting long and sensitive interviews and writing thorough summaries. Most of the clinical descriptions in this book are based on those transcripts. Other clinicians, however, merely went through the motions; their interviews were inordinately short or the summaries so brief and schematic that they could not be used.

THREE WAVES OF MEASUREMENTS

There were three waves of measurements, in the summers of 1982, 1983, and 1984. The procedure was similar in each and so were the research instruments, with certain modifications and additions. Clinical interviews were not conducted the second year on account of insufficient funds. In the third year, we also conducted lengthy interviews with several groups of soldiers who had fought in multiple wars with different psychological outcomes. This time, however, we had the benefit of our experience during the first year, and we prepared a far more structured interview format with a detailed questionnaire for the clinicians to fill in after the interview. We also prepared the interviewers more thoroughly in order to ensure greater standardization and had all interviews tape-recorded and, later on, transcribed. The interviews conducted in the first and third years were analyzed using a content analysis.

The subjects in the two major groups, the CSR casualties and the pairwise-matched non-CSR controls, were summoned all 3 years of the study. But one of the interesting things about our sample is that it grew steadily. The first year's sample consisted of casualties who had requested or been referred for IDF mental health assistance between June 6, 1982, and February 28, 1983. But as soldiers continued to apply to the army's mental health facilities for treatment, the casualty population more than doubled over the 3 years of the study. Some were fresh CSR cases; because the IDF was effectively in Lebanon for about 3 years, our soldiers continued to be exposed to fighting, and not a few of them sustained acute stress reactions well after the first cutoff point. Others had suffered from emotional disturbances since the early days of the war but had delayed asking for help. These veterans showed up at our clinics when they could no longer bear their distress. There were also those who had reactivated or delayed reactions. So our files steadily expanded, and the target population grew all the time. Soldiers who approached IDF facilities after the cutoff point for the first wave of measurements were included in separate groups in the second and third years.

SUBJECTS' REACTIONS

Most of the men who filled out the questionnaires did so without any practical impediment. A very small number had trouble reading or writing, so a room was set aside with an examiner who read the questions aloud and filled in the answers for them. Emotionally, however, completing the questionnaires was not at all easy for many of the respondents. During one of the sessions, for example, one of the examiners drew my attention to a man who had been sitting over his questionnaire for half an hour without writing a word. I went over to him; his eyes were closed, but he was not sleeping. I asked if I could help. He opened his eyes, and I saw that he was trembling all over. I suggested that we go to an empty room where we could sit and talk. It turned out that the young man, who before the war had graduated with honors from the Haifa Technion (a top Israeli university) and was currently working as an engineer in civilian life, was having a very hard time concentrating. He had looked over the questionnaire and filled out his background details without any difficulty. On the second section, medical history, he felt slightly uncomfortable but was able to complete it. When he reached the questions on the war, though, he got dizzy and could not reply.

Many of the subjects demonstrated a less extreme form of avoidance. In the waiting area, before the soldiers entered the test rooms, we would distribute newspapers. Some of them read the papers all the way through, but others looked only at the sports sections so as to avoid the news, which in Israel often relates to the army.

Many subjects were extremely restless. Perhaps the most striking example is one subject who got up in the middle of the testing and asked permission to leave the room and take a run around the base. His therapist, the subject explained, had suggested that he work off his tension by jogging.

Many of the subjects were highly sensitive. Every sonic boom literally made them jump from their chairs. So did the noise of the helicopters that sometimes land at the nearby Tel Hashomer Hospital. Their sensitivity was particularly marked in the first year of the study. One incident stands out in my mind: I happened to be in a room when a metal ashtray fell to the floor with a sharp sound. Many of the subjects jumped; one of them got up in panic and ran to the corner for shelter. The feeling was that the war was still on.

The subjects were seated randomly, with CSR and control soldiers taking the tests together. Yet even before the data were gathered and processed, we could discern from our casual encounters which of them were still suffering from the impact of their war experiences, and which less so.

To my relief, I also found that their coming together for these tests also proved profitable for a good number of those in distress. One of the most moving incidents during the gathering of the data was a group discussion that arose spontaneously during the first wave of measurements. The assessments were organized so that men who had served in the same army units were summoned on the same day. Thus, most of the men who took the tests together were army buddies. Most of them had fought in Lebanon together, and some of them had even been treated for CSR in the same mental health facilities at the same time.

One morning, soldiers arrived from the unit that had sustained both the largest number of physically injured and the largest number of CSR casualties. Without any urging from us, they started talking. One of the men in the group was a CSR casualty who stuttered so badly as a result of his injury that it was difficult to follow his words. At first, he sat on the side and merely listened. Then the men called him to join in, and they all launched into a discussion of his injury and the problems created by his stuttering. No mental health professional intervened. I let the conversation go on for about an hour.

Many of the subjects who filled out the questionnaire came to talk to me afterward. People whose sad stories I knew only from their medical files suddenly became flesh and blood. Quite a few were suffering very badly. Some were open and freely told how impotent and helpless they felt; others maintained a stern facade.

I remember one officer in his late 20s. He looked like the typical good Israeli boy: muscular, handsome, well educated. Speaking an excellent, educated Hebrew, he informed me that although he personally had no problems, he believed there were some serious flaws in the questionnaires. As tactfully as possible, I explained to him that we had worked very hard on the questionnaires, but that I would be very glad to hear what he had to say. It was a scorching summer day, and we were sitting under the trees on the lawn. The young man looked at the questionnaire, thumbed the pages, found a random question, and with a striking lack of interest pointed out what looked like a flaw to him. When I explained why the question was phrased as it was, he smiled, agreed without further argument, and immediately turned to the subject that he really wanted to discuss.

It turned out that David, as he was called, was one of the few officers who had experienced CSR in Lebanon (most of the casualties were from the ranks). He had been treated in a frontline treatment station in the battle zone and returned to his unit, only to drop out again and be sent home. Ashamed of his breakdown and determined to put it behind him, he refused to go for further therapy and returned to work and to the university, where he tried to go on with the courses for his master's degree. But from the time of the war right up through our conversation under the trees, he was disturbed by residual symptoms. Especially troubling were the memory and concentration problems that threatened the continuation of his studies.

Behind the facade of competence and well-being, what David wanted was to clarify with me his need for therapy, and his fear of the stigma. No one in his family knew of his CSR, and I was apparently the first person to whom he could bring himself to go for advice.

Quite a number of soldiers approached me as David did. Some had complaints about untreated somatic problems; such soldiers I referred to the appropriate section of the medical corps. Many more came to ask about emotional problems connected with their military service. Some had already received treatment for combat stress reactions but had stopped. Some had dropped out on their own initiative. In other cases, the treatment was terminated by the therapist or by the IDF, which at that point was providing therapy for a short 6 months only and transferring chronic cases to the Ministry of Defense, Israel's equivalent of the U.S. Veterans Administration. Now, many such soldiers from the CSR group felt that they were not coping with their distress and wanted help. I referred them for treatment again.

I was also approached by quite a number of soldiers from the control group, which had been chosen precisely for not having had identified emotional problems. Like David, they too came to me to try to gauge their need for therapy and to check out how they could apply for it, whether it would be kept confidential, where it would be given, and so forth. On the days when subjects were summoned, the therapists in the CSR unit of our clinic worked long and exhausting hours.

OVERVIEW OF THEMES

In the years since the war, we have invested a great deal of effort in analyzing the data that we gathered from the interviews and questionnaires. Part of that work serves as the basis for this book. The focus of the book is the emotional price paid by some of our soldiers for their participation in combat. We begin by describing the process by which the soldier is stripped of his coping resources and breaks down emotionally, and by looking at the typical picture of a battlefield combat stress reaction. Then we follow the soldier when he leaves the battlefield. We examine the psychiatric residues of his breakdown and its impact on his somatic health, future military functioning, and day-to-day life in his family, work, and community.

Next we turn our attention to the implications of Israel's unique circumstances, which require many men to participate in war a number of times. What happens to soldiers who are exposed to war more than once? Do they become stronger and more resistant to battle stress, or does the recurrent exposure to combat make them more vulnerable in the future? We also examine the transgenerational impact of trauma as it relates to the effect of the Nazi Holocaust experience on the adult sons of survivors. Do such traumatic experiences in the past cast a shadow on or possibly strengthen the children of survivors?

The unique and tragic circumstances of life in Israel raise these questions, and also enabled us to answer them. These issues are at the focus of this book.

3

Psychological Breakdown on the Battlefield

Combat stress reaction (CSR) is one of the most elusive of psychiatric disorders. Unlike other emotional disorders, CSR is not defined by any necessary and sufficient combination of symptoms. Disorders such as depression, paranoia, posttraumatic stress disorder, and others all have typical clinical pictures that can be used for diagnostic and treatment purposes. CSR does not.

The difficulty of defining and describing CSR can perhaps be appreciated by looking at the conclusions of a prestigious American psychiatric commission following an extensive tour of post–World War II Europe:

> This picture of psychological disorganization does not correspond, either in its moderate or its extreme form, to any recognized or established psychiatric syndrome. . . . It certainly is not a neurosis in the ordinary sense. . . . It certainly is not merely a state of exhaustion. It certainly cannot be adequately described as anxiety or fear. . . . It comes closer to a situation psychosis than anything else, but its subsequent clinical course is quite different. (Bartemeier, 1946)

A major cause of the lack of clear definition is the polymorphous and labile quality of CSR, that is, the variability and rapid changes of its somatic, emotional, cognitive, and behavioral manifestations. Some casualties become apathetic and withdrawn; others rant and rage. Some freeze on the spot or hide in a trench, while others run amok or charge against a hidden enemy. Moreover, whatever the predominant symptom, it can be rapidly replaced by others that, in turn, can yield to yet others. For example, a casualty who runs amok may in a very short time, sometimes within hours, become withdrawn and detached, or vice versa.

The following two descriptions by casualties of their CSRs convey the multiform, changing character of the disorder. The first is by Avi, a tank driver who broke down when he was recalled to reserves shortly after completing a 30-day stint of duty in Lebanon, his third war. The stress reaction began when he received the summons and developed when he reached the base where his unit assembled:

> I had a shock on the spot. . . . My knees began to tremble. I began to shake. I said, "That's it. . . . Now it's my turn to die. . . . [When] I got to the base, I saw the tanks. It was the end. I couldn't walk. My legs wouldn't walk. The commander started to tell us that we were going to do such and such. . . . With his talk, I'm more and more certain of death. Death is coming. Death is coming closer. It got into my head. . . . We were there two days. I didn't eat, didn't sleep. I was like a piece of wood.

Overwhelmed by the apprehension of death, Avi went from trembling and shaking to the opposite: a brief paralysis of the legs, which gave way to general withdrawal and emotional and physical numbness and the inability to eat and sleep.

The second description is by Micki, who broke down during the Yom Kippur War at age 19, "the first time I ever saw dead people":

> I became very frightened. . . . I think the most shocking part was seeing people I knew slaughtered by hundreds of Egyptians, and screaming. . . . And at that point, I stopped fighting. I lay in the trench more than I fought.
>
> I must have fainted or something, because when I woke up it was getting dark and no one else but me was there. I began to run. I heard all sorts of Arabic voices. But since it was getting dark, I threw the smoke bomb I had and began to run. I think I ran all night. I didn't know where to run. I didn't have a map. I ran in the sand.
>
> As dawn was breaking, I reached a road. I saw some Israeli army vehicle. They took me to the base and told me to wait. I didn't eat for a day and a half. Actually, I couldn't eat. I sat and waited . . . and I didn't talk to anyone. . . . The guys kept away from me. And I wanted to have as little to do as possible with anyone.
>
> There was an aerial bombing, and I felt how the bullets were falling half a yard away. I went into the bunker and didn't move for 5 or 6 days. Other than drink, I must have eaten two crackers all that time. I had terrible diarrhea. I couldn't do a thing. . . . At one point, there was a terrible daylong shelling, and I was afraid to go out. I even defecated in the stronghold. After that, I said, when I can, I'll go out. And everyone began to laugh. . . .
>
> One night we were supposed to go out on a mission, and I told my commander that I wanted to rest a bit because I can't go on. . . . I was trembling terribly. I was really afraid. . . . I wanted to commit suicide. I said to myself, "There's no chance I'll get out of here."

Micki's CSR shows the same polymorphic lability as Avi's, with many similar symptoms: paralyzing fear of death, emotional and physical numbness, lethargy, withdrawal, depression reaching the level of suicidal ideation, inability to eat, and trembling. It also contains other manifestations, however: fainting that gives way to uncontrolled flight (which differs from calculated desertion in that it is an unthought-out, disoriented flight into unknown, unsafe territory without a map or even the knowledge of where one is going), loss of bowel control, and a terrible sense of loneliness that had both external and internal derivations— external in that he was new in his unit and the men rejected him on account of his bizarre behavior, internal in that he withdrew and wanted nothing to do with the others.

HISTORICAL PERSPECTIVES OF CSR

The multiplicity and variability of the symptoms, both within a single soldier and from casualty to casualty, make it very difficult to capture the elusive nature of CSR. This difficulty is reflected in the succession of appellations the phenomenon has borne, each encapsulating a different conception of its etiology and essence. In the American Civil War it was called "nostalgia," reflecting the notion that the psychopathology was caused by the soldier's yearning for his distant home. In World War I, the term became "shell shock," expressing the belief that CSR is a disorder of the central nervous system brought on by the soldier's exposure to intense shelling and bombing. In the postwar vogue of Freudian thought, the favored name became "war neurosis," conveying the view that CSR is caused by a reawakening of subconscious conflicts dating back to the soldier's childhood. This theory resulted in soldiers being evacuated from the battlefield for prolonged psychoanalysis, which brought on a virtual "epidemic" among American troops in the early years of World War II. To curtail the evasion, in 1943 General Omar Bradley ordered that soldiers showing psychopathological reactions be placed under observation for 7 days and that their condition be classified as "combat exhaustion," a term that was used along with "combat fatigue." The assumption behind these rubrics is that the combat breakdown is a short-term response to transient battlefield conditions rather than the consequence of a predisposing personality defect, as implied by "war neurosis." Their disadvantage is that they fail to capture the complexity of the disorder, as was noted by the Bartemeier (1946) commission.

The term used by the Israel Defense Forces, *combat reaction*, preserves the nonjudgmental tone of "combat exhaustion" (and its assumption that the disorder is an outcome of combat) without limiting the scope or manifestations of the response. Our term, *combat stress reaction*, which is taken from Mullins and Glass (1973), expresses the conviction that the breakdown is the result of the massive stress to which the soldier is exposed: the imminent threat of death and injury, first and foremost, but also the sight of death and injury in others; the loss of commanders and buddies; the physical deprivations of food, water, and sleep; the discomfort of the burning sun and cold nights without adequate shelter; and the lack of privacy, on the one hand, and of the support of family and friends, on the other.

Because of the difficulties of defining CSR clinically, however, the diagnostic criteria that are used in practice are functional. They are based on Kormos's (1978) definition: "Combat reaction consists of behavior by a soldier under conditions of combat, invariably interpreted by those around him as signalling that the soldier, although expected to be a combatant, has ceased to function as such." The two criteria are that the soldier ceases to function as a combatant and that others—in our case, authorized mental health personnel—recognize that he has.

This functional definition serves well on the battlefield. In most cases, the casualty's inability to function is in fact recognized. Avi tells that his buddies at the base were "astonished" by his behavior: "Cheerful Avi, suddenly something like this." The soldiers with Micki saw the state he was in and either made fun of him or kept their distance.

As Kormos (1978) acknowledges, however, the definition makes no distinction between soldiers who are unable to fight and those who are unwilling. Its neutrality, which is useful medically, unfortunately still leaves the CSR soldier open to accusations of weakness, cowardice, evasion of duty, and desertion, which have detrimental implications for his treatment and recovery. Nor does this definition address the still-outstanding need for a clearer clinical definition. This chapter will look more closely at the major components of CSR and offer a preliminary taxonomy.

CSR IN THE LEBANON WAR

Like their colleagues in other wars (Neuman, 1981), the clinicians who treated CSR casualties of the Lebanon war found a very wide range of symptoms and behaviors. They found casualties who were anxious, depressed, apathetic, unresponsive, tense, and/or phobic. They found a range of cognitive disturbances, including lack of concentration, the inability to understand or to communicate (i.e., the words not coming out, or the inability to give orders), being scattered and forgetful, and the performance of "magical" rituals such as not showering or changing in the hope that these would save them.

Somatic symptoms—ranging from heavy perspiration, vomiting, nausea, diarrhea, and loss of appetite to rapid pulse rate and heart palpitations, headaches and dizziness, and tics and tremors—were quite common. A number of hysterical or conversion reactions (in which there is a loss of functioning in some part of the body without any organic impairment) were also reported, namely, paralysis of the limbs and mutism. There were many cases, too, of partial amnesia, but none in which there was total amnesia.

The behavioral expressions of CSR that these clinicians observed were also numerous. There were casualties who became listless and passive, who withdrew into themselves, sitting off to the side, gazing into space, not talking to anyone, not fighting. There were casualties who became very restless and irritable, their frustration threshold plummeting. Some exhibited strong startle reactions. Some burst into rage out of all proportion to the supposed provocation; some picked, criticized, and complained about every trivial detail, especially those that had anything to do with the planning, organization, or implementation of the various military tasks. Others worried unduly about their equipment. Rumor mongering and generally looking for every and any excuse to panic were also observed among the casualties.

For the most part, the CSR manifestations that our clinicians observed in Lebanon were the same as those observed in other wars and other armies. There were some exceptions (i.e., the conversion reactions of blindness and deafness that were found in the British, French, and American armies were not noted in the Lebanon CSR casualties, nor was total amnesia), but the differences are few. The problem with the observations is that, like those that preceded them, they do little to clarify the nature of CSR. Essentially, they add up to a list of symptoms that tells us neither how prevalent any of the manifestations are nor in which combinations they tend to occur.

A TAXONOMY OF CSR

Several attempts have been made to formulate a taxonomy of CSR. In World War I, the medical forces of the U.S. Army developed a standard taxonomy, and discussed the relationship among clinical subtypes, treatment strategies, and prognosis (Bailey, Williams, Komora, Salmon, & Fenton, 1929). After World War II, Grinker (1945) and Cavenar and

Nash (1976) proposed five types of CSR depending on the dominant expressions, and Bartemeier (1946) suggested a model based on the severity of the symptoms (incipient, partial, and complete disorganization). All of these taxonomies, however, were based on clinical impressions gathered during and after war.

We, too, attempted to construct a taxonomy, but one that was based on an empirical approach. In cooperation with Dr. Tuvia Yitzhaki, an IDF psychiatrist, we first conducted an exploratory study using clinical records made on or near the front and filed in our psychiatric register (Yitzhaki, Solomon, & Kotler, 1991). One hundred files were chosen at random. The files were read by two experienced psychiatrists, who compiled a list of all the CSR manifestations. These were then divided into eight categories: (a) anxiety, (b) depression, (c) cognitive disorders, (d) dissociative states, (e) somatic complaints without physiological basis, (f) excessive or retarded motor activity, (g) polymorphic symptoms, (h) labile states. The files were then reread, and except for the cases showing polymorphic or labile symptoms, each case was classified in accordance with the one symptom that seemed to characterize it.

Analysis of the data yielded two major findings. First, it confirmed the labile, polymorphic nature of CSR observed by others (McGarth & Brooker, 1985): 48% of the cases were polymorphic, and 11% were labile. Second, it emphasized the predominance of anxiety and depression in those CSR cases that were not polymorphic. Anxiety states characterized 13% of the sample, depression 9%, and all the remaining manifestations added up to no more than 10% altogether. Moreover, in the 48 cases of polymorphic CSR, which contained a total of 20 different symptom combinations, anxiety was the most prevalent symptom (29 out of 48 instances), with depression following next (21 out of 48). In the labile cases, the most prevalent change was from anxiety to depression. Usually, anxiety was the first manifestation of the CSR, whereas depression was the last.

The salience of anxiety places CSR in the category of anxiety disorders. It confirms Grinker's (1945) contention that "the basic problem in all cases of war neurosis is anxiety and its management." As varied as the manifestations of CSR are, this finding suggests that what is behind most, if not all, of them is the fear of death. It makes it plain that the soldier who runs amok and the soldier whose legs lock are both acting out, albeit in different ways, the same terror of dying.

The casualty's depression may have many meanings and sources. It may be induced by the numerous losses of war: of friends and acquaintances, of one's sense of youth and innocence, and of one's positive view of the world as a safe and good place. Depression may also derive from the sense of helplessness that the casualty experiences as he is unable to keep his anxiety in check or to control the way he acts on it.

The transition from anxiety to depression may be explained by their being related states that often occur in tandem (e.g., in postpartum depressions). Delay and Ishaki (1981), for example, found that there was also secondary depression in 36% of the anxiety disorders they examined.

With reference to CSR, the following sequence may be postulated. The soldier's anxiety (or, more accurately, as Grinker suggests, his inability to handle the emotion) causes his breakdown. It also brings about his removal from the scene of the danger. All the files examined in this study belonged to soldiers who reached treatment stations either behind lines or at a relatively protected location on the front while the war was still in progress. Once out of danger, casualties could hardly escape the thought that they owed their lives more to fear than courage. This is a humiliating, guilt-provoking conclusion. As one evacuated casualty put it, "I felt like a child. I was ashamed of myself. I thought that I wouldn't fight any more." And another, who walked about for weeks after his breakdown with a mixture of fear and self-disgust, said, "Maybe my weakness is that I didn't know I'm afraid to die." The end result of such unwelcome self-knowledge seems to be a radical loss of self-esteem and ensuing depression, the symptom most frequently diagnosed in the last examination at the treatment station. It is possible to conjecture that the transition from anxiety to depression occurs mostly in casualties who break down on the battlefield itself, rather than in those whose CSR occurs after they have served their terms and been honorably discharged, as happens in many cases.

The findings of the Yitzhaki study are based on clinical records made in wartime, many of them on the front. Such records have the advantage of currency—that is, the manifestations are recorded quite close to the time of their occurrence—but the disadvantage of being partial and unsystematic. It is difficult enough to treat CSR under battle conditions, let alone study it. Battlefield clinicians invest all their efforts in treatment and generally give the recording of data low priority. Records made in the storm of battle tend to be skimpy and are not always preserved.

Thus, to explore the subject further, we examined the 104 clinical interviews conducted in the first year of the study (Solomon, Mikulincer, & Benbenishty, 1989). As the reader may recall, these subjects were chosen randomly from among those that participated in the first year of the study. In these interviews, casualties had been asked to describe in as much detail as they could remember the sequence of events leading up to their breakdowns along with how they felt and acted before, during, and after. The interviews were read by experienced clinicians, who made up a list of 25 distinct emotional, cognitive, somatic, and behavioral manifestations of CSR. Some were quite rare, others more common.

Seventeen manifestations were reported in 10% or more of the interviews. Several of them were particularly widespread: acute anxiety was cited in over 48% of the cases, fear of death in about 26%, and crying in about 21%. Psychic numbing was reported in about 18% of the cases, and a feeling of total vulnerability in about 17%.

In order to identify CSR patterns, we performed a factor analysis on the 17 manifestations with prevalence of more than 10%. Factor analysis is a statistical method that examines the strength of the relationship among various variables and builds groups of variables so that each group contains those variables that are related. Each group is termed a *factor,* and the name chosen for it attempts to convey the common quality of the variables it contains.

The analysis enables us to draw up a prototypical combat stress reaction, with each factor representing a component that makes up a certain proportion of the whole. An individual soldier may report anywhere from one to all of the factors. The analysis also tells us which manifestations a soldier is likely to report together (i.e., if he reports crying, what other manifestations he is likely to report with it), and so helps to grasp the essential expressions from among the multitude of separate symptoms, feelings, and behaviors.

As can be seen in Figure 3.1, six main factors were derived that together explain about 62% of the variance. This is a significant proportion of explained variance, and it indicates a relatively high validity for the classification in this analysis. The six main manifestations of CSR were distancing, anxiety, exhaustion and guilt over poor performance, feelings of loneliness and vulnerability, loss of self-control, and disorientation.

Distancing is the term we assigned to the reporting of psychic numbing, fantasies of running, and engaging in thoughts about civilian life. It explained 20% of the total variance. All three are means by which the soldier tries to block the intrusion of unbearably threatening battlefield stimuli and/or to distance himself mentally and emotionally from the fighting (Beebe & Apple, 1951; Klinger, 1975; Shontz, 1975). Psychic numbing, a blunting of one's senses and perceptions, is the soldier's distancing himself from his inner self. It is the common denominator underlying Avi's feeling like "a piece of wood," Micki's lethargy and uninvolvement, and the robotlike behavior that so many combatants report. Some thoughts about civilian life—namely, worries about the

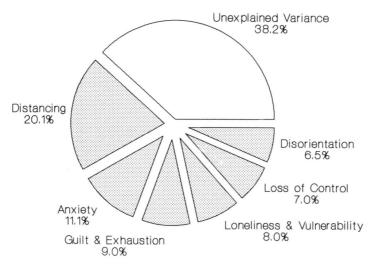

Figure 3.1. CSR factors.

wife and children at home—may be considered to be sources of anxiety in themselves (although they may still serve to distract the soldier from more severe anxiety over threats to his life); others, such as recollections of good times or fantasies of pretty girls, are clearly attempts at escape.

Anxiety explained 11% of the total variance. As a category, anxiety included reports of paralyzing anxiety, fear of death, and thoughts of death. Its association with sleeplessness suggests that the problems casualties had in falling and staying asleep were caused by their fear. Anxiety can be seen in Avi's image that "death is coming" and his subsequent inability to walk, in Micki's terror during the aerial bombing and his fear of leaving the stronghold, and in the nightmares that combat soldiers report.

Guilt about poor performance and exhaustion explained 9% of the total variance. The double appellation is necessary to convey the fact that fatigue was reported together with guilt feelings and thoughts about poor performance in combat. Our assumption is that this concern with poor performance refers largely to our casualties' feelings about their breaking down in combat, that is, to their inability to function effectively as combatants. It is notable that our casualties felt guilty about their CSRs, as opposed to the survival guilt found in other catastrophes (Lifton, 1968). The finding, however, accords with Grinker and Spiegel's (1945) suggestion that soldiers who break down in battle feel guilty because they view their breakdown as a sign of weakness.

Loneliness and vulnerability explained 8% of the total variance. Loneliness may derive from being away from home and family, from being new in a unit, from the loss of friends and buddies in combat, and from the recognition that, however one lives, in death one is alone. The feeling of vulnerability develops from the reality that the soldier has few means of effectively countering or evading the threat. Often he has no place to hide or take shelter; an armored personnel carrier (APC) can become a trap, and he cannot predict or control where or when the bombs will strike (Maier & Seligman, 1976; Silver & Wortman, 1980). The sense of utter vulnerability is vividly expressed in the statement of a casualty who went to his commander and cried, "I want a roof!" The two emotions are related in that the battlefield deaths that bring on feelings of loneliness also reduce the instrumental support available to the surviving soldier and, on a psychological level, do more than anything else to bring home his diminished chances of survival.

Loss of self-control, which accounted for 7% of the total variance, covered weeping, screaming, and a range of impulsive behaviors (e.g., running amok, bursting into rage). It also describes bodily reactions such as vomiting, wetting, and diarrhea. All of these actions are indicative of the casualty's inability to control his response to the threat of injury and death. Shaw (1983) has also observed a loss of bodily and emotional control among combat soldiers.

Disorientation, fainting, and trembling explained 6.5% of the total variance. Disoriented casualties have difficulties concentrating, focusing their thoughts, and making mental associations. At the extreme, they may not know where they are, what unit they are in, or what time or day of the week it is. They may not recognize their commanding officers or the men in their units. Some go about in a daze. In their disoriented state, they are cut off from the reality around them; fainting might be considered the epitome of being cut off. Disorientation, too, was noted in previous wars (Bartemeier, 1946; Cavenar & Nash, 1976; Grinker, 1945). Because the disorientation of the CSR casualty superficially resembles that in a brief psychotic episode, various observers, such as Bartemeier (1946), have suggested that CSR is closer to a situational psychosis than to any other clinical disorder. In contrast to psychosis, however, the disorientation in CSR is transient, however, and usually passes by the time the casualty is brought to treatment.

The findings of our second study (Solomon, Mikulincer, & Benbenishty, 1989) essentially corroborate the preliminary work we did with Yitzhaki (Yitzhaki et al., 1991). Either separately or in combination, acute anxiety, fear of death (which is the major source of anxiety in combat), or thoughts about death were reported by about 87% of our sample; next to distancing, anxiety contributed to more variance than any of the other factors. Anxiety may also be seen as underlying other factors. Distancing, through both psychic numbing and conscious thoughts of being elsewhere, has been recognized as a means of blocking anxiety (Horowitz, 1982; Lifton, 1968). One may wonder whether anxiety would account for a higher percentage of the variance were it recognized by the casualties who blocked it with avoidance. Similarly, anxiety would seem to be behind the conceptual confusion of the disoriented casualty who is so busy coping with his abundance of fear that he cannot think straight. According to Grinker (1945), disorientation is an indication of the regression to an infantile level that may occur when adult methods of coping with anxiety fail, as they do in CSR casualties. The impulsiveness and weeping we found as the fifth factor in our analysis lend support to Grinker's contention, and these may be considered expressions of anxiety as well.

While depression was not assessed directly, as in the Yitzhaki et al. study, it can be seen as expressed in several of the major CSR components found in this investigation. Depression, which is often a concomitant of mourning, might underlie the loneliness of CSR casualties. Grinker (1945) reported that many World War II combat veterans developed depressions related to the death of some person to whom they had been closely attached during combat. The fatigue and guilt reported by CSR casualties are familiar symptoms of depression, with guilt appearing as feelings of worthlessness and inadequacy over poor functioning during the war.

Taken as a whole, the current taxonomy of CSR is not dissimilar to earlier theoretical classifications. The factors we isolated appeared in Grinker's and then Cavenar and Nash's taxonomies under different names—our depression corresponding to their depressive type of CSR, our distancing corresponding to their passive-dependent type, our loss of control overlapping with their psychosomatic and hostile-aggressive types, and our disorientation being equivalent to their psychotic type. And although Grinker did not define anxiety as a separate type, he regarded it as the core of all combat stress reactions. Among other manifestations, Bartemeier (1946) noted that anxiety, depression, and psychosomatic symptoms develop following the evacuation of the CSR casualty to rear facilities. These considerable similarities were found despite the fact that our taxonomy was made in a different culture, with a different population, and following a different war. The resemblance in the taxonomies drawn up in different circumstances indicates that CSR, by whatever name it is called and however difficult it is to define, is a pathology with a consistent set of symptoms and expressions. Although it may be colored by personal and cultural factors, essentially it is a war-induced pathology wherever and whenever that war takes place and whoever the fighters are.

The reactions that we found to the stress of war are not limited to CSR casualties. It is the rare soldier who does not feel fear, however good his defenses are. A certain amount of anxiety is, in fact, beneficial on the battlefield, in that it helps keep the soldier alert. Distancing and emotional withdrawal are perfectly normal defenses for the preservation of ego integrity, and they enable many soldiers who do not break down to cope with the abundance of mutilation and death. Similarly, soldiers who do not break down also mourn the friends they lose in combat and also feel lonely and depressed as a result. Fatigue is natural to combatants, who are frequently compelled to make strenuous physical exertions with inadequate sleep and irregular food intake. A certain amount of disorientation and confusion can be expected in soldiers who are bone tired and who have been ranging at night over unknown terrain. Combat conditions may similarly induce a certain loss of self-control.

What distinguishes these feelings and behaviors in the combat stress reaction is the extremity to which they are carried. The soldier who finally sustains a combat stress reaction is so anxious and vulnerable that he feels he can no longer function effectively. His fear is intense enough to impair his judgment, paralyze his limbs, make him lose consciousness, or cause him to engage in counterphobic activities that lead to unnecessary risk taking. His psychic numbing is so pervasive that it blocks not only pain, horror, and grief but also the perceptions needed to make realistic judgments. His fatigue, depression, and withdrawal impair effective action and make him dangerous to himself and his fellow fighters.

The functional definition of CSR thus has validity in that it distinguishes normal responses to the stress of combat from pathological ones. We hope, however, that the clearer definition we have suggested will aid commanders, physicians, and CSR casualties themselves in understanding, identifying, and responding to the disorder.

4

Naked on Dizengoff

Whereas the previous chapter presented a historical view of combat stress reactions (CSR) along with our findings from the Lebanon war, this chapter will discuss the psychological processes underlying and contributing to this phenomenon.

For those of us who are fortunate enough never to have been in combat, it is difficult, if not impossible, to grasp what happens to the soldier who breaks down under the strain of the ubiquitous life threat. But to understand what brings on the breakdown, it is necessary to understand first the remarkable fact that the vast preponderance of soldiers remain psychologically intact despite the awesome destructiveness of modern warfare. They feel fear, and most of them exhibit at least some of the symptoms of stress that can develop into the CSR manifestations described in the previous chapter. But they continue to function effectively enough not to constitute a menace to themselves or their fellow fighters.

THE PROTECTIVE ILLUSION OF SAFETY

Most soldiers go into battle with the expectation of coming out alive. Along with the many implements for physical protection with which soldiers are outfitted, they are armored with a psychological sense of safety. Nurtured from earliest infancy, this is the sense that the world is safe for us and that we are able to meet, by ourselves or with help, the challenges of living. It is the sense that enables us to leave our homes in the mornings with the expectation of returning in the evenings, to cross the street, drive a car, fly in a plane, use sharp instruments and power tools, go out to the movies in the dark of night, and take the million and one other "risks" we take every day without the paralyzing fear of becoming a police statistic or an accident victim. It is the sense that enables the soldier to keep his head while he is being bombed or shelled, to shoot when shooting is called for, to rescue casualties under fire, and to use his wits to keep out of harm's way when that is the right thing to do.

This sense of safety is composed of both rational and irrational elements: the experience and skills we have accumulated in living (e.g., we have all learned to cross the street and have done so successfully in the past) on the one hand, and the inability of human beings to conceive their own nonbeing on the other.

Soldiers bring to the battlefield the same sense of safety that enables us to function adequately from day to day. To help them preserve their sense of safety through the peril of combat, soldiers are well outfitted, trained to the hilt, inculcated with a well-defined set of values and beliefs, made part of a larger group of other well-trained and well-motivated troops who lend them support, and led by commanders whom they have been taught to trust. Together, their physical implements, their mores and fighting skills, and their identification with a group stronger than their individual selves foster a sense of mastery and assist soldiers (both physically and psychologically) to cope with the onslaught of dangers they face.

In addition, soldiers bring to the battlefield the irrational part of the sense of safety, which the American military psychiatrist Jon Shaw (1987) has termed a protective "illusion of safety" and which enables them to deny to themselves the eminent knowledge of death and injury. According to Shaw, the illusion is sustained by three defense mechanisms: (a) the myth of personal invulnerability, (b) the delusion of having an omnipotent leader who will in some magical way ensure their survival, and (c) the feeling of being part of an all-powerful group that will never fail to protect them. Together, these defenses allow the individual to repress conscious awareness of his biological vulnerability. In combat, the illusion is perhaps capsulized by the common battlefield phrase, "There's no bullet with my name on it." The shell will strike, the bomb will fall—but elsewhere. Others may die, but not I.

But just as the soldier's steel helmet and flak jacket can be penetrated and fall far short of offsetting the vulnerability of the human body, the sustaining sense of safety is also far from impervious. While it provides effective insulation for most soldiers in many battle situations, it may be penetrated or destroyed. It is when this happens that the soldier breaks down.

Continuous close range exposure to violent death, especially of comrades and commanders, inevitably forces the awareness of one's diminished chances of escaping unharmed into consciousness. So does injury to the military unit (whether through multiple casualties or deterioration in morale), since the soldier's well-being and survival depend on the emotional and instrumental support of his comrades. Similarly, any breach in the soldier's trust in the fighting capacity of his unit, in the efficacy of his military training and equipment, or in the concern and competence of his officers or army commanders may also undermine his sense of security and strength.

As casualties mount and as the soldier feels more and more isolated on the battlefield, his sense of safety may itself fall victim to the war. A combat stress reaction occurs when the soldier, stripped of this defense, feels overwhelmed by the threat that he is powerless to distance or avert and is inundated by feelings of helplessness. Filled with fear, he loses the ability to cope effectively and develops a sense of existential insecurity. As Shaw (1987) describes it:

> The threatened emergence into conscious awareness of the feeling of helplessness to cope (internal danger) before the fear of injury and death (external danger) is the sine qua non of the combat reaction. . . . The unmasking of the illusion of safety represents a traumatic moment when the individual becomes aware of . . . the reality of one's biological vulnerability to an imminent and pressing danger.

CSR: SHATTERING THE ILLUSION OF SAFETY

The feeling of utter helplessness can develop very quickly, as it did in Ron, a well-built fifth-generation Israeli who sustained a combat stress reaction in his first heavy fighting of the Yom Kippur War. For his compulsory military service shortly before the war, he had volunteered for the parachutists, an elite and demanding corps, and during the war he served as a squad commander in a unit he had helped train. He went into the war feeling strong, fortified by the conviction that "I'm with quality people I can count on." He soon discovered that he could not, however, count on himself. His description of his CSR illustrates the essence of the breakdown—the soldier's utter helplessness in the face of his inability to cope with the threat:

> What we went through in Yom Kippur wasn't pleasant. . . . I saw a lot of wounded, and a lot of guys who died of their wounds because we couldn't reach them. They cried out for help. The shelling was heavy, and you can't get to them. And all the

while, they're slaughtering us, and the wounded are dying like flies. . . .
   I remember the feeling of utter impotence. In just another minute, they'll
finish me off. I'll die. And there's no way out. I was waiting for a miracle. I asked
myself, "Why the hell did you volunteer for the parachutists, of all things? Who
needs it? What am I doing here?" I saw dying men, soldiers of mine, who'd been
training for several months, call me to help them. I want to go over, but I can't! My
legs won't carry me. Even if it might have been possible to reach them, I couldn't
have gone. I wanted to walk, but I found myself crying. I was sweating, crying, and
trembling. I was shaking, shaking like a leaf. A madness of fear. . . . I was rooted in
one spot. I was lying there and couldn't get up.

Torn between his desire to do his duty by his buddies and his fear-filled
desire to save his life, Ron cannot move. His legs lock, and his paralysis,
although not among the most common manifestations of CSR, serves as
an image of the utter helplessness the breakdown entails.

   The key statement in Ron's description is that he felt utterly impotent. His recognition that he is powerless to avert or avoid enemy fire
brings on his combat stress reaction. His inability to reach the men who
were calling for assistance, both because of practical impediments of
crossing through enemy fire and because of his paralyzing terror, confirms his helplessness, while his loss of control over his bodily movements—
his sweating, shaking, trembling, crying, and, above all, virtual
immobility—both confirms and augments it.

CSR: GRADUAL AWARENESS OF VULNERABILITY

   In other CSR casualties, the awareness of vulnerability takes longer
to penetrate, and the sense of utter helplessness develops gradually as
stresses pile up one after the other. The truth is often brought home
when the soldier knows the person who was killed or had just spoken to
or touched him, or when circumstances make him feel that he had been
saved at the last minute or that someone had been killed instead of him.
Then it is very hard for the soldier to escape the knowledge that he can
be killed or injured as readily as the next man.

   Many other factors may also contribute to the development of the
sense of helplessness. Disorganization or bad relations in the unit, problems in the steady flow of equipment and supplies, and mistakes by
officers, by the army high command, or by the government that sends
the soldier to the front can all make the soldier feel alone and unprotected.

   In the following account of Michael's breakdown, we can see the
step-by-step erosion of the sense of safety that helps the soldier preserve
his balance under extreme peril. Michael came to Israel from Tunis in

1961, during his late adolescence. After studying Hebrew at a kibbutz near Hadera, he was drafted into a mortar unit and participated in numerous retaliatory operations against positions on the Syrian border. On the whole, he felt all right in the army and was more bothered by the fact that the rough-and-ready Sabras he served with ribbed him about his good manners than by his military duties.

During the 1967 Six-Day War, Michael served as a reservist and also fared well. The brevity of the war and the relatively easy victory enabled him to keep the awareness of the threat at bay and his illusion of safety intact. As he puts it: "It was like a short trip. I saw a few dead, but it was so quick. . . . We had two wounded, one who got shot in the back, the other in the shoulder. And the war was over. We were discharged, and everything was fine."

When the Yom Kippur War broke out 6 years later, he still felt "the confidence of the Israeli superman" derived from the smashing 1967 victory. In the course of the war, his confidence was steadily chipped away until he felt that he could no longer cope, and he broke down.

The first blow to his assurance came with the surprise of the Arab attack on Yom Kippur, the Day of Atonement—the holiest day of the Jewish year. In 1967, Israel's preemptive strike had placed Israel in control of the fighting from the beginning and had given IDF soldiers the feeling that they were marching to certain victory. The surprise attack on Yom Kippur resulted in massive troop losses during the first days of the war, which left many Israelis fearful that the country would be overrun and feeling that the politicians, who had censored news of enemy troop buildups and had yielded to American pressure not to attack first, were playing with their lives.

Like so many others, Michael began to feel uneasy even before he was called up. Yom Kippur is a very special day, with an ambiance all its own. It is an extraordinarily still day. More Jews are in synagogue than on any other day of the year. There is no Israeli radio, no television. Driving is tacitly forbidden. All non-life-essential labor is at a standstill.

The boom of planes breaking the Saturday morning quiet was the first sign that all was not well. "Why are planes suddenly flying on Yom Kippur?" Michael asked himself. Looking up, he saw that they were armed and flying in groups of four. He hurriedly picked up his infant (his wife was working as a nurse at the nearby hospital) and rushed over to the main road to see what was going on. At the sight of convoys of tanks and other vehicles, he "felt that something was about to happen." It still did not dawn on him, though, that there had been an attack. "I said to myself, we're probably going to do some retaliatory operation and come back."

By early afternoon, the tanks, which were on trailers when Michael first saw them, were moving north, and the road was full of traffic. "It can't be," Michael said to himself. "It's Yom Kippur. Something must be happening." He was worried enough to switch on Radio Monte Carlo, which announced the concentration of Syrian and Israeli forces. Nervously playing with the dial, he by chance tuned in to the army station, usually inoperative on Yom Kippur, just as the siren was sounding. Shortly afterward, the army spokesman began announcing the code names of units being called up, and Michael realized "something's about to start, something's wrong. . . . It looked to me like a war."

Like many Israeli men, Michael spent the afternoon eagerly waiting to be called up to take his place on the front. By the time his summons arrived that evening, and by the time he finally reached his base just before dawn, he was quite tense. On the way to the base, he could already hear and see the flares of the Syrian bombs falling nearby, and he realized that they could hit the base.

Then, what he saw when he reached the base made him feel shakier still:

> We didn't have enough ammunition. The weapons weren't ready. The mortars weren't prepared. It looked like no one had been taking proper care of the equipment. Everything was a big mess. Lots of things were missing. People were running right and left. They made us sit until dawn doing nothing. And all the while we heard and saw the flares of the Syrian and Israeli bombs.

The closeness of the bombing gave Michael his first inkling that he could be hurt. The disorder at the base—with equipment missing or unready, people running every which way, and the seemingly pointless waiting—made him feel that "there was no one to take care." In the course of the war, Michael's exposure to danger and his sense that there was no one to care for or protect him both mounted steadily, undermining the sense of security that he needed to retain his equilibrium.

The intuition of danger and sense of abandonment were reinforced for Michael the next morning, when he had his first encounter with large-scale death. Traveling up to the Golan Heights, his unit passed an open truck "full of dead soldiers lying there like sardines in a can." The sight was especially disconcerting because the corpses were uncovered. "I think that if they were dead, they should have covered them," Michael complained. "It's very hard to forget something like that."

The corpses being brought back from the direction in which Michael's unit was going were a warning of what lay ahead. What made the dead bodies so terrible was that seeing them, as opposed to only knowing that they were there, made them much more real. As with the events at the base, both the physical threat (implicit in the corpses) and the sense that the people responsible were not looking after things properly combined to erode Michael's confidence.

During the first week of the war, Michael served with the support forces on the Golan Heights. There was heavy Syrian bombing, and Israeli planes were downed. "It was an awful feeling to see our planes downed. . . . I saw a plane fall and crash into smithereens, and we all stood there stunned. In the battery we all thought, how could it be that they hit a plane of ours?" Michael's fear at that moment was of being hit by a stray splinter. No less important was that the reassuring belief of Israeli superiority was beginning to crack. Like other Israelis, Michael had been taught to regard the air force as the ultimate guarantor of Israel's safety. As long as Israeli planes ruled the skies, Israeli men, women, and children were safe on the ground, the reasoning went. With the shattering of the plane, yet another bit of Michael's sense of safety was chipped away.

For the most part, however, the fighting of the first week was at a distance, and Michael and the others could keep their fear at bay. "I still had the feeling that it was another trip, like the Six-Day War, that we'd be in and out." Death was still sufficiently far away for the men to be able to joke about it and to console themselves with the cold comfort that should they die, the IDF would look after their wives and children. Michael could keep up his morale by thinking about his family and occasionally eyeing a picture he had of two girls wearing bikinis in the snow, and telling himself, "This is what's waiting for us when we get home."

These ploys all crumbled, however, the second Saturday of the war, when the deputy battalion commander misread the maps and directed the unit into a Syrian ambush. This was the first in a series of errors that Michael believed could have been avoided. It resulted in the men being totally exposed, riding in open half-tracks, when the first Syrian shell landed right in the middle of the battery. Michael's commanding officer was hit in the throat and fell on Michael.

Feeling afraid, Michael stooped for cover, but just then another shell fell 2 yards away, totally covering the half-track with sand and stone. With the smell of gunpowder in his nose and the explosion still ringing in his ears, Michael jumped out of the vehicle to look for shelter.

No one seemed to be in charge. The wounded were screaming, crying out for help. Michael saw a soldier with his hand almost totally severed, connected by only a few strands of flesh and sinew, and paused to comfort him. "Close your fist and hold it with your left hand and lie still," Michael told him, "because there's nothing we can do here with them shelling us."

Michael's feeling that "there's nothing we can do" mounted steadily.

They were in the direct line of Syrian gunfire. The area was full of smoke and odors and splinters. The shells were "falling like rain . . . four to five a minute." Retreat was hampered because the vehicles were too close together to maneuver, and when they tried to escape through the adjacent field, they found it was mined.

One of the things that upset Michael during the ambush was the IDF policy of rescuing casualties at all costs, even under fire. The idea governing this policy is that soldiers who know that they can count on their buddies to save them will be more confident and motivated to fight. On Michael, the policy had a different effect: It made him feel that healthy soldiers were risking their safety for casualties who either could wait or were beyond help anyway, and for him it was yet another sign that the IDF was not taking proper care of its men.

As the shells were flying and soldiers began rescuing the casualties, Michael lay down on the ground and shouted, "Don't evacuate while they're shelling. Don't evacuate and don't move, because shells are falling. Lie down." His warnings were ignored, making him feel powerless to avert tragedies as he saw them about to happen. Just as he was calling out "Lie down," he saw another officer hit. Asked what he felt during this attack, Michael answered, "First of all my helplessness, my fear of getting hurt, a lack of security, as though you're walking naked down Dizengoff [Tel Aviv's main street]. You have no confidence that anything can protect you."

The image of "walking naked down Dizengoff" is an image of utter exposure and vulnerability. It expresses the soldier's terrifying recognition that the flesh is perishable, that the soldier can be wounded or killed, and that all the protections on which he had relied can fail him.

Michael's sense of helplessness here has two components: his awareness of his personal powerlessness to ensure his or his comrades' survival in the circumstances of the battle and the sense that there was also nothing outside himself to protect him. Together, these produce the feeling of being utterly exposed and vulnerable that so many CSR casualties recount.

Both these feelings mounted as other mishaps followed. After finally extricating themselves, Michael's unit moved on a few miles, where they stopped to set up a field hospital—yet another error, in Michael's view, as there they were subjected to "even worse" shelling. Michael's encounters with death at this point were close and intense. While the shells were falling, Michael helped the medics carry the wounded and collect and cover the dead. Poles were set up with saline solution and blood transfusions, and the casualties were hooked up to them. One of the casualties was the commanding officer who had fallen on top of

Michael in the half-track after being hit by the first Syrian shell. When Michael called the medic, the latter checked his pulse and said dryly, "That's it. Take him down."

The officer was a personal friend, whom Michael had known from the kibbutz where he lived when he first arrived in Israel. The death of a commanding officer on the field is usually an extremely upsetting event because of the leadership that the commander provides. It often leaves soldiers with the feeling that they have lost a guide and protector, a kind of father figure whose strong presence promises that all will be well. The fact that the officer was also a friend whom Michael had known and trusted made his death all the more devastating.

This close encounter with bodily injury and death, especially of friends and officers, finally shattered the reassuring and somewhat sustaining myth of Israeli invincibility that had prevailed since the Six-Day War: "All I saw was red, blood, the dust of shells. I felt insecure all the time. I'd come here, fought in the Six-Day War, and it was as if we were supermen, and suddenly I saw that the Syrian soldier can shoot well, and hit."

Michael continued to function by acting like an automaton and not permitting the meaning of the events to penetrate intellectually or emotionally. "I was a total robot. I was reacting automatically, without any thought. Pick up a casualty. Pick up a dead man. Lie down. . . . I didn't have time to think." When he saw his friends die, he didn't allow himself to cry. At one point, he helped the medics put back the insides of a buddy whose abdomen had been torn open, and he didn't allow himself to feel disgust either.

The image of being a robot expresses the psychic numbing discussed in the previous chapter. While such numbing helps the soldier to keep out feelings of unbearable grief, fear, and horror, it also blunts his senses and impairs his judgment. Thus, that evening, when he was on guard duty, Michael permitted an Israeli armored personnel carrier to drive into an off-limits area, contrary to both orders and good sense. The field was mined, and 5 minutes later he heard the explosion. Michael blamed himself ("Why did I let him go in?") and could not fall asleep that night.

Michael dates the beginning of his CSR to the following week, when the immediate danger had let up:

> I felt it begin the second week, with the news that the IDF forces were starting to recover. . . . With every passing day I felt more and more exhausted. I couldn't move, I couldn't function, I couldn't write down orders, I couldn't fall asleep at night. When I did fall asleep, I had nightmares. I tossed and turned in my sleeping bag. I jumped up. I didn't want to take off my clothes, even though that week the

battalion commander came with a smile and said, "Friends, it's not yet time to open up the champagne, but it's all right. We're on our way to Damascus." . . . The minute he said this, I felt weak. I couldn't move, I couldn't function. And then, I think, I cried.

With the passing days, he became increasingly weak physically and more and more lonely, alienated, and withdrawn. Images of the Saturday shellings repeatedly ran through his mind. Noises made him jump. He could not eat, sleep, write down orders, or function at all. Feeling utterly helpless, he applied to the medic in charge, who sent him home for the weekend with a referral to the Haifa hospital, where his CSR was diagnosed and treated.

Michael's sense of helplessness developed as the props and supports that had sustained him fell. Beginning with the surprise Yom Kippur attack, the bombing in the vicinity of his base, and the sight of the uncovered corpses, and ending with the large casualty count during the ambush, the death of friends and officers, and his assisting in evacuations, Michael was exposed to increasing doses of death, so to speak, and his initially distant and symbolic encounters became increasingly close, real, and concrete. Each encounter with death made it that much clearer to Michael that he, too, could die.

At the same time, the delay in his being called up, the disorganization at the base, the careless exposure of the corpses in an open truck, the commander's disastrous misreading of the maps, and other errors— along with the IDF policy of evacuating casualties under fire—all made him feel that the powerful institutions and people who should have protected him were unconcerned and inept, while his exposure in the open tank and the ignoring of his warnings to take cover added to his feeling of being powerless to affect events. In short, the various crutches that had enabled him to face the danger (from high morale and confidence in the leadership to the illusion of safety) were taken away. As this happened, he became less and less able to cope and more and more frightened and anxious.

Both Ron and Michael had entered the war with feelings of mastery based on their training and experience, the proven power of the IDF, and the responsibility that they both felt for their buddies. Michael (unlike Ron, who had become paralyzed with the first heavy fighting he encountered) had been able to function with considerable feelings of helplessness before he broke down when the IDF was regaining control and the situation had become relatively safe. By that time, however, he had internalized the reality of the danger, and it was too late for the improvement in external circumstances to restore his lost sense of mastery.

Once the soldier starts to feel this tremendous sense of helplessness, another process starts to get under way: the internal conflict between fight and flight. This basic conflict becomes stronger the longer he is on the front. On the one hand, the danger is formidable, ever present, and impossible to ignore or deny totally, however strong his sense of safety. The soldier's personality, motivation, military assignment (more non-coms than officers break down), and standing in his unit all affect his perception and interpretation of the danger and his assessment of his ability to cope with it; ultimately, though, his fear of getting hurt impels him to want to escape the battle zone. On the other hand, numerous counterforces keep him fighting. These include his soldierly pride and self-image as a man; his ties to his buddies and officers; his dependence on, identification with, and sense of belonging in his unit; and his belief in the justice and aims of the war he is fighting.

The soldier's emotional ability to withstand the threat depends on the balance of his fear and these counterforces that promote his doing his duty. So long as the latter outweigh the former, the soldier will continue to fight. When the perception of danger increases and/or the sustaining convictions, morale, and personal ties weaken, the soldier's anxiety mounts until it reaches a peak. At this point, the soldier is overwhelmed by anxiety that he can no longer keep in check.

In Ron's CSR, the conflict between fight or flight was quite obvious, as he heard his men calling him, knew he should go to their aid, yet felt too afraid to move. "Why the hell did you volunteer for the parachutists?" he asked himself. Michael does not articulate the conflict directly, though he expresses it in his resentment at IDF policy of rescuing injured soldiers under fire and in his robotlike behavior toward the end of the long day of fighting. In both cases, however, as in all other combat breakdowns, the CSR enables the soldier to resolve the conflict. At least in the IDF, such breakdown usually results in his removal from the field, either behind lines or to a treatment station in a more protected spot in the combat zone.

This in no way means that the conflict is mainly conscious (even in Ron, it is not), or that a CSR follows upon the soldier's conscious decision to save his life in this way. A CSR is neither malingering nor pretense; it reflects the soldier's inundation by his anxiety. Nonetheless, the soldier may pay a very high price over a very long time for his escape from danger.

5

Does the War End When
the Shooting Stops?

As all-encompassing and disruptive as a combat stress reaction is, we know remarkably little about its aftereffects. Combat stress reactions have been known since biblical times and have been noted in professional literature since the American Civil War. Since the middle of the last century, quite a number of wars have been accompanied by an outpouring of studies, conducted during and immediately after the hostilities, on soldiers' reactions to the stress of battle. But there has been almost no systematic study of the long-term psychological sequelae of combat stress reactions.

Military authorities, who hold most of the relevant data, have been understandably reluctant to address the possibility of a problem that is an affront to the fighting ethos and have nervously pushed aside the notion that a CSR might have long-lasting consequences. Their interest in combat stress reactions has been motivated largely by the desire to minimize the manpower loss they cause, for which studies of the short-term impact seemed to be most to the point.

In Israel, other factors may also have contributed to the issue having been given short shrift. The idea that participation in combat might leave a searing imprint clashed with the image of the Israeli superman so assiduously cultivated by Israel's founders and pioneers and so eagerly adopted by subsequent generations. The image was of "the new Jew" living in his own land who would be everything that the stereotypic diaspora Jew, despised and persecuted, was not. The new Jew would be proud, free, and, above all, strong—physically and emotionally. In this collective belief system, weakness had no place (Margalit, 1987).

The fact that much of Jewish history can be read as a saga of persecution also worked to aid and abet denial. A hefty proportion of Israel's population have had to rebuild their lives in the shadow of a major traumatogenic event. This is true of both Holocaust survivors and of the Jews from Moslem countries whose Arab neighbors turned on them when the state of Israel was declared. Traumatized individuals are often the last to admit that their experience has damaged them. Such an admission would add force to already humiliating feelings of victimization and seem to counter their forward-looking efforts to get on with their lives.

Coming against this background of persecution, the succession of wars by which Israel has been battered since its inception has ironically made the notion that man's inhumanity to man can have lasting psychological consequences even more threatening. Indomitable giants, not mere flesh and blood subject to the ignonimities of psychological disturbances, seemed to be required to meet the exigencies of existence. There was the vague, not quite articulated fear that by looking too closely at our weaknesses, we would sap our strength.

Thus, in Israel as elsewhere, the question *How long and profound are the wounds of war?* remained largely unanswered. The professional consensus is that exposure to the extreme stress of combat may upset a soldier's emotional balance, but opinion is divided as to the probable severity, breadth, and duration of these psychological wounds. Is the damage a short-lived transient reaction to "insane" circumstances? Or is it a long-term, persistent debilitating disorder?

The literature does not allow for an unequivocal determination of the impact of CSR on subsequent mental health and adjustment. Most of the studies on combat-related trauma focus on the postwar effects without linking them to wartime psychopathology (i.e., whether or not the soldier suffered a breakdown on the battlefield). Furthermore, their conclusions are inconsistent. Figley (1978a), in a comprehensive overview of studies assessing psychosocial adjustment of Vietnam veterans, summarized what he considered to be the two major views that emerged from that war. The *stress evaporation hypothesis* argues that while there are immediate widespread detrimental effects, much of the reaction is superficial, nonpersistent, and rarely dysfunctional. In this view, the distressing residuals persist only among a small proportion of veterans. In contrast, the *residual stress hypothesis* claims that the deleterious effects of combat stress are widespread, deep, persistent, and long lasting. In especially severe cases, these residuals create serious emotional distress that impairs functioning and adjustment and requires professional treatment.

Empirical studies of the impact of combat have brought support to both views. Some studies have found the stress of combat to produce highly pervasive, deeply internalized, and essentially negative psychological effects (Strayer & Ellenhorn, 1975; Stuen & Solberg, 1972). Other studies have found that the detrimental effects of combat are generally superficial and transient (Helzer, Robins, Wish, & Hesselbrock, 1979).

The contradiction in the findings may be accounted for by the studies' numerous methodological shortcomings. Prior to the publication of the DSM-III (American Psychiatric Association [APA], 1980), there was no clear standardized definition of posttraumatic stress, so the earlier studies used a variety of definitions and assessment criteria for the psychological aftereffects of combat. Moreover, the subjects in many of these studies were mostly patients who had come for treatment; the samples were small and seldom representative of the target population, and only a few of the studies employed adequate control groups. In addition, the time interval between the original trauma (i.e., combat) and the assessment of posttraumatic stress disorder (PTSD) varied from study to study and in some instances was not even clearly specified (Figley, 1978a). These shortcomings make it difficult to generalize from the findings.

For the IDF, the problem of generalization was further complicated by the fact that these studies were not conducted in Israel. Studies of war-related trauma are inevitably carried out in connection with specific wars, on specific national populations, and in specific societies whose features may bear on the shape of any mental disorder. Thus, there was a question of how applicable the findings of any study conducted in a very different context would be to Israeli soldiers (i.e., what would be similar, and what would be different).

The few studies that focused specifically on the long-term effects of CSR are similarly flawed. The Swedish psychiatrist Kettner (1972) followed up 35 Swedish CSR casualties serving in the United Nations forces in Zaire and concluded that they adjusted no worse in the long run than a group of comparable controls. His elegant design, unfortunately, is marred by his small sample size and by the highly selective nature of these recruits. A preliminary study by our own group (Solomon, Oppenheimer, & Noy, 1986) of CSR casualties of the 1973 Yom Kippur War is likewise impaired by doubts as to the representativeness of the sample and the use of an inadequate outcome measure—the soldiers' military profile, which is an exclusively Israeli measure of combat fitness and not a valid indicator of mental health. Thus, doubt is also cast on its optimistic conclusion that most CSR casualties recovered within a year.

The host of questions left unanswered by the literature remain pertinent and pressing. What are the residuals of combat participation in general and of a combat stress reaction in particular? How severe might they be? How long lasting? The distressed combatant is not an isolated individual, but a part of a larger community of immediate and more distant family members; of friends, acquaintances, and colleagues; and of the nation in whose army he served and in which he was traumatized. The personal consequences of his breakdown inevitably touch the lives of many other people, who are affected by his distress and who also have a moral responsibility to try to repair whatever damage he may have incurred on their behalf. Knowing whether and what kind of postwar sequelae can be expected following a CSR is obviously the first step in helping the afflicted individual and society at large to deal with it.

The questions are particularly relevant in Israel, which is a small, closely knit society in which most citizens serve in the army and an inordinately high proportion of men have had to fight in one or more wars. There are relatively few Israelis who are not associated, with a greater or lesser degree of intimacy, with someone who has been in combat. Thus, even if only a very small number of soldiers sustain CSRs, any aftereffects affect the lives of a relatively large circle of people.

Moreover, the reserve composition of the Israel Defense Forces gives the question a very specific urgency. Unlike veterans in the United States, a sizable percentage of Israeli combatants continue to serve in the regular army or active reserves even after they fight a war. While the discharged American soldier is unlikely to return to the army or to engage in combat again, the Israeli veteran frequently does both. Any change in the veteran's health or functioning, mental no less than physical, requires reconsideration of his military status and reserve duty assignments.

To answer these questions we assessed the emotional psychological sequelae of the Lebanon war 1, 2, and 3 years afterwards, comparing CSR casualties with non-CSR controls who resembled them in military background, sociodemographic variables, and combat exposure in that war.

POSTTRAUMATIC STRESS DISORDER

The most common and conspicuous long-term sequela of combat stress is posttraumatic stress disorder. Whereas CSR is an acute reaction that occurs on the battlefield, PTSD is a complex of distressing emotional reactions that can follow the experiencing of any kind of traumatic event, such as an accident, severe illness, natural disaster, rape, or combat. It can ensue directly from a breakdown in the course of the traumatic event (a CSR in the present instance), or it can develop independently after the event has come to an end and the individual is no longer in danger.

In either case, PTSD casualties remain embroiled in the traumatic event. They continue to suffer from the anxiety it induced and to relive the experience in frequent nightmares and intrusive images, thoughts, and recollections that bring back the strong, painful emotions of the traumatic moment. Continuing to live in the world of the trauma, most PTSD casualties lose interest in activities they had previously found pleasurable or significant, withdraw from social contact, and shut themselves off emotionally. They tend to be nervous, irritable, and to have various and sundry difficulties in sleeping, concentrating, and remembering.

To a greater or lesser degree, the lives of PTSD casualties revolve around the traumatic incident. The persistent intrusion of trauma-related imagery into their lives is thought to reflect their struggle to master the traumatic event through repetition. Their apathy, social withdrawal, and emotional anesthesia in part reflect attempts at avoiding those painful reminders. As they struggle to master the traumatic experience on the one hand and to put it out of heart and mind on the other, the trauma continues to absorb much of their interest and life energy.

In our study, we adopted the definition of PTSD provided by DSM-III (APA, 1980). Since the publication of DSM-III, clear criteria have been available for the diagnosis of PTSD (see Box 5.1). Its uniform definition permits, for the first time, meaningful comparison of data gathered by different researchers and clinicians.

Our study employed a 13-item PTSD inventory based on DSM-III criteria. Each item describes a PTSD symptom adapted for war trauma. The respondent was asked to indicate whether or not he had experienced the described disturbance in the past month. The 13 statements were divided into three categories of symptoms corresponding to DSM-III criteria for the diagnosis of PTSD: (a) reexperiencing of the trauma,

BOX 5.1

DSM-III Diagnostic Criteria for Posttraumatic Stress Disorder

A. Existence of a recognizable stressor that would evoke significant symptoms of distress in almost everyone.

B. Reexperiencing of the trauma, as evidenced by at least one of the following:

(1) recurrent and intrusive recollections of the event

(2) recurrent dreams of the event

(3) sudden acting or feeling as if the traumatic event were reoccurring, because of an association with an environmental or ideational stimulus

C. Numbing of responsiveness to or reduced involvement with the external world, beginning some time after the trauma, as shown by at least one of the following:

(1) markedly diminished interest in one or more significant activities

(2) feeling of detachment or estrangement from others

(3) constricted affect

D. At least two of the following symptoms that were not present before the trauma:

(1) hyperalertness or exaggerated startle response

(2) sleep disturbance

(3) guilt about surviving when others have not, or about behavior required for survival

(4) memory impairment or trouble concentrating

(5) avoidance of activities that arouse recollection of the traumatic event

(6) intensification of symptoms by exposure to events that symbolize or resemble the traumatic event

(b) numbing of responsiveness, and (c) a combined group of miscellaneous symptoms.

To be diagnosed with PTSD, a person must first of all have experienced a prior traumatic event. All our subjects, in both the CSR and control groups, met this criteria in that they were all in combat units on the front in the Lebanon war. A soldier was considered to have PTSD when he reported at least one symptom each from the reexperiencing and numbing categories and two from the miscellaneous list. (The inventory, along with detailed information on its validity and reliability, is presented in Appendix B.)

This PTSD inventory was used to assess the sequelae of CSR during the 3 years following the onset of the 1982 Lebanon war. Employing it, we examined the rates of PTSD, the duration of the syndrome, the average number of symptoms, and the symptom profiles of CSR and non-CSR veterans.

PTSD Rates

First, we determined the prevalence of PTSD in the CSR and non-CSR control groups (Solomon, 1989a). The results, presented in Figure 5.1, indicate that among identified CSR casualties, PTSD rates were quite high throughout all 3 years of the study. Sixty-three percent of the CSR soldiers suffered from diagnosable PTSD 1 year after the outbreak of the 1982 Lebanon war, 57% 2 years after, and 43% 3 years after. In other words, nearly half of the soldiers who sustained a CSR on the battlefield were still suffering from pervasive *diagnosable* disturbances 3

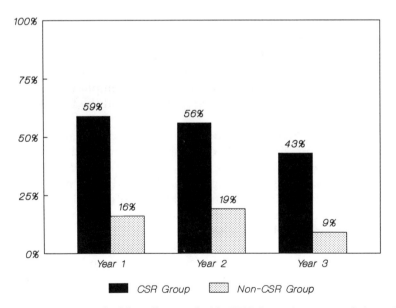

Figure 5.1. Percentage of soldiers diagnosed with PTSD by study group and time of assessment.

years after their participation in battle. Clearly, for a large proportion of CSR combatants, the war does not end when the shooting stops. For many of the CSR casualties of the Lebanon war the breakdown was not just a transient episode but rather crystallized into chronic PTSD from which recovery, if it came at all, was slow. In the control group, 14% of the veterans were diagnosed with PTSD in the first year of the assessment, 17% in the second year, and 10% in the third. The differences in the PTSD rates of the two groups were statistically significant at all three points of time.

Three trends are apparent from the above figures. The first is that both CSR and non-CSR veterans showed substantial rates of PTSD. Since the literature does not offer norms for comparison to CSR casualties of other wars, it is difficult to gauge how representative our rates are. Recent studies of Vietnam veterans have found PTSD rates ranging from 24% to 48% (Egendorf, Kadushin, Laufer, Rotbarth, & Sloan, 1981; Walker & Cavenar, 1982), but these calculations were made without reference to whether or not the subjects had sustained a prior CSR. The rates we found are astonishingly high, however, considering that nearly all of the CSR casualties had received quite intensive treatment; 3 years after the war, 43% of them were diagnosed as still suffering from PTSD. The rates for the control group are no less alarming, because these men were chosen for our study from the same units as the CSR casualties on the basis of their having been healthy. Although none were known to have broken down on the battlefield or to have applied for treatment, we found a significant number of them to be suffering from PTSD at all three points of time. It should be emphasized that these rates reflect not sporadic or residual symptoms, but the full-blown diagnosable disorder.

These figures point to the detrimental impact of war on men who weathered the immediate stress of combat without a visible breakdown and resumed their lives without ever applying to a mental health agency. Undoubtedly many were not aware that they had a definable disorder, or they believed that their symptoms were a natural and inevitable outcome of their harrowing experiences on the front. Others were reluctant to seek help. Similar reluctance to seek treatment has been found among psychiatric casualties of the Vietnam war (Figley, 1978a). It is all too likely that these "silent" PTSD veterans signify a much larger number of psychiatric war casualties whose distress is similarly unidentified and untreated.

Although the observation that PTSD is a disorder that often goes untreated is well documented, in the current Israeli context, the disinclination to seek treatment is surprising. Had these Israeli PTSD casualties sought help for their war-related disturbances at any IDF mental health clinic, they would have averted the very real risk of being sent back to the front.

Two possible explanations come to mind. One has to do with the fact that the control group differed from the CSR group not only quantitatively in terms of their PTSD rates, but also qualitatively. As will be shown in more detail in the following sections, their PTSD had different clinical features. Our findings suggest that the PTSD in the control group was less severe and less distressing than in the CSR group. Earlier studies (Ingham & Miller, 1982) have shown that seeking treatment for psychiatric disorders and adopting the sick role are related to symptom severity.

Another possible explanation is that veterans who did not identify themselves as PTSD casualties by seeking treatment were highly motivated to continue serving in the army and were not interested in obtaining the possible secondary gains of illness. In Israel, masculine identity is very strongly associated with army service. Identifying oneself as ill may well entail a heavy price in both self-esteem and social acceptance.

Veterans who experience a psychiatric breakdown and seek psychiatric help have to contend with its serious implications, with the shame and guilt of having let down their buddies, and with betraying the trust placed in them by nation and family. With the great importance attributed to the army in Israel, their sense of failure and the injury to their manhood and self-esteem is certain to weigh heavily and to act against any inclination to reveal their distress and ask for help.

The second trend to be observed is that during all 3 years of the study, the percentage of subjects diagnosed with PTSD was overwhelmingly higher among soldiers who sustained a combat stress reaction during the Lebanon war than among those who had not. In other words, more CSR subjects suffered from PTSD than non-CSR subjects. It appears that the war, and especially a breakdown in war, leaves an imprint that is not easily erased. Since this seems to be one of the most significant findings of our study, an entire chapter (Chapter 10) will attempt to cast light on its meaning and implications.

The third trend is that in both groups there seems to be a decline in PTSD rates as the interval from the war increases, with the largest drop occurring in the third year. Time and circumstances seem to have combined in fostering healing. Similar improvements over time have been found in PTSD following other catastrophes (Davidson, 1979). Moreover, shortly before the third wave of measurements was carried out, Israel finally pulled most of its troops out of Lebanon. Hence, the very real threat of being sent back to Lebanon, where periodic flare-ups continued, was lifted, and many PTSD veterans could breathe a sigh of relief and embark on the road to recovery. Still, Israel's defense problems are far from resolved, and these casualties are still surrounded with threatening stimuli, so whether or not they continued to recover remains to be seen.

The Duration of PTSD

Another issue that was addressed was the duration of PTSD among CSR and non-CSR veterans. Figure 5.2 shows how long the PTSD lasted in the CSR and non-CSR groups. Among CSR subjects, 28% were diagnosed with PTSD all 3 years of the study; 32% for 2 years (18% the first 2 years, 6% the last 2 years, and 8% the first and third years), and 15% for 1 year (8% during the first year, 5% in the second, and 2% in the third). Twenty-five percent did not have PTSD at all.

Among non-CSR subjects, only 3% were diagnosed with PTSD all the 3 years of the study; 7% for 2 years (2% the first 2 years, 3% the last 2 years, and 2% the first and third years); and 18% for 1 year (7% during the first year, 9% in the second, and 2% in the third). Seventy-two percent did not have PTSD in any of the 3 years of the study.

These findings indicate that there was some fluctuation in the two groups, and that not all veterans diagnosed as having PTSD fulfilled the entire set of DSM-III criteria at all three points of time. In both groups, a certain proportion suffered from a diagnosable disorder in all 3 years; some seemed to have recovered but later deteriorated; others recovered and stayed that way; and yet others had delayed reactions after a period in which there was no diagnosable disorder. The patterns in the two

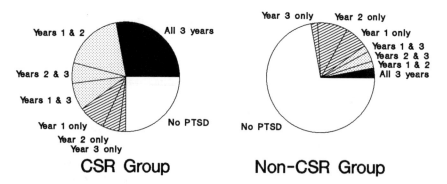

Figure 5.2. Distribution of subjects according to years in which PTSD was diagnosed.

groups are similar, but the rates are markedly different. In the CSR group, 75% were diagnosed as having PTSD at least at one point during the three years, as compared to 28% in the control group. The data thus show a clear difference in the scope of the disorder in the two groups. Moreover, the percentage of those diagnosed as PTSD at all three points of time is much lower in the control group than in the CSR group. In other words, the veterans that did not apply for treatment had not only lower rates of PTSD, but also disorders of shorter duration. The shorter periods of distress in this group may also have contributed to their avoiding treatment.

Number of PTSD Symptoms

To assess further the psychological sequelae of the war, we compared the *number* of PTSD symptoms displayed by the two groups. The above examination of PTSD rates provided global information as to the number of veterans who met the DSM-III criteria for PTSD. Although this method does provide important epidemiological data, it is also somewhat crude, because in order to be classified as suffering from PTSD, the veteran had to meet *all* the DSM-III criteria. If he met many or even most of the criteria, but not all of them, he was classified as non-PTSD. Assessment of the *number* of symptoms, irrespective of diagnosis, allows for a more sensitive comparison between the two groups. Results showed that in the CSR group, the average number of symptoms reported was 6.86 the first year, 6.44 the second year, and 5.01 the third year. In the non-CSR group, the average was 2.59 PTSD symptoms the first year and 2.45 and 1.47 in the second and third years, respectively (for further details, see Appendix C).

These figures are consistent with our findings on the PTSD rates; just as PTSD rates declined in both groups, so did the number of symptoms. If the number of symptoms can be regarded as a rough index of distress, this decline also seems to indicate that following a brief period of readjustment, the suffering of the PTSD casualties decreased and a gradual healing process occurred. At the same time, the figures also show that at all three times of assessment, CSR veterans endorsed more PTSD symptoms than non-CSR veterans. This difference, which the dichotomous DSM-III criteria for PTSD overlook, suggests that PTSD among CSR casualties was not only more prevalent but also more distressing in all 3 years of the study. Although the healing process can be seen in both groups, the number of PTSD symptoms in the third year is still very much higher in the CSR group than among the controls.

The Symptoms Profile

Finally, we used the DSM-III inventory to delineate a symptom profile of PTSD. Figure 5.3 presents the symptom profiles of four groups of Lebanon war veterans—PTSD veterans with an antecedent CSR, PTSD veterans without an antecedent CSR, non-PTSD veterans

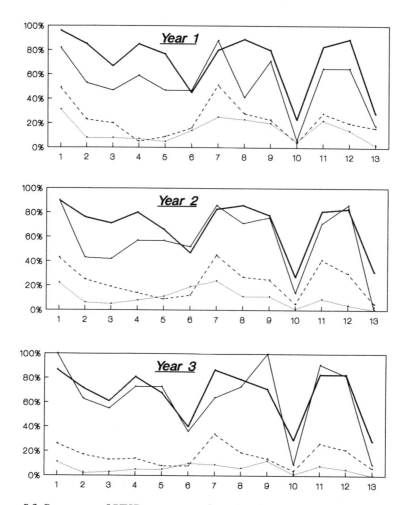

Figure 5.3. Percentage of PTSD symptom endorsement in each group. *Key:* (1) recurrent scenes and thoughts; (2) recurrent dreams and nightmares; (3) feeling of being back in the war; (4) loss of interest; (5) feeling remote from people; (6) constricted affect; (7) hypersensitivity; (8) sleep difficulties; (9) memory difficulties; (10) survivor guilt; (11) avoidance; (12) intensification of symptoms; (13) guilt about functioning.

with an antecedent CSR, and non-PTSD veterans without an antecedent CSR—at all three waves of assessments.

The four curves in all three figures are similar in shape but different in height. The similarity in shape shows that all our combatants, whether they had a wartime CSR or not and whatever their current PTSD status, reacted to the war with a similar constellation of responses. Whether symptoms were highly endorsed or not, within each group they were endorsed with the same relative proportions at all three points of time. These graphs inform us that PTSD is less an extraordinary response to the pressure of combat than an amplification of responses that are clinically nonpathological. It thus appears that it is quite normal for all the combat veterans of the Lebanon war, and probably of other wars as well, to ruminate about their experience, to remain sensitive to noise and other stimuli, to avoid reminders of the war, to feel disengaged from the outside world, and to have trouble sleeping. These symptoms testify to the impact of the war on all the men who fought in it.

With this, the graduated heights of the curves reflect the different intensity of the impact. The large gap between the similarly shaped curves of the PTSD and non-PTSD veterans shows that the posttraumatic disorder lies not in the kind of response to combat, but in its frequency. In keeping with the data presented above, the highest curve is that of the PTSD veterans with prior CSR, followed closely by that of the other PTSD casualties. Their heights, especially those of the CSR veterans, are a visual indication of the intensity of these veterans' suffering and the degree to which they are still living—to borrow a phrase from Kardiner (1947)—in the "emotional environment of the traumatic event."

Second, whereas the DSM-III gives identical weight to each of the symptoms, our findings indicate that not all symptoms are equally endorsed, and that some are more prevalent than others. Some symptoms, such as recurrent recollections of the war, were endorsed by most of the veterans over the 3 years, while others, such as survivor guilt and constricted affect, were endorsed by relatively few.

Endorsement of PTSD Symptoms

The last point made by these symptom profiles is that while the PTSD symptomatology of non-CSR veterans remained fairly stable over the 3 years of our study, the content and composition of the syndrome in the CSR veterans did change. As is readily observable from Figure 5.4, in PTSD casualties without prior CSR, time brought about both a decline in most of the symptoms and a change in their relative weights. During the first 2 years of the study, their PTSD was characterized

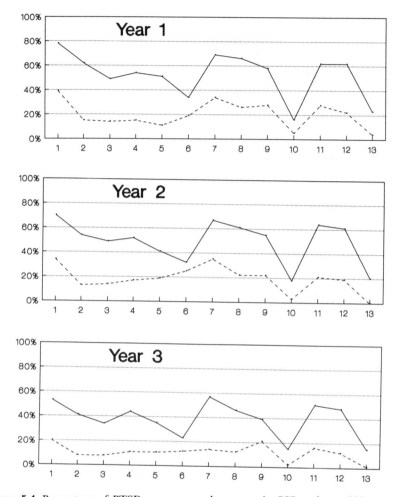

Figure 5.4. Percentage of PTSD symptom endorsement in CSR and non-CSR veterans. *Key:* (1) recurrent scenes and thoughts; (2) recurrent dreams and nightmares; (3) feeling of being back in the war; (4) loss of interest; (5) feeling remote from people; (6) constricted affect; (7) hypersensitivity; (8) sleep difficulties; (9) memory difficulties; (10) survivor guilt; (11) avoidance; (12) intensification of symptoms; (13) guilt about functioning.

mainly by recurrent recollections of the war, hyperalertness, concentration difficulties, avoidance of activities reminiscent of the war, and intensification of symptoms upon encountering war-evocative stimuli. On the whole, the intrusive symptoms were more prominent than the symptoms of avoidance, withdrawal, and psychic numbing. By the third year, the balance had shifted. Although recollections of the war, hyperalertness, and sleep difficulties were still prominent, the decline in their endorsement is very large relative to the other symptoms, leaving the avoidance symptoms (i.e., loss of interest in previously significant or enjoyed activities, social alienation, and avoidance of activities reminiscent of the war) proportionately more salient than they initially were in the composition of the syndrome.

No such change occurs in the composition of the PTSD of the casualties with antecedent CSR. The content of their PTSD remained pretty much the same as it was the first year of the study, when it was characterized in this group mainly by intrusive dreams and recollections of the war, hyperalertness, sleep difficulties, avoidance of stimuli reminiscent of the war, and intensification of symptoms upon exposure to such stimuli. By the third year, there was a statistically significant decline in recurrent recollections of the war, recurrent dreams of the war, social alienation, and sleep difficulties, and a nonsignificant general decline in most of the other symptoms. More or less, however, the relative weights of the various symptoms remained similar, with the two major intrusive symptoms continuing to receive stronger endorsement than the avoidance symptoms.

This differential picture of the specifics of the PTSD of the CSR casualties and the non-CSR controls may be interpreted as yet another indication of the greater difficulties that CSR soldiers have in working through and overcoming the trauma of combat.

STRESS RESIDUES: INTRUSION AND AVOIDANCE

Although PTSD, as defined by DSM-III, is recognized as the most common and conspicuous form of postcombat pathology, the psychological sequelae of war can be assessed by other criteria as well. According to Horowitz (1982), the period following a traumatic event is usually characterized by alternating responses of intrusion and avoidance, which oscillate over time. *Intrusion* refers to the penetration into consciousness of thoughts, images, feelings, and nightmares about the stressful event, and to a variety of repetitive behaviors. *Avoidance* reflects the tendencies of psychic numbing, conscious denial of meaning and consequences, behavioral inhibition, and phobic activities related to the event. Horowitz (1982) describes a process in which the relative salience of intrusion and avoidance changes according to the individual's idiosyncratic pattern until the trauma is "worked through" or resolved. The amount of intrusion and avoidance of wartime thoughts, feelings, and imagery a veteran reports may thus serve as an indicator of how well he has resolved the inevitable stress of combat or, conversely, of how distressed he still is by it.

To deepen our understanding of the stress residues of war, we traced our subjects' postcombat intrusion and avoidance responses employing the Horowitz, Wilner, and Alvarez (1979) Impact of Event Scale (IES), adapted to the trauma of combat. The IES, as we used it, describes 15 emotional reactions to the trauma. Intrusion is tapped by such items as "I thought about the war when I didn't mean to," "Pictures of the war popped into my mind," and "Any reminder brought back feelings about the war." Avoidance was tapped by such items as "I tried not to think about the war" and "My feelings about the war are kind of numb." Respondents were asked to indicate on a 4-point scale (ranging from "not at all" to "often") how frequently they had experienced each reaction during the previous week. The intrusion and avoidance in the Horowitz IES scale correspond roughly to the "reexperiencing the trauma" and the "reduced involvement with the external world" categories of the PTSD inventory.

The analyses of data gathered by the IES yielded results that were consistent with those obtained on the PTSD inventory. As can be seen from Figure 5.5, intrusion and avoidance responses were amply endorsed by subjects from both the CSR and non-CSR groups. What one sees in PTSD is the intrusion into consciousness of thoughts and images of the trauma and symptoms of apathy, social distancing, and emotional anesthesia that function (among other things) to ward off the threatening imagery. The PTSD casualty is in a state of continual conflict between these two tendencies. The findings on the IES show that memories of the war continued to force themselves on our casualties, who persisted in investing a large portion of their energy in efforts to ward them off.

Figure 5.5 also shows that soldiers with antecedent CSR showed more distress at all three points of time than comparable controls with no history of CSR. The added pressure the CSR casualties suffered was reflected in both more intrusion and more avoidance. Moreover, as with the number of PTSD symptoms, the number of intrusion and avoidance responses (especially intrusion) also declined over the 3 years of the study, with the most significant decline in the CSR group.

Furthermore, the differential trends in the relative salience of intrusion and avoidance in the two groups that were evidenced in their PTSD symptoms profiles are seen even more clearly in the longitudinal data gathered via the IES, which also revealed that time had a differential impact on the balance of intrusion and avoidance in the two study groups. During the first year of the study, intrusive symptoms received

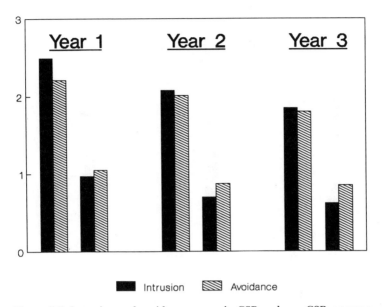

Figure 5.5. Intrusion and avoidance scores in CSR and non-CSR veterans.

significantly higher endorsement than avoidance symptoms in the CSR group. In the second and third years, however, intrusion was not significantly greater than avoidance in this group. There was a greater decline in intrusion than in avoidance in both groups over the 3 years (see Figure 5.5).

The change in the balance of intrusion and avoidance is consistent with the views of Horowitz (1976) and Zilberg, Weiss, and Horowitz (1982), who see PTSD as a vacillating syndrome whose two major components, intrusion and avoidance, tend to oscillate in alternating phases. It is also consistent with the observation by Horowitz et al. (1979) that intrusion is the dominant reaction shortly after the traumatic event, whereas as time passes, working through reduces the intensity of intrusive distress and allows greater utilization of avoidance responses.

Figure 5.6 presents the intrusion and avoidance scores for the two groups of PTSD casualties (those with and without prior CSR) over the 3 years of the study. The view that the process of working through starts with intrusion and continues through avoidance implies that the shift in the balance of intrusion and avoidance symptoms among PTSD casualties without prior CSR is a sign of their progress toward recovery. Titchener (1986) warns that too-early avoidance can inhibit the working through of intrusive memories and thereby may usher in a process of

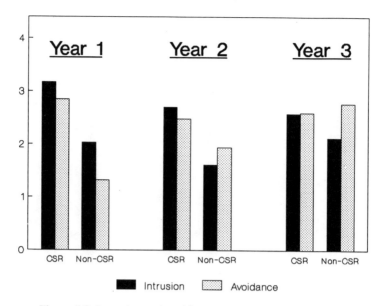

Figure 5.6. Intrusion and avoidance scores in PTSD casualties.

"posttraumatic decline" marked by hypochondriasis and the multi-faceted constriction of feeling and activity (see Chapter 6). It might also be argued, however, that a certain degree of avoidance—when it comes in due time, after the intrusive memories are dealt with—is a sign of mastery. It at least has the virtue of assuaging intense suffering. The fact, seen in Figure 5.6, that such a strong shift in symptoms does not occur among PTSD veterans with antecedent CSR is yet another indication, if Horowitz is correct, that the process of healing is slower in the more traumatized group.

The data gathered via the PTSD inventory and the IES scale thus indicate a decline in PTSD rates and symptoms as well as a reduction of distress pointing to gradual recovery. This amelioration can be attributed to the healing effect of time, treatment, or the natural course of the disorder. The findings are consistent with Horowitz's findings of a major reduction in the distress of bereaved offspring with time. There is evidence indicating that spontaneous recovery from mental disorders occurs among patients waiting their turn for treatment (Endicott & Endicott, 1963) and among Nazi concentration camp survivors (Davidson, 1979). Horowitz, Weiss, and Kaltreider (1984) have suggested that a reduction of cues reminiscent of the traumatic event reduces both intrusion and avoidance tendencies. The passage of time may thus work as a healer by decreasing the salience of the traumatic event.

PSYCHIATRIC SYMPTOMATOLOGY

I noted earlier that the DSM-III's uniform criteria for the diagnosis of PTSD enable objective research with generalizable results. But this very useful standardization is also something of a drawback. To obtain it, the DSM-III task force studied posttraumatic syndromes following a large variety of traumatic events. It examined the symptoms of concentration camp survivors, World War II and Vietnam veterans, ex-prisoners, and survivors of rape and assault and of natural disasters such as earthquakes and floods. The diagnostic criteria arrived at included only the symptoms common to the posttraumatic response for all the events that were considered, whereas the symptoms particular to only one or even several events were listed separately as "frequently associated features." These features, which include anxiety, depression, hostility, and other responses, are not essential to PTSD diagnosis. Their exclusion precludes the ability of any instrument based on DSM-III criteria to provide a detailed or distinctive picture of the posttraumatic reaction to any specific traumatic event.

To obtain a more detailed picture of the long-term psychological sequelae of CSR in the Lebanon war, we employed the revised Symptom Checklist-90 (SCL-90; Derogatis, 1977), which assesses a much wider range of psychiatric symptomatology. The SCL-90 is a self-report measure that inquires about a very large range of psychiatric symptoms during the 2 weeks preceding the assessment. It is composed of 90 self-report items rated on a 5-point distress scale. The scale has nine symptom dimensions: somatization, obsessive-compulsive problems, interpersonal sensitivity, depression, anxiety, hostility, phobic anxiety, paranoid ideation, and psychoticism. The SCL-90 is a well-validated and widely used measure that permits (a) global evaluations of the magnitude and severity of pathology, (b) a detailed psychic profile of nine problem areas, and (c) the comparison of subjects' scores with norms for other groups.

The more profound distress of veterans with antecedent CSR, which was evidenced in both the PTSD inventory and the IES, was again demonstrated in the scores on the SCL-90. CSR soldiers endorsed more symptoms and rated each as more distressing than non-CSR controls at all three points of time. Moreover, this difference remained stable over all 3 years of the study. Similarly, we also found that at all three points of measurement, CSR veterans endorsed more severe symptomatology on all nine subscales than non-CSR controls (see Solomon, 1989c). The differences in subscale endorsement can readily be seen in Figure 5.7. The CSR veterans suffered from more psychiatric symptomatology than the controls on all of the nine SCL-90 subscales, especially those for obsessive-compulsive symptoms, anxiety, depression, and hostility.

The SCL-90 also provides normative scores reflecting the severity of disturbance in various groups. Because of the tremendous investment of effort on the part of IDF mental health officers, only two out of the several hundred CSR casualties of the Lebanon war were hospitalized (both for short periods of time). We thus chose the scores for psychiatric outpatients as a baseline for gauging symptom severity. The comparisons parallel the pattern on the DSM-III and IES: A higher percentage of CSR soldiers had scores exceeding psychiatric outpatient norms than non-CSR soldiers. This difference was found to be significant for each of the SCL-90 global scores and psychiatric subscales at all three times of measurement.

In contrast to the amelioration of distress directly linked to the war (as measured by the PTSD inventory and the IES), however, there was no alleviation of our subjects' general psychiatric distress as measured by the more comprehensive and sensitive criteria of the SCL-90.

As can be seen from Figure 5.7, the curves of both groups remain approximately the same height throughout; so do the percentages of soldiers in each group whose endorsement of symptoms in each category exceeds psychiatric outpatient norms. Time had no effect on the level of their psychiatric symptomatology. The initially severe psychiatric symptomatology among our CSR casualties remained as severe 3 years after their breakdown as it had been only one year after.

This stability contrasts sharply with the decline in the prevalence and severity of PTSD and PTSD-related symptoms in both groups. The contrast tells us that despite the mitigation of their PTSD over time, our CSR veterans had not necessarily gotten well, and that non-CSR veterans also continued to suffer from as much distressing symptomatology as they had the first year after combat. In other words, the results on the SCL-90 indicate that in many areas of the veterans' lives not tapped by the PTSD inventory, the war continued to have an impact. It also appears that the formal PTSD criteria do not encompass the full post-traumatic picture, and that there are still many areas in which the "recovered" CSR casualty still fares much worse than his non-CSR counterpart, even though he may no longer be eligible to be diagnosed as suffering from PTSD.

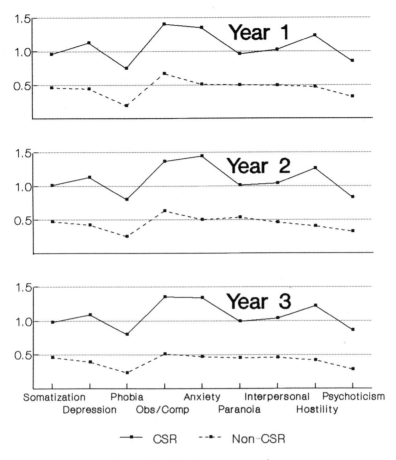

Figure 5.7. SCL-90 symptom scales.

In some cases, though, it did seem that there was a positive shift taking place. Ron said that shortly after the war, he was very sensitive to sounds and color, and his dreams about the war were all very vivid. He added that "today the colors are darker, the sounds less sharp," though he was still more sensitive to sound and color than before the war.

Despite the positive developments (and the IDF's exit from Lebanon, which encouraged and enabled such a process to take place), however, the fact remains that 43% of the CSR group and 10% of the non-CSR group still suffered from PTSD 3 years after their ordeal. For these men, the war did not end when they were removed from the traumatic scene. As Aaron, a veteran who sustained a CSR in both the

1973 Yom Kippur War and the 1982 Lebanon war, recounted the 9 years between the wars:

> What I remember is that those 9 years never seemed like 9 years. The events of the war were engraved in my mind so strongly that the 9 years seemed like only 1 year to me. As if it happened only a year before. Everything is deeply engraved in my mind. Nothing has faded.

Our findings thus indicate that the question of how lasting and profound the wounds of war are does not have an unequivocal answer. A good proportion of our CSR subjects seem to have bounced back. For them the trauma of the war was a relatively transient crisis. For an almost equal proportion of our CSR subjects, however, the trauma was still fixated three years after it occurred. A similar division is found among the PTSD casualties without an antecedent CSR.

Thus, the conception of the stress evaporation and residual stress hypotheses as mutually exclusive is an inadequate account of the facts. For a little over half of our veterans, the stress evaporation theory is more applicable; for a little less than half, the stress residual theory applies more. All in all, for too large a proportion of fighters to ignore, the wounds of war are deep and difficult to remedy. Furthermore, when more sensitive and comprehensive measures were employed, more general and widespread residuals were found, even in men who seemed to have recovered in terms of PTSD.

Overall, data gathered by three separate measures (the PTSD inventory, the IES, and the SCL-90) led to the conclusion that participation in combat has long-lasting psychological sequelae that are especially persistent and distressing in soldiers who sustained a CSR on the battlefield. PTSD is found in more than negligible rates among all our subjects, including combatants who did not break down on the battlefield and did not seek help at IDF clinics. At the same time, during all 3 years of the study, CSR casualties reported (a) higher rates of PTSD and more PTSD symptoms, (b) more intrusion and avoidance, and (c) a much larger amount of general psychiatric symptomatology than non-CSR casualties.

In short, combat stress reaction casualties are no less casualties than the physically injured. They may be in possession of all their limbs, but the fact that their injuries are not as visible does not mean that these men are well and able. They are not. Moreover, they are more seriously injured than men who suffer from PTSD without an antecedent CSR.

6

Posttraumatic Stress Disorder
The Inner Landscape

Posttraumatic stress disorder, as defined by DSM-III, is the most common and conspicuous residue of combat-induced stress. But though the core of PTSD symptoms is similar in casualties of a large range of catastrophic events, clinical studies show both variations within the posttraumatic syndrome and a large variety of symptoms above and beyond those included in classic PTSD. Each catastrophic event leaves its own particular mark, and even different wars have somewhat different psychiatric aftermaths derived from their own distinguishing characteristics. This chapter delineates the characteristic manifestations of posttraumatic disturbances among Israeli veterans of the Lebanon war.

Returning to the profile of PTSD symptoms in Figure 5.3, it becomes evident that whereas in DSM-III all symptoms have the same weight, they are differentially endorsed by the PTSD casualties of the Lebanon war. Some symptoms (i.e., recurrent recollections of the war, sleep difficulties, increased sensitivity to noise, and reduced interest in the outside world) are endorsed by the vast majority of the Lebanon PTSD casualties, whereas other symptoms (i.e., survivor guilt, guilt about conduct in the war, and constricted affect) were reported by very few. Uneven endorsements were similarly made on the IES and the SCL-90. On the IES, although PTSD casualties endorsed both more intrusion and avoidance responses and a higher level of general distress (as measured by the sum of these responses) than noncasualties, their intrusive symptoms were, for the most part, more salient.

On the SCL-90, PTSD casualties reported more psychiatric symptomatology in all nine categories than their unafflicted counterparts:
more somatic problems, paranoia, anxiety, depression, phobic thoughts
and actions, hostility, obsessive-compulsive behavior, and psychotic tendencies. But again, their endorsement of these symptoms is uneven (see
Figure 5.7). The most strongly endorsed symptoms are obsessive-
compulsiveness and anxiety. Although, as a general measure, the
SCL-90 assesses obsessive-compulsiveness in a wide range of behaviors,
the prominence of this trait parallels and supports the salience of intrusion found in the other two measures insofar as the PTSD casualty
experiences intrusion of wartime thoughts and images in an uncontrolled and recurrent manner. The second most endorsed symptoms are
hostility and depression. Third in the order of endorsement come interpersonal sensitivity, paranoia, and somatization. The fourth and least
endorsed symptom group includes phobic anxiety and psychoticism.

Putting these measures together, we see that the clinical picture of
the posttraumatic sequelae among Israeli veterans of the Lebanon war is
characterized by strong intrusion and avoidance tendencies, relatively
little guilt, a great deal of anger and hostility, and considerable anxiety
and depression. It seems that this particular distribution reflects the
specific impact of the Lebanon war. Although our veterans naturally had
a great deal in common with the survivors of other catastrophes, they
also differed in accordance with their unique experience. Each of these
symptoms will be dealt with separately in the course of this chapter.

INTRUSION

In traumatogenic situations like war, people are flooded by an excess of aversive stimuli that are difficult either to block out or integrate.
Thus, after a war ends on the field, it still continues in the men's minds.
Practically all the soldiers I know are to some degree still haunted by
their war experiences, both when they are asleep and off guard and
when they are awake and in more conscious mental control. Even men
without PTSD may wake up from nightmares of exploding tanks or find
themselves ruminating about lost buddies in the middle of a business
meeting.

In the traumatized individual, the defenses used to ward off aversive stimuli were overwhelmed, and he continues to relive them more
frequently and in a more obsessive and uncontrolled manner than the
others. PTSD veterans experience and reexperience their ordeal long
after the war has ended.

Vivid memories of being strafed and shot at, images of bloated and charred bodies, the faces of fallen friends, and sometimes questions (e.g., "Did it have to happen this way?") assail them. Veterans mull over the fate of their friends, the actions of their officers, and their own behavior, especially if they broke down on the battlefield. The smell of dust and explosives sticks in their noses, the sounds of shooting and crashing objects in their ears. The recollections crop up at odd moments—in the middle of a class, in the middle of work, in the middle of a conversation. They throw the veteran back into the war, distract him from his current activity, interfere with his memory and concentration, upset his peace of mind. They keep him from falling asleep at night and often wake him up once he does.

Many of the nightmares and flashbacks represent an accurate reliving of actual experiences. Others contain horrible scenes that reflect the dreamer's fears and anxieties. One common dream is the dream of being dead, of being mistaken for dead, or of being buried alive or mourned as dead. Another recurrent theme is of being stuck (either because one's legs will not move or because conditions on the field prevent passage) and of being unable to protect oneself or to reach a friend who calls for help. Also widespread are dreams of being bombed and shot at, of planes exploding in air, tanks going up in flames, and other scenes of war. Dreams of swollen or burnt corpses and of bodies missing the head or limbs are also common.

One of the more severe forms of intrusion is the feeling of being back in combat, even when one is far from the front. Although it was less marked than other intrusive symptoms, it also received endorsement. One casualty told of driving in the country with his wife and children and suddenly ducking because "they're shooting at us." Another casualty, who finds his war experience even more difficult to put behind him, reported that "scenes come back to me. It takes me a while to realize where I am."

These highly disturbing intrusions of the war may nevertheless provide a certain relief. Van der Kolk (1986) reports that in his study of Vietnam veterans who sought treatment in a VA hospital for PTSD, at least 20% reported that they often saw combat movies or exposed themselves to danger. Van der Kolk contends that reexperiencing traumatic situations provokes the production of endogenous opioids with psychoactive tranquilizing properties that reduce paranoia and feelings of inadequacy and depression. He suggests that this opiate release might account for the sense of calm on reexposure to stress that is reported by many traumatized individuals.

Another view, developed by Freud (1920) and elaborated on by others, suggests that the frequent intrusions of the traumatic experience represent the victim's attempt to gain mastery. By replaying the trauma, with all its attendant terrors, in his mind, the victim attempts to absorb and digest his experience. Freud believed that the reexperiencing of the trauma "decathects" and undoes it. Horowitz (1976) and Rangell (1976), who follow Freud, believe that this type of working through is so essential to the posttraumatic process that they have given what they see as the victim's addiction to the traumatic event the oxymoronic name of "traumatophilia."

In contrast with the above approaches, which have emphasized the physiological and emotional function of intrusive imagery, Meichenbaum and Fitzpatrick (in press) have highlighted the impact of intrusive tendencies on cognitive reintegration. They believe that intrusive imagery may be viewed as an attempt by an individual to make sense of or to construct meaning about a stressful event or to formulate a narrative account of what happened and why.

Something of the working-through process can be seen in a repeated nightmare of Eli, who developed PTSD after participating in intense fighting in the Lebanon war. Among the many harrowing experiences that he underwent, one that cut very deeply was of being shot at by 10-year-old "RPG kids," named after the automatic weapons they carried. What made this experience so terrible for Eli (and other Israeli soldiers who described it) was not only the inherent threat of injury and death but also the moral conflict it evoked in these soldiers, who were trained not to harm children. With the onset of his PTSD, Eli began to have repeated nightmares of RPG kids shooting at him; these were so frightening that he would jump out of bed with the image before his eyes. The nightmare appeared with all sorts of variations, quite frequently at first, then less and less so. Parallel to the decrease in frequency, a process of working through took place in which Eli found "practical solutions" to the problem. In the early versions of the nightmare, he generally stood by helplessly as he was shot at. In later versions, he took cover or cocked his weapon.

In our experience, similar efforts at working through can be seen in the recurrent thoughts and nightmares of other emotionally injured veterans. The process can take a very long time, however, and often it is not completed. Full working through should result not simply in a reduction, but in an end to intrusive imagery. Despite his not-to-be-slighted improvement, 3 years after the war Eli had not yet resolved the dilemma of his encounter with the RPG kids. Many of our injured veterans still had their sleep punctuated by terrifying dreams and their daytime occupations interrupted by unwelcome thoughts and images of combat, which continued to disturb their equilibrium and disrupt their lives.

PSYCHIC NUMBING, AVOIDANCE, AND WITHDRAWAL

Avoidance and psychic numbing constitute the opposite pole of the intrusive reaction to trauma. Psychic numbing is an emotional state, avoidance a set of behaviors. As overlapping responses, they both have the purpose of blunting the pain of the traumatic experience. Psychic numbing often begins during the war itself, when it helps the soldier face the threat of death and the horrors of combat. Many soldiers describe feeling and acting like robots so that they can perform on the battlefield. Called by Egendorf et al. (1981) "a trained inability to feel" and by Smith (1981) "sanction and sealing over," this numbing protects the soldier from what would otherwise be unbearable feelings of horror, fear, and guilt.

Its usefulness in combat can be seen from the account of Ami, who served on the front in both the Yom Kippur and Lebanon wars. Ami, who in his youth had been active in drama circles and an avid filmgoer, went into the Yom Kippur War with "the feeling that I was going to play the part of a soldier in a war movie." This fantasy sustained him throughout the war:

> I accompanied convoys and served as a supplier of gasoline for ammunition, but I felt more or less all right. . . . I said to myself, it's not so terrible. It's like a war movie. They're actors, and I'm just some soldier. I don't have an important role. Naturally, there are all the weapons that are in a war movie. All sorts of helicopters, all sorts of tanks, and there's shooting. . . . [But] basically, I felt that I wasn't there. That is, all I had to do was finish the filming and go home.

When Ami was called up for the Lebanon war, he put his fantasy back into motion. Again, he went into the war with a feeling of unreality. The fantasy this time began with being on a tour:

> The Lebanon war broke out about 2 weeks after I came back from Egypt. And I saw it as a sort of continuation of my tour of the Middle East. That is, I was in Egypt with Galilee Tours; I'll be in Syria now, in Lebanon. I see a pretty view of mountains, pretty little villages, pretty women. And they throw rice and cherries at us.

Soon, however, both the fantasy of the tour and the fantasy of being in a movie that accompanied it were put out of operation by the press of events against which they were meant to defend. Beginning with the third day of the war, Ami encountered massive destruction: soldiers killed; civilians, including children, dead; houses and buildings toppled, with dogs sniffing the corpses underneath. He was exposed to "Katyusha bombs landing like fireworks" and involved in heavy face-to-face fighting. The last straw was a particularly horrific scene in Beirut of stables piled with the corpses of prize Arabian racehorses mingled with corpses of people. The scene filled him with a sense of apocalyptic destruction, and he collapsed: "I went into a state of apathy, and I was not functioning." Ami explains the process as follows:

> [In the Yom Kippur War] I put my defense mechanism into operation and it worked fantastically. I was able to push a button and start it up. . . . In Lebanon, the picture was clearer. In the Yom Kippur War, we didn't fight face-to-face or shoot from a short distance. . . . If I saw a corpse, it was a corpse in the field. But here [in Lebanon] everything was right next to me. . . . And of all things, the thing with the horses broke me . . . A pile of corpses . . . and you see them along with people who were killed. And that's a picture I'd never seen in any movie. . . . I began to sense the reality [that] it's not a movie anymore.

Serviceable though it may sometimes be, however, psychic numbing can readily become dysfunctional. In wartime it can prevent the soldier from absorbing and responding to vital information and, if it is deep enough, can itself constitute a breakdown in functioning.

This is evident in 28-year-old Ze'ev's description of his CSR in the Lebanon war. Serving as a communications aide to his battalion commander, he was often caught in the middle of heavy fighting. In the course of one particularly gruesome incident, a corpse's head rolled onto his foot while he was helping the medics evacuate the many dead and wounded. That incident "broke" him, he reported. For a while, he continued to pick up the wounded in between bouts of vomiting. Then, a gasoline truck was hit and went up in flames, and the driver, whom Ze'ev knew personally, began to scream, "Get me out of here!" Like Ron, whose CSR was described in Chapter 4, Ze'ev wanted to help, but his legs locked and refused to move. He was so afraid that when he heard the "horrible boom" of the truck exploding, he convinced himself that he had been killed:

> I thought I'd been killed and that I only think I'm alive. Because I wanted to run and help, but couldn't. I had the feeling of a person who [has] died and sees everything from the other side. . . . All night there was shelling. But I wasn't afraid of anything anymore. Because I was dead, and a dead man can't be killed.

Once "dead," Ze'ev was no longer afraid of being killed, but, in that state, he was obviously no longer able to defend himself or fight for his buddies.

After the war, psychic numbing can interfere with many aspects of the injured PTSD veteran's personal life. In order not to feel the pain of their experience, PTSD veterans tend to stifle their feelings altogether. As DSM-III points out, "emotional anesthesia" results and is evidenced in constricted affect, estrangement from other people, and an inability to sustain intimate relationships. Very many of the injured veterans in our sample suffered intensely from feelings of alienation and isolation, deriving in part from their not entirely unfounded belief that people who had not undergone it could not understand their experience, in part from their shame and humiliation at having broken down, and in part from their defensive numbing and withdrawal.

Ami's life after the Yom Kippur and Lebanon wars illustrates some of the devastating consequences of the PTSD veteran's persistent psychic numbing. After the Yom Kippur War, which he had weathered with the help of this defense, Ami was unable to turn off his photographer fantasy. Upon his discharge, he took a trip to Europe:

> Abroad too I begin to see myself playing the role of a photographer. I see the Eiffel Tower, and the Seine and London and Amsterdam, and I say to myself that again I'm not really there. That they are only background pictures. In fact, the story keeps going on. I don't have the feeling of reality at all. I begin to feel like on some tour, and it goes on for a long time.

The colorful and wryly self-mocking quality of the description should not obscure the pain of Ami's emotional anesthesia. He experiences everything from a distance, and his ability to enjoy life and to live fully is impaired. The numbing, expressed in distancing and detachment, is intended to preserve his equilibrium, but it costs him a very high price.

One of the marked features of Ami's life after the two wars was the constriction of his social ties. Though he was in the same reserve unit for 10 years, he "didn't have a single friend there." On duty, he joked with the other soldiers, drank coffee, and passed the time with them, but unlike many Israeli men, he studiously avoided socializing with them afterward. Limiting the scope of his involvement, he kept them as "friends for that time and no more." After his CSR in the Lebanon war, his social life was constricted even further. He became "less open, less ready to join in and share."

Especially affected were his intimate ties. Between the wars, he married and fathered two children. After his CSR, he kept himself as distant and remote from his family as from friends. "I sometimes travel in order to cut myself off," he said. "I prefer being by myself to being with people. Even with my family. Because if I'm with other people or even with my family, whom I love very much, I'm afraid they'll bother me, [and] I go off alone. And if I'm alone, no one bothers me."

Although many people seek out quiet and privacy at times, the extent of Ami's need to be by himself was unusually strong. His fear of and aversion to being bothered in any way and his need to keep his family at a distance were staunch barriers to intimate involvement and interaction. Before his injury, Ami was a very different sort of person, one who sought and enjoyed company, and his injury changed this.

Psychic numbing is a definite emotional handicap. The PTSD veteran suffers from a partial but nonetheless limiting disability. The disability can be covered up and is not necessarily visible to casual acquaintances, but it reaches into the depths of his personal life. Between the casualty and other people, there is an invisible barrier, a glass wall.

Avoidance, like psychic numbing, has a functional intent and often dysfunctional outcome. Usually starting after the war, avoidance is intended to ward off the insupportable intrusion of wartime imagery. Although avoidance is a more conscious process than psychic numbing, the PTSD veteran has hardly any more control over one than the other. He is driven by his fears and suffering to avoid any number of stimuli, both external and internal.

External stimuli may include a potentially infinite number of objects and experiences that are associated directly or symbolically with combat. There are PTSD casualties who cannot bring themselves to eat tomatoes or watermelon because the color red makes them think of blood, others who are nauseated by meat because it reminds them of flesh or who will not go near chocolate because it evokes the image of a burning body. Many emotionally injured veterans skip over newspaper accounts of the war, leave the room when the war is mentioned on the TV or radio, or stay away from memorial services for war dead, because all these arouse associations with the war. There are yet others who avoid even less direct associations, such as murder or detective novels that they had once enjoyed and movies featuring war or other forms of aggression. "I go straight into the story, and as I see myself there, all the thoughts come up," one veteran said in explaining his aversion.

Not a few refuse to ride buses for fear of a terrorist attack, and some are afraid to drive their cars lest they come across a dead cat on the road or even a rag, which may remind them of mashed and mutilated bodies. The more seriously impaired are afraid of the dark and will not leave their homes at night for fear of being attacked by terrorists or by some stray bomb or shell. Men who had been trapped in burning tanks may become phobic about closed places: One of our subjects refused to explore a cave on an organized outing; another would not go abroad because he could not bring himself to get into an airplane; yet another regularly walked up and down the four flights of stairs to his apartment so that he would not have to get into an elevator. Almost all of our PTSD casualties were afraid of weapons and reserve duty, and not a few, even those who did not request a military discharge, employed a battery of evasion tactics.

Few, if any, of these phobic reactions were present in our subjects before their injury. With the exception of military stimuli, most of the stimuli that the casualties avoided were neutral or benign. Eating tomatoes has never harmed anyone; in most cases, neither has watching the news on TV. There is a generalization of the threat, so that anything can potentially symbolize the trauma and frighten the traumatized veteran.

The internal stimuli that our casualties avoid are thoughts and recollections of the war. Most try not to think about it and to shove unwelcome thoughts forcibly out of their minds. Many find some avenue of escape; frenetic work is one such avenue. Dror, an energetic and forceful personality who had served as a medic in the Yom Kippur and Lebanon wars, tells how after sustaining a CSR in the latter, he threw himself into his work as a self-employed carpenter so as to avert the pain of memory:

> For me, work is health. I work at an astonishing pace. People who know me say: "When Dror starts to work, you can't stop him." Work is my relaxation. Even when I get home at 11 at night . . . I say to myself, "Dror, go to work." . . . Work is my salvation. Maybe it's not so good, I don't know. The truth is that only after work do the sadness and loneliness come. When you're at work, the machines work, the telephones ring, clients phone up. I don't think about anything. And then when the let up comes—night, quiet—it's like the song by Dani Sanderson [a popular Israeli singer], "When the stars shine, the jackals wail." I begin to let out all the pain, all the bitterness, and all the frustration . . . but during the day, I don't think about it. Because during the day, I have laborers at my side, and there are telephone calls, and every second there's someone to ask, "Where's my closet? When are you going to finish my table?" I can't think. The problem is that when the stars come out, you're by yourself.

Working hard and well in enjoyed labor often brings the benefits of economic well-being and pride in achievement, and more will be said about this in Chapter 7; what is notable here is the driving impulse to escape unbearable pain, bitterness, frustration, sadness, and loneliness. Other injured veterans seek out different escapes, such as music or, in a relatively few cases in Israel, drugs. The pressure to keep disturbing thoughts and feelings at a distance also affects the PTSD veteran's sleep. The problems that many afflicted veterans have in falling asleep sometimes derive from their inability to stem intrusive thoughts; at other times, the difficulties reflect their efforts to avoid dreaming about the war.

Traumatized individuals may gain some sense of subjective control by shunning all situations and emotions related to or evocative of the trauma. But in fact, as Krystal (1968) emphasizes with regard to traumatized Holocaust survivors, there is a surrender of the individual to his helplessness in the face of external danger and threat. In blocking the feeling of pain, the personality is narrowed and constricted to the point of "emotional death." As one very unfortunate casualty put it: "I don't care about anything. I don't feel anything about anything. As if the feelings I had dried up or evaporated. Now I simply exist until I die."

The end result of avoidance is the radical reduction of both feeling and activity. The casualty encapsulates himself in a double shield: one between himself and the world, the other between himself and his feelings. The long list of mental prohibitions, the activities not engaged in, and the thoughts pushed out of mind make it impossible for PTSD casualties to enjoy life or to live fully.

The dominant quality of the posttraumatic disorder is determined by the relative weights of the intrusive and avoidant tendencies. Some casualties are more troubled by dreams and nightmares, whereas in others psychic numbing, withdrawal, and avoidance are dominant. What is clear is that both intrusion and avoidance are maladaptive reactions once the traumatic events of war are over. For the PTSD casualty who oscillates between these poles, the war is still going on, not outside on the battlefield but in his distressed soul.

GUILT

In planning our PTSD inventory, we consulted with numerous IDF clinicians who had treated PTSD casualties of previous Israeli conflicts. The one piece of advice they all gave us was to look out for guilt feelings, which most of them found featured prominently in the PTSD of the veterans of the Yom Kippur War. On the basis of their advice, we divided the guilt component in the DSM-III into two: guilt over wartime conduct and survival guilt, both of which have been widely observed among victims of other catastrophes.

Guilt over wartime conduct, according to Hendin and Pollinger-Haas (1984), is a key component of the PTSD of many Vietnam veterans. As these authors explain it, the guerrilla combat in Vietnam, with ununiformed "civilians" often participating in ambushes, fostered the rampant feeling that the whole country was the enemy and blurred the distinction between combatants and noncombatants. The results included the killing of women, children, and the elderly, as well as the acting out of diffuse aggression and the commission of atrocities. More than one-third of the veterans Hendin and Pollinger-Haas interviewed had profound guilt feelings over actions such as rape, mutilating enemy dead, or killing enemy prisoners; some reported guilt over "fragging"— the killing of their own officers. Even when killing is necessitated by the circumstances, Hendin and Pollinger-Haas suggest, it may leave the soldier feeling profoundly guilty.

Survivor guilt is the guilt that one may feel in outliving someone either physically or emotionally close. It has been noted among survivors of various types of catastrophes. It has been reported among survivors of the Buffalo Creek flood, where 127 people in a small Appalachian town were drowned (Erikson, 1976; Titchener & Kapp, 1976). Robert J. Lifton (1968) claims that such guilt was central to the survivors of the atomic bombing of Hiroshima and Nagasaki. Niederland (1968) and Sigal, Silver, Rakoff, and Ellin (1973) found it to be widespread among Jewish concentration camp survivors.

To our surprise, neither guilt over wartime conduct nor survival guilt were highly endorsed by our subjects. A number of subjects even criticized us for posing the questions, maintaining that they had acted as well as soldiers possibly could in a war. Thinking that perhaps a questionnaire is not a sensitive enough instrument to assess something as complex as guilt feelings, I checked the clinical reports; the clinicians who interviewed about 180 of our subjects reported a similar paucity of guilt.

It thus seems that guilt—of any kind—is indeed not a major component of the PTSD following the Lebanon war. This intriguing finding can be accounted for by numerous features of that war and of the social context in which it was fought.

Guilt about Wartime Conduct

Guilt about wartime conduct may be rare among our soldiers because they have little to feel guilty about. Unlike their Vietnam counterparts discussed by Pollinger-Haas and others, no IDF soldiers participated in the massacre of civilians or in the murder of helpless prisoners or their own officers (Glover, 1984; Haley, 1974). Few, if any, were involved in the mutilation of enemy dead, looting, sexual abuse, or other barbarities reported in other wars. On the contrary, Israeli soldiers, including many of our PTSD casualties, went to inordinate lengths to avoid harming civilians.

One of the key concepts of military training and indoctrination in the Israeli army is the concept of "purity of arms," which refers to the preservation of humane conduct in war. It entails refraining from unnecessary bloodshed and avoiding harming civilians in general and women and children in particular. It also implies avoiding damage to sacred buildings, treating POWs in a humane way, and refraining entirely from looting, rape, and other atrocities (Pa'il, 1970). Expounded by the medieval Jewish philosopher Maimonides, the ideal of purity of arms is deeply ingrained in Jewish religious thinking and secular values. In Israel, it is a widely accepted cultural norm and an inherent part of every soldier's basic training.

Lest lapses occur in the heat of combat, the IDF maintains strict vigilance. Throughout the Lebanon war, it constantly issued detailed directives for avoiding harm to innocent civilians. Something of the flavor and scope of these directives can be gleaned from the following description by a senior combat officer, taken from the daily Hebrew newspaper *Yediot Aharonot:*

> I can [state] unequivocally that we had a large number of casualties caused directly by the instructions not to harm civilians, women and children. Usually when you wage a battle, you first neutralize the target with artillery fire in order to minimize your casualties. Here in Lebanon we are forbidden to do that for fear of hurting civilians. Every target was carefully checked before being attacked. We dropped leaflets, announced it on the loudspeaker. We certainly could have advanced more quickly, captured more terrorists and most importantly saved lots of our own lives [had we not exercised these cautions]. The terrorists knew all of this and deliberately mingled with civilians; and there was nothing we could do because of the strict instructions . . . not to open fire unless we were absolutely certain that terrorists were there. . . . Where is the red line by which a commander must decide what is more important—protecting the lives of his own troops or first considering the lives of civilians, some of whom support the terrorists? It seems to me that Israeli commanders have gone far beyond the red line in favor of protecting civilian lives even at the expense of the lives of their own soldiers. (Gal, 1986)

As can be seen from this account, purity of arms was insisted upon even at the expense of Israeli lives. The directives the commander describes (as well as similar measures for the same purpose) were widely enforced, and humane behavior was maintained in Lebanon. Even the foreign media, which covered events with Argus's eyes, did not find the kind of violation of human rights common in other wars. In Israel, the Kahan Commission, formed as a result of public pressure, was charged with the task of investigating the massacre in the Sabra and Shatilla refugee camps in Lebanon, which were under Israeli control at the time. Although the commission was critical of many aspects of the war, it reported that despite the fact that atrocities were daily occurrences in Lebanon, Israeli soldiers maintained the purity of arms (Kahan, Barak, & Efrat, 1983).

Soldiers who drop warning leaflets and refrain from opening fire in a war where armed terrorists deliberately mingle with civilian popula-tions have little to feel guilty about. On the contrary, the natural reaction is anger. As one military reporter expressed it, "They have turned the army into a punching bag" (Amikam, 1983).

The reader may recall that guilt over wartime functioning is a major component of CSR (Chapter 3). Its differential importance in CSR and PTSD may reflect differences in the kinds of performance guilt that were actually assessed in the two groups. Although CSR casualties felt guilty about their breakdowns, PTSD casualties without a battlefield CSR had no cause to feel guilty on that account. Their presence in this sample may have influenced our findings here, whereas the PTSD casu-alties as a whole had no cause for feeling guilt over inhumane conduct in which they did not engage. Our findings suggest that combat-related guilt is a more complex phenomenon than we initially expected, and that measures used in future should try to take into account more of its possible components.

Survivor Guilt

The paucity of survival guilt, though initially surprising, is actually not inconsistent with earlier findings of its presence in similar life-loss situations. As Lifton (1968) explained, survivor guilt is strongly associ-ated with proximity: the closer the survivor is to the person who has died, the stronger the guilt; the more distant the relationship, the less intense the guilt. Lifton was referring to physical as well as emotional closeness. But Hendin and Pollinger-Haas, who found comparatively little survivor guilt among the Vietnam PTSD veterans they interviewed, emphasize the role of the emotional relationship, indicating that combat soldiers vary in how close they feel to their comrades.

In situations where survivor guilt has been highly prevalent, the deaths were massive and tended to include large numbers of close rela-tives and friends. In both the atomic bomb attacks in Japan and the Nazi Holocaust in Europe, whole communities were decimated, and few fami-lies remained intact. Much the same holds true for the Buffalo Creek flood. In the Yom Kippur War, the determining factor may have been the number of losses. There were cases where almost complete battalions were wiped out, with the exception of only one or two survivors. In contrast to these catastrophes, the losses in the Lebanon war were rela-tively moderate and, on the whole, did not include the soldiers' families.

Yet another possible explanation for the low endorsement of surviv-al guilt may have to do with the ongoing nature of the threat in Israel. As repeatedly pointed out, Israeli soldiers can rarely be sure that any current war is their last. Their survival is thus always contingent. Some soldiers have expressed the almost superstitious feeling that every war they survive increases their risk of being killed or maimed in the next— in short, the sense that their luck is bound to run out. It may be that when survival is so tentative, guilt is less readily developed. Ami, whom we quoted above about his psychic numbing, makes this somewhat cynical suggestion as he tells the following story in response to the interviewer's question about feeling guilty for surviving:

> After the Yom Kippur War, I took a trip abroad. The day before the flight, the mother of a friend of mine who had been killed said to me, "What, are you alive?" and I said to her, "Yes, I'm alive and I'm going abroad." And she said to me, "Great. Are you emigrating too?" [a bitterly sarcastic and critical remark] I said, "No, I'm only going to see what the rest of the world looks like. Because there can be another war and I won't get the chance." That is, I don't feel guilty that I'm alive.

Along different lines, our subjects' low endorsement of guilt may be related to their high endorsement of anger. As is well known, guilt may be interpreted as the internalization of anger. The issue of anger and hostility will be treated more thoroughly in the next section. Here, the point to be made is that our subjects' experiences were different from those of at least two of the groups in which survivor guilt was found to be salient. Unlike both Japanese atomic bomb victims and Jewish concentration camp inmates, our subjects were permitted to express their anger freely. The helpless survivors of Hiroshima and Nagasaki could do little to harm the Americans who had dropped the atom bomb. In the concentration camps, any form of overt aggression was life threatening, and many of the victims reacted to their persecution with overwhelming fear and a profound sense of helplessness. In both groups, the blocked anger was internalized and took the form of guilt. Israeli veterans of the Lebanon war did not have to make such a conversion, because both the nature of the traumatic event they underwent (i.e., open warfare) and the norms and values of Israeli society allowed them to give ample vent to the whole gamut of angry feelings from irritation to rage.

The relatively rare cases of survivor guilt reported by our subjects tended to occur among soldiers who felt that they were somehow responsible for the death of one or more of their buddies. Guilt was reported by men who felt that their survival had been paid for by another soldier's death, or that if they themselves had not survived, others more deserving might have. Such feelings tended to follow upon situations where the surviving soldier had failed to heed cries of help or where he had changed assignments or roles with someone who was subsequently killed. "It haunts me till this very day," says Ron of his hiding behind a rock in an ambush in Lebanon. "Fear, shame, guilt. Because guys were wounded in that ambush and I ask myself: if I'd been functioning, maybe . . . maybe I would have been in their place." In some cases, the veteran's guilt feelings are less conscious and are expressed in his dreams. Some of the commonplace dreams of being dead or injured probably reflect guilt as well as fear.

ANGER AND HOSTILITY

Aggression is a sine qua non of combat, the means by which the soldier survives and the military attains its aims. Soldiers are trained and encouraged to direct their aggression against the enemy. Through experience, they learn that aggression can be efficacious and, in some cases, pleasurable. After a war, veterans may continue to externalize their aggression, even though the need for it has passed.

In Lebanon, the expression of anger received additional legitimization. The Lebanon war was the first Israeli war whose justification was seriously disputed in the country. Criticism of the war's motives and methods and of the politicians who started it was rampant from the very beginning. The war was debated in the Knesset (Israel's parliament) and argued against by significant portions of the military establishment. In an unprecedented act, a high-ranking career officer, Colonel Eli Geva, even resigned his commission as a statement of protest. It is safe to say that about half the general public was opposed to the crossing of the Litani river in Lebanon and to the movement of Israeli troops northward. The soldiers who fought the war, many of them reservists, were as involved in the debate as anyone else. And because the war was in such dispute, those who opposed it could voice their indignation freely.

Moreover, Israeli culture is notably tolerant to expressions of aggression that more temperate cultures frown upon. It values straightforwardness and is egalitarian in its disregard of position and rank. Individuals are thus permitted a good deal of leeway in what they may say, how, and to whom, and friction in public life is open. There is little censure of shouting and pushing in public, and the safety campaign the authorities have been waging against aggressive driving has fallen on an unreceptive audience.

Together, the nature of combat, the disagreement over the Lebanon war, and the tolerance of Israeli culture for aggression all made it possible for the traumatized soldier to acknowledge and express hostility. This was evident in the PTSD inventory, where our respondents indicated that they didn't inhibit the externalization of anger; in the SCL-90, where our CSR casualties significantly exceeded psychiatric outpatient

norms for hostility; and in the clinical interviews, where they spoke of
their anger and hostility freely and movingly.

None of the veterans in our sample had a known precombat history
of antisocial behavior. Like the intrusion of wartime imagery and the
struggle to avoid reminders of the war, the hostility of our PTSD veterans represented the extension of the war into their postwar lives. In their
report of intense and sometimes explosive rage, they were quite similar
to traumatized Vietnam combat veterans (Figley, 1978a). Hendin and
Pollinger-Haas (1984) suggest that PTSD veterans divide between depressed individuals who remain "tied to the war through their bond with
those who died in combat" (p. 12) and "those with a paranoid adaptation
who remain tied to the war in how they treat civilian life as an extension
of combat" (p. 12). PTSD veterans who regard civilian life as an extension of combat are likely to cope with it in the same way—by striking out.

Moreover, during war, aggression is channeled against the enemy as
not only an obvious means of survival but also a way of coping with fear.
It is quite likely that PTSD veterans, especially those with an antecedent
CSR, were more afraid (or more in touch with their fears) than other
soldiers on the front. After the war, these PTSD casualties may generalize the aggression they had used to dampen their terror on the battlefield to the many other situations that evoke anxiety.

Similarities notwithstanding, the Lebanon PTSD casualties seemed
to be less hostile than their Vietnam counterparts. Our casualties were
irritable, on edge, impatient with their wives and children, readily an-
noyed with friends and coworkers. They lost their tempers over
trivialities—a child's noise or bad appetite, a glass of spilled milk, a
chance remark, an inconvenient interruption and so forth—that they
had previously taken in stride. The feeling of being just on this side of an
explosion was common. Numerous casualties described themselves as "a
smoldering volcano." Yet, though a great many of them reported aggressive urges, few reported overt expression of those urges. In contrast to
their Vietnam counterparts, none of the known Lebanon PTSD casualties were involved in truly destructive acts. There were no murders or
assaults causing grave bodily harm.

Roughly, the aggression our PTSD veterans reported can be divided
into three levels. The vast majority were unacted-on *fantasies of violence.*
For example, Jacob, a medic in the Lebanon war, recounted the following fantasy he had at home one day several months after the formal
cease-fire, while IDF soldiers were still in Lebanon. Going to do some
errands in town, he became enraged when he passed men and women
sitting in cafés, enjoying the fine weather and clear blue sky. "How dare
they enjoy themselves like that when people in Lebanon are being

killed?" he fumed, feeling a tremendous desire to hurt them. "If I had a submachine gun, I would powder them with bullets."

The next category consists of various degrees of *near-violence* that is curbed just in the nick of time either by the veteran himself or by someone in the vicinity. Some of the more gruesome examples we had were directed toward Arabs. Dror, the carpenter quoted above concerning how he threw himself into his work so as to avoid intrusive thoughts of the war, placed an Arab laborer in his carpentry shop on an electric saw and turned on the switch, fortunately to be forcibly restrained by three other workers who came to the poor man's rescue. Ron, who owned a silver goods and jewelry plant, threw an anvil at an Arab laborer after hearing on the news that Israel had released a thousand imprisoned terrorists in exchange for hostages; luckily, the anvil missed its mark, too. Yossi, who fought in bloody battles in both the Yom Kippur and Lebanon wars, also became infuriated by a security item on the evening news, took a Kalashnikov rifle and ammunition, put them on, and went out to hitchhike to the largely Arab town of Nazareth. "It was fortunate that I never got there," he said. "Some of my friends saw me and wouldn't let me go."

Both the fantasies of violence and the near-violence generally left their "perpetrators" extremely shaken up. On the whole, the men were not violent before the war and were taken aback and frightened by the force of their rage and the damage they could do. They were grateful when their acting out was checked, and it is probable that they had a part in seeing to it that it was checked (by blowing up when there were people around to stop them, or by missing their mark).

Many of them worked out ways of controlling their impulses by themselves, mostly by leaving the scene of the irritation—that is by avoidance. Yossi recalls becoming so angry when his small son spilled some milk that he almost punched him, but he ran out of the house instead. Another veteran, a CSR casualty of the Yom Kippur War, used to beat his wife; they both decided that when they noticed the signs coming, she would say "Out!" and he would go elsewhere to cool off. The tactic of averting physical damage by withdrawing has the disadvantages of leaving the already alienated casualty even more alienated and isolated and of preventing the working out of family problems.

In contrast to a great many descriptions of near-violence, there were only isolated instances in the third category of *actual physical violence,* most of them in the family. Wives and children were the targets most readily at hand. Coworkers were also sometimes victims; more rarely, strangers were, too. For example, Yossi told of beating up some guys who were blocking the road. Even here, though, the violence was monitored in that it usually consisted of hitting or punching with bare hands or throwing and smashing things. Several veterans describe crushing table glasses with their bare hands, and verbal abuse (shouting and cursing) was rampant, but we had no reports of weapons being used. The ultimate aim seems to have been the relief of pent-up fury rather than paranoid self-defense, as was reported among the more severely disturbed Vietnam PTSD casualties (Hendin & Pollinger-Haas, 1984). As one veteran (Aaron) put it, "I would blow up like a volcano. Not necessarily when anything happened. The main thing was to blow up."

There is evidence, too, that some veterans learned to exploit their aggressions to attain control over the environment. Ron, for example, who threw the anvil at the Arab worker, told that after his second CSR (the first was in Yom Kippur, the second in Lebanon), "everything made me mad" and recounted a whole series of violent outbursts: he cursed and shouted, flung dishes at his mother, threw a neighbor across the room and sent her crashing into the refrigerator, smashed thousands of dollars worth of industrial equipment in his plant, grabbed and shook up workers so that four men left his employ, and beat his wife and children. Many of the outbursts were sudden and unpremeditated, and they took him as much by surprise as they did his victims. They also frightened him. At the same time, he turned his violence to his own use:

> If I were talking with you and you didn't answer the way I wanted you to, I could grab you and break your arm. I knew I was strong and took advantage of it. . . . I exploited my strength in order to shut people up. For example, right after the war, I slept with my wife's sister in order to prove to myself that I could perform. . . . She was the easiest prey, and she was nearby and I had a lot of influence on her. . . . Afterward I threatened her. I slapped her, sent her flying onto the bed, and warned her that worse would happen if she ever told. I flex my muscles a lot.

Although there were some extreme cases of violent behavior such as this, the large majority of our subjects did not display aggression to this degree. The relative control of their anger that our casualties showed is in keeping with their relatively low endorsement of paranoid ideation. Although the seeds of paranoid ideation were found in our sample, they were comparatively minor. In contrast to their Vietnam counterparts, many of whom met criteria for paranoid disturbances, our soldiers on the whole ranked much lower than the norms for psychiatric outpatients and did not meet those criteria.

Perhaps this is because the Lebanon war was shorter and less brutal than Vietnam, and also because IDF units were organized so as to reinforce group cohesion and trust. American soldiers in Vietnam were rotated in units with men they did not know, or they were left to fight in the jungle by themselves. Most Israeli soldiers were in organic units.

They knew their buddies and officers, had trained with them, and in many cases had fought with them in previous wars. Problems like fragging and racial tension were practically nonexistent. Moreover, unlike their American counterparts, Israeli soldiers were not blamed for fighting a dirty war. Hendin and Pollinger-Haas (1984) suggest that what they term "the paranoid adaptation" of Vietnam veterans is characterized by a denial of guilt and a refusal to accept blame or responsibility for their actions in combat. Israeli soldiers did not need that adaptation.

DEPRESSION

Depression is usually associated with loss: the death of a loved one, the termination of a close relationship, a blow to core values, or a loss of parts of the self. War, by its very nature, causes terrible destruction in which everyone loses, the victors as well as the soldiers on the defeated side. Victors and vanquished alike inevitably take part in and witness the loss of life and the large-scale destruction of nature and manmade goods. The loss of friends and loved ones and of limbs and body functions are the most obvious losses combatants face, but there are many less tangible losses as well. Most men who go to war come out very much less innocent, less naive, less optimistic than they were when they had gone in. The belief in a just world, faith in one's fellow man, and the comforting anchor of peacetime morality are all difficult to maintain under the haphazard barrage of enemy fire. Lifton (1976) points out that traumatic experiences cause a complete breakdown of the symbol system by which the person has lived.

It is thus not surprising that many soldiers report depressive responses both during and after combat. In fact, in our population, depressive reactions seemed to be a universal response in the 6 to 12 months following the war. Identified psychiatric casualties as well as veterans with no diagnosable disorder told of feeling sad, grieved, and low as they mourned the deaths of army buddies and officers, friends, or close relatives—losses that almost every combatant experiences.

The extent of the depressive reaction related to mourning is conveyed in the account that a young combat veteran gave of himself and his kibbutz after the Yom Kippur War, in which he did not sustain a CSR or PTSD:

> I was constantly bothered by thoughts of what happened to the others. What happened to the guys here on the kibbutz—guys who were killed, classmates who were killed? Then the stories began to come out. One was killed, another missing in action. It's hard, hard, hard. It had an effect on me. I remember about half a year,

maybe a year, all of us in my age group on the kibbutz were very sad. It was a feeling
of mourning all the time. . . . We were really sad for about a year. I remember about
a half a year after we were discharged, it was Purim [a holiday of masquerade and
abandon]. We didn't celebrate. Nothing. No one on the kibbutz my age felt like
doing anything. Socially, it was really depressing.

The kibbutz, Israel's prototypical communal agricultural settlement, is
by definition a small, close-knit community in which many of the members have grown up together and most of those who have not have
known each other for years, working together in the same concern,
eating together in the same communal dining room, socializing in the
same clubhouse. After a war, they also grieve together.

Such postwar grief, however, is also palpable in Israel's towns and
cities. It stems from a shared sense of loss that extends beyond personal
friends and family to all the fallen. The tiny size of the Jewish population and the even tinier size of the Jewish population in Israel give
weight and resonance to each and every war death, to the extent that in
the months after a war one may find a great many Israelis suffering
from subclinical depression.

In PTSD soldiers, this depressive reaction can be intensified to a
painfully high pitch, sapping not only the desire to socialize or revel but
also the very marrow of life. The extremity of the depression described
by Avi after his CSR in the Lebanon war was not unusual in our worst-hit
PTSD casualties:

After the war there was a period where I really didn't like life. I told myself: What
do I care? I might as well die. I'll get rid of all my suffering. . . . There was a period
that I couldn't laugh. Two months, a year, two years, I couldn't. I couldn't even
smile. There was no joy in my heart. . . . Sometimes, I would pick up [from work]
and go to the beach, and cry and cry. . . . I was on the verge of despair. I wanted to
kill myself. It wasn't living. I had all kinds of ideas in my head how to finish it off.

This, in contrast to the sadness and grief described by the *kibbutznik,* is a
full-blown depression, all-encompassing and incapacitating. The uncontrolled bouts of crying that Avi recounts, the utter absence of positive
feeling, and the near-total despair and suicidal ideation corroborate our
statistical finding of the greater severity and duration of depression in
PTSD soldiers than others.

Although DSM-III names depression only as an associated feature
and not as a necessary condition for the diagnosis of PTSD, the literature indicates that depressive responses are a quite common psychological aftereffect of catastrophic events. Indeed, our finding that 1, 2, and 3
years after the Lebanon war, CSR casualties had depressive reactions
exceeding outpatient psychiatric norms by 26%, 28%, and 23%, respectively, is consistent with observations of survivors of other catastrophes.

Survivors of the Nazi concentration camps (Eitinger, 1969; Niederland, 1968), of the atomic bombs dropped on Hiroshima and Nagasaki (Lifton, 1968), of the Vietnam War (Helzer et al., 1979; Hendin & Pollinger-Haas, 1984; Nace, Meyers, & O'Brien, 1977), and of the lesser disaster of the Buffalo Creek flood (Titchener & Kapp, 1976) all tended to suffer from serious depression.

The depression of our casualties can be traced to two main sources. One is the same as the major source of depression among veterans, whether psychiatric casualties or not: the encounter with death. This is the most obvious loss of war, and it is made all the more terrible by the accidental, meaningless, massive, and grotesque way that death strikes on the battlefield. Soldiers do not die neat, clean deaths. Limbs are severed, body parts mutilated, and flesh burnt beyond recognition. There is no moral order or meaning in who is struck down and who survives. Bombs, shells, and bullets are blind, hitting one and sparing another through impersonal chance. Obviously, the meaning a soldier assigns to the deaths he encounters will vary with his relation to the victim. The death of a close, significant person will be more painful than the death of a stranger. The death of an officer has special significance. The deaths of fellow fighters whom the surviving soldier does not know personally, of civilians caught in the fire, or even of enemy troops, however, can all be traumatic.

The descriptions of our soldiers reveal that the seeds of their depressive reactions are often planted when they witness absurd losses and destruction. As the reader may recall, Ami, who could not shake off the psychic numbing he had tried to use as a defense, broke down when he saw stables piled with the corpses of dead Arabian horses. Another soldier broke down subsequent to driving over attacking Egyptian infantry in the Yom Kippur War. The death of a young person is generally more upsetting than the death of the aged, and many of our seasoned soldiers told of feeling terrible at the sight of 18- and 19-year-old conscripts being killed. More than a few soldiers reported feeling surrounded by death. This feeling was not uncommon following a battle with heavy troop losses. It was particularly widespread among soldiers whose job it was to care for the wounded and among those who collected the corpses and body parts and brought them to burial. Medics, ambulance drivers, and corpse bearers who are in close and constant contact with the dead (often burnt or mutilated dead) are, in fact, especially prone to combat stress reactions and posttraumatic responses.

Most of these themes come together in the depressive reaction of Moshe, a fireman in civilian life and a seasoned veteran who participated in all of Israel's wars since the Six-Day War in 1967. Moshe broke down in an uncontrollable fit of crying in the Lebanon war, in which he was stationed with the medical corps. In the interview with our clinician, he cried as he told the story:

> In Lebanon I collected the dead. It broke me. They were kids, so many dead kids. It was awful. I can't describe it. We loaded the corpses. It was hard. Mutilated corpses. I'd be lying if I told you that I actually saw the corpses. I didn't come close enough. I only saw them being put into large plastic bags, piled on stretchers, and loaded on the trucks. It was so painful that I couldn't take it. I felt that I was breaking down. . . . I couldn't sleep at night. . . . I couldn't eat. During the daytime we went on gathering the injured. There were over 100 wounded, and more than 30 fatalities. Many of them were burnt beyond recognition. . . . They brought a kid in, a young soldier with a bullet in his lung, and I had to watch him drop dead in my arms. For me this was the end. Kids 18 years old.
>
> We got an order to evacuate the dead, who had been placed around 200 meters away. There were loads of them, and they had been lying there for a long time. The smell of corpses was something terrible, indescribable. I went to the battalion commander and I told him, I really can't . . . I have to talk to someone. I couldn't go on. I was finished. They brought a mental health officer, and then I really burst into tears. I cried and I cried. I cried so much that he wanted to evacuate me. . . . I cried and cried and couldn't stop. When I came home after the war, I cried all the time. I couldn't stop. I started crying in the entrance hall. I cried when I saw my wife and the kids. . . . My wife wanted to know what had happened during the war. Sometimes I would tell her and then I would burst into tears.

Not every soldier sees as many mutilated and distorted corpses as Moshe saw, or has a younger soldier expire in his arms. Many do, however, and not all of them become clinically depressed. What distinguishes the depressed PTSD casualty from the others is that he has internalized the deaths he encountered. There is no distance between Moshe and the boy who died in his arms; that dying boy, the flesh in the linen bags, the distorted and burnt bodies he saw, and the stench of rotting corpses have all become part of his inner landscape.

This internalization of the reality of death in all its senselessness and grotesqueness gives rise to the feeling in depression of "What's it all for?"—to the widespread loss of purpose and inability to find meaning in life among PTSD veterans. In the more seriously affected soldiers, it leads to an identification with death. This identification often shows itself in images and dreams of the dead that the soldier finds difficult to throw off, as well as in a pervasive inner sense that one is not quite alive oneself.

Some of the PTSD casualty's very common dreams of being dead are not only expressions of anxiety but symbolic enactments of that state. This can be seen in a repeated nightmare reported by a veteran who had lost his good friend and next-door neighbor in the Lebanon war. Circumstances had it that when the war broke out, Shimon, as this man was called, had met that friend in the elevator and handed him his draft notice. Needless to say, this act later provoked feelings of guilt that tied the living man to the dead one and made him feel unworthy of life. Then a mix-up, in which the dead man was identified as Shimon, added to the latter's identification with his dead friend and neighbor. In his recurrent nightmare, Shimon repeatedly saw the memorial album that had been issued in honor of his friend—only in the dream the album contained Shimon's photograph, which, as he dreamt, gradually faded and disappeared. In his dream, Shimon was mourning what he experienced as his own death.

Lifton (1968) has termed this phenomenon the "death imprint" and has noted that people who are afflicted by it tend to live as though they are dead, denying themselves pleasure and curtailing their own vitality. According to Lifton, the emotional anesthesia (discussed above) that is often a part of a more general depressive reaction functions not only to keep the pain of the war at arm's length, but also to keep the veteran in a state resembling death.

The other source of depression is relevant mainly to CSR casualties and helps to explain why their depression is usually more severe than that of veterans with PTSD alone. This is the terrible blow to one's self-esteem, masculine pride, and sense of social belonging that generally follows upon a CSR. Freud (1920) has pointed out that the loss behind depression is not necessarily the loss of an external object. It can be any number of intangibles, not least of which are the values and positive worldview that readily fall victim to the brutalities of combat. Brown and Harris (1978) suggest that what is important about a loss in the genesis of depression is "that it leads to an inability to hold good thoughts about ourselves" (p. 233).

That inability to hold good thoughts about oneself is one of the major consequences of a CSR. As we have seen, CSR entails strong feelings of helplessness, which readily develop into feelings of hopelessness and incompetence. The CSR casualty almost inevitably loses his sense of mastery and, with that, much of his self-esteem. In Israel, where social acceptance and masculine identity are strongly linked to combat performance, this consequence of CSR may be particularly pronounced. The following account by an officer in the Six-Day War of the attitude of his fellow kibbutz members to the returning soldiers conveys something of the centrality of military functioning in the value system that most of our soldiers have internalized:

> Combat is the supreme test. The veteran who performed well in combat is almost a god. He is esteemed beyond all proportion. The veteran who performed poorly is devalued in a similarly exaggerated way. As far as social standing is concerned, he's

finished. . . . There are no compromises. Men who fall short on the battlefield are considered inferior, surely in their own eyes and in the eyes of their peers. (Spira, 1968)

This officer was talking about run-of-the-mill poor soldiering, not about a failure as total as a CSR. One can imagine how much worse the CSR soldier, who broke down in a vital task when others were counting on him, feels. The failure to live up to both others' and his own expectations can leave the CSR soldier bereft of all positive estimation of himself, certainly as far as his military ability is concerned, but also in many aspects of his civilian life.

Depression in the CSR veteran may thus reflect his mourning for the loss of his positive identity. "The last thing I expected was to feel so pressured and exposed," one veteran explained his depression after his CSR. "I expected more. I expected too much of myself. Maybe my weakness was that I didn't know how afraid I was, that I didn't know I wouldn't be able to take it."

Uri's depressive reaction contains both elements. He started crying during the war in grief over the premature deaths of boy soldiers. He continued to cry at home, now mourning not only the dead but the strong fighter self that he had believed himself to be and had perhaps once been, and that he lost irrevocably with his breakdown. In an interview 3 years after his CSR, Uri was still unable to talk about his breakdown event without crying:

> The truth is that I didn't want to quit. And I tried, I really tried, to hang in. I kept saying to myself, "what's with you? Do you want to be a deserter? What are you, a chicken, running away?" But it was such a nightmare. No matter how much I wanted and tried, I couldn't. I couldn't anymore.
>
> I'll tell you the truth, I was ashamed to ask for help. I was ashamed in front of the guys, in front of my commanding officer. At work [in the fire department], I'd been through a lot. I saw people injured and killed. . . . I constantly see accidents. So I was very surprised that I couldn't take it in the war. . . .
>
> Even when I talk I cry. I feel like a baby. I'm so ashamed of myself that I couldn't go on. . . . Especially since I know other people stuck it out. It's a lousy feeling. I've been feeling angry and disgusted with myself for a very long time.

Our casualties' depressions were characterized by a general loss of energy and interest. Some PTSD soldiers tell of exhaustion that lingers well beyond any physical justification. Many lose interest in their work, families, and friends. Many have no desire to go out and have a good time. The sexual problems of which many PTSD casualties complain stem in part from their depression. Among the more severely depressed soldiers, there is a general feeling that life is meaningless. Quite a number of them share Avi's feeling (quoted earlier) that "I didn't like life," that there is no point in living, and that death would put them out of their misery. The exhaustion and sense of futility involved in depression make it severely limiting. "I'm not functioning," said one depressed PTSD casualty. "I don't go out. Nothing interests me. I'm tired of everything. I don't go to friends. I don't want anything."

The dislike of life and the temporary cessation of functioning were the most severe expressions of depression among our subjects. To our knowledge, none of the psychiatric casualties of the Lebanon war reached the epitome of depression: completed suicide. As with their hostility, their acting out of depression was relatively contained. There was considerable suicidal ideation, similar to Avi's. There were also several suicide attempts, which in my estimation were more expressions of despair and cries for help than serious efforts at self-annihilation. This can be seen, for example, in the suicide attempt made by Ron. The attempt followed upon extensive suicidal ideation that was often prompted by difficulties he was having with his studies, which intensified the anxiety and sense of worthlessness he had felt ever since his CSR (when he failed to come to the aid of his calling crew):

> There were lots of moments when I felt I was falling apart. Failures in school . . . things that were hard for me to learn . . . made me more anxious even than I usually was. And then thoughts of suicide would come. I said to myself that it had to be a quick death without any pain and the only way was by shooting myself. Shooting wasn't a problem, because as a student policeman I had a gun. I had the chance.
>
> Once I almost did. The Druse guys I was working with stopped me. I don't know how they could tell, but apparently there were clear signs. . . . It seems my survival instinct told them.

Ron himself realized that with all the opportunities he had to do away with himself, he made sure to give advance notice of his intentions so that he would not be able to carry them out.

Thus far, the survival instincts in our PTSD subjects have been stronger than their depression. There have been only a small number of suicide attempts, and no known completed suicides among them. The restricted, contained nature of the depression in the PTSD casualties of the Lebanon war is in sharp contrast to the depression of Vietnam veterans, whose suicide rates were staggering. According to an article by Deborah Golomb (1985), more than 115,000 Vietnam veterans had died since their return to the United States—more than twice the number killed in action—and as many as 30% of those deaths were suicides. Empirical studies of Vietnam veterans report high rates of both suicidal ideation and suicidal acts. Several factors may have contributed to the difference.

One is the freedom, noted above, with which the veterans of the Lebanon war could express their anger, both in direct criticism of the war and in the form of diffuse aggression, which Israeli society permits. To the extent that suicide is the epitome of hostility turned against the self (Menninger, 1938), the ability to externalize their aggression may have saved at least some of our casualties from taking their own lives. The process is similar to that whereby the opportunity to express aggression may have helped to mitigate guilt among the PTSD casualties of the Lebanon war.

A second factor may have been the warm welcome that soldiers returning from Lebanon, as from every other Israel-Arab war, almost always received. Though many and loud voices were raised against the Lebanon war, few, if any, were raised against the soldiers who fought it. In our beleaguered state, few, if any, Israelis have anything but profound appreciation for the men who sacrifice their lives and well-being for the safety and survival of us all.

On the whole, the Lebanon soldier returned to a highly supportive, containing environment. Unlike in the Vietnam experience, there was little separation in Israel between home and front—in Israeli military history, the two are never more than some hours away. Nor was there the gaping abyss that opened up after Vietnam between soldier and civilian. Because of the largely reserve composition of the Israeli Army, most male civilians are, will be, or have been soldiers; most soldiers are civilians; and most people have friends or relatives who have been or will be soldiers. In such circumstances, there is no way there could have developed in Israel the us-versus-them attitude that so profoundly split the United States during and after Vietnam.

The warm welcome to a containing environment may have softened for the PTSD soldier, especially for the casualty with a prior CSR, the ego blow of his war-induced psychopathology. To be sure, many PTSD casualties we interviewed complained of not being understood, many felt painfully inadequate, and most were deeply alienated. No Lebanon soldier that we know of, however, encountered anything approaching the ostracism and contempt to which Vietnam veterans were so commonly subjected. A Lebanon PTSD casualty may have had to step down a few rungs on the social ladder, but he was never flung, as was his Vietnam counterpart, beyond the pale. At the bottom line, the black-sheep sons of the Lebanon war remained sons: erring, unheroic, but nonetheless sons. To the extent that suicide is an expression of a sense of worthlessness so profound that a person is driven to take his life, the core acceptance of the soldier in Israel may have shored up PTSD casualties enough to keep them from reaching that extreme.

The third factor may be the thoroughly institutionalized nature of mourning work in Israel. The extensive experience of tragic death acquired in Israel in the course of seven wars in 40 years of statehood has led to the development of an extensively institutionalized system of grief work.

Memorialization of the dead is institutionalized on both a religious and national level. In Jewish law, the funeral is followed by a 7-day period of *shiva*, in which the bereaved family remains at home to receive callers who offer condolences and join them in their grief. That is followed 3 weeks later by an *azkara*, in which family and friends return to the cemetery to place the tomb on the deceased's grave. After that, annual memorial services are held at the cemetery on the anniversary of the death. These observances are usually carried out even by people who do not follow other religious regulations, and the army actively encourages soldiers to participate in the rites for fellow veterans as well as close friends and family. In this way, the bereaved soldier, like the bereaved family, is given a set and accepted way of expressing his personal grief in the company of others who share his sorrow.

On a national level, every May, on the day before Israel's Independence Day celebrations, there is an annual Memorial Day for all the fallen soldiers. In respect for the soldiers whose "deaths bought our lives," a countrywide siren is sounded. For 1 minute while the siren sounds, traffic stands still, people stop what they are doing, and everyone stands at attention—on the street, in the supermarket, in school, office and factory—to honor the memory of the dead. Family and friends of the fallen make organized visits to the cemeteries where they are buried. On the eve of Memorial Day, close friends of a deceased soldier often gather to commemorate him, reminiscing about his personality, recounting his deeds, and looking through his memorial album.

The perpetuation of the memory of the dead is also a national matter. One of the constant features of Israel's landscape are memorial mounds. These may be tombstones or mounds of rocks and stones bearing the deceased's name and placed by his friends and family along the roads and at picnic sites, on moshavim and kibbutzim, and wherever else people pass or gather.

As with the rituals of mourning, the Ministry of Defense encourages many of the commemorative activities. It finances the cemetery treks and memorial albums, and in many other ways acknowledges the vast debt that the Israeli public feels toward the soldiers who fell in its defense. This public acknowledgment and payment of the debt is comforting to soldiers who survived their comrades in arms. With the grief work for the war dead interwoven into Israel's social fabric, on a national level mourning is not an isolated act, but a collective act in which the bereaved soldier can deal with his private loss in a socially organized fashion. The various rites and rituals enable surviving soldiers to work through their grief and find meaning in their losses. In so doing, they alleviate the worst of their depressions (and guilt) and apparently keep whatever suicidal impulses they have from reaching completion.

Lest I create too sanguine an impression of our PTSD casualties' depression, I would like to end this section with an account of an unusual but shockingly illustrative suicide dating back to the victim's combat in the 1971 war of attrition and in the 1973 Yom Kippur War. The case was reported by Dr. Ilan Kutz (1987) at a conference on traumatization and retraumatization held at the Van Leer Institute in Jerusalem:

> I was asked to see the family of a person who had killed himself. He had killed himself out of the blue, without any notice. Taking a can of gasoline, driving to the dunes near the Tel Aviv airport, pouring the gasoline on the surrounding vegetation, tying his own legs, pouring the gasoline on himself, he ignited both himself and the plants. Crawling onto the road like a flaming torch, he was spotted by some passersby and brought to the hospital.
>
> In the 2 days that he lived, he talked about the Sinai dunes and his war experiences. Afterwards, his wife and father came to see me to help them understand what had happened; the connection became very clear. In the war of attrition, he had been decorated with one of the highest medals for rescuing soldiers from a burning tank. Two years later, in the Yom Kippur War, he was himself caught in a burning tank and suffered 40% burns and spent several months in the hospital.
>
> After he recovered from his burns, he went back to university, married, and fathered. He worked at various jobs, holding each for only a few years before quitting on account of small irritations that occur at every workplace. But apart from this and one minor depressive episode, he seemed perfectly all right throughout the 13 years between the burn and his suicide. Neither wife nor friends suspected that anything was seriously amiss.
>
> Only one small quirk could be seen to point to his tragic ending. Every Friday evening, he would gather all the twigs and branches from his own and his neighbors' yards into a blazing bonfire. The meaning of this act, however, became apparent only after his self-immolation. While he was alive, it became a joke on the moshav where he lived, and his friends would even bring him cardboard and sticks to burn in his weekly bonfire.

The immediate trigger for this man's suicide was pressure at work with which the perfectionism and rigidity of his character made it difficult for him to cope. Behind this precipitating cause, however, were profound despair and severe depression associated with the feelings of helplessness he had when his comrades went up in flames. This man did not suffer from an identified CSR or PTSD, but the pathological depression induced by his war experience made him vulnerable to the unpredictable and uncontrollable stresses that are part of all our lives.

The form his suicide took points to his identification with his dead comrades, not in the safety of dreams but in all of its fatal implications. Here was a striving, idealistic young man who killed himself in a replica of his comrades' deaths in order to be at one with them in their final end.

This is a bizarre and unusual incident; however, it points to the persistence of unassuageable grief over fallen comrades despite a supportive social environment and institutionalized mourning procedures. Although there are as yet no known Lebanon war veteran suicides, an incident such as this, which occurred more than a decade after the combat experience that led to it, warns against complacency.

7

From Front Line
to Home Front

Most mental disorders create in their wake a host of problems in the sufferer's day-to-day functioning—in his or her family, community, and work (Dohrenwend & Shrout, 1985). PTSD, it seemed to us, would be no exception. The PTSD symptoms described in the previous chapters can be quite encompassing and absorbing. It appeared likely that the PTSD veteran who was bombarded by or frantically warding off intrusive reminders of his war experience would have little energy or peace of mind left to meet the demands of daily life effectively.

The literature, however, does not provide an unequivocal picture. Studies to date have looked at the consequences of combat and other disasters on the social functioning of the survivors, but none, to our knowledge, has examined the functional implications of CSR or PTSD. Thus, even where the studies find impairment in social functioning, they leave unanswered the question of the source of that impairment (i.e., whether it stems from the experience of the catastrophe itself or is a result of the posttraumatic psychopathology).

Findings on Vietnam veterans, for example, are inconsistent. A number of early studies found that veterans who served in Vietnam had no or few more problems in subsequent social functioning than other veterans (Borus, 1973; Worthington, 1977). It was only somewhat later that Wilson (1978) and Egendorf et al. (1981) found that Vietnam combat veterans reported more problems in intimacy and stronger feelings of detachment from others than noncombat veterans, and Penk, Robinowitz, and Roberts (1981) found that Vietnam veterans who reported having experienced intense battle-related stress had more problems in close personal relationships than combat veterans who reported less stress. On the whole, however, the difficulties that Vietnam veterans were found to have in their interpersonal relationships were attributed less to their exposure to the stress of combat than to their alienation from a country that had become disillusioned with the war and no longer accepted them as full members of their communities (Walker, 1981).

Findings in disaster research similarly indicate that social dysfunctioning often follows upon the experience of a catastrophe. Both Holocaust survivors and survivors of natural disasters have been shown to have more than their share of difficulty in relating to family and friends (Chodoff, 1962; Erikson, 1976; Titchener & Kapp, 1976). This research, however, also raises the question of whether their problems were a direct result of the disaster or of the social disintegration that followed. In their study of the mental health consequences of the Buffalo Creek flood, which swept through an Appalachian valley in West Virginia in 1972, taking 127 lives and leaving thousands homeless, Titchener and Kapp (1976) found that survivors displayed enduring changes in personality following the disaster. These changes were reflected in a decline in sociability, ambition, and interest in former hobbies and sports. Erikson (1976), however, points out that the flood was a communal disaster that uprooted the survivors from their homes, took them away from their neighbors, and destroyed the social tissue that gave direction and purpose to their actions, served as a source of nurturance, and provided the mold that shaped their personal relationships. He argues that many of the survivors' social problems "are as much a reaction to the shock of being separated from a meaningful community base as to the disaster itself" (p. 302). The same argument can be made for Holocaust survivors, most of whom lost all or almost all of their families and friends in the conflagration and who had to start life anew in strange countries.

The Lebanon war was different. Unlike the Vietnam veterans, the Israeli soldiers were welcomed back as defenders of the country, for the criticism of the war in Israel was never extended to the men who had to fight it. And unlike the survivors of other disasters, most of the Lebanon veterans returned to their homes, communities, and jobs. Although many of them lost relatives and friends, their larger social fabric remained intact, and they remained part of it.

Two questions thus remained open with regard to the Lebanon war veterans: Would they too suffer an impairment in their day-to-day functioning? And if they did, would the impairment be associated with exposure to the stress of combat in general or, more specifically, with psychic traumatization in combat—that is, with having a CSR or PTSD?

To examine these issues, my colleagues and I constructed the Social Functioning Problems Scale (SFPS), a self-report measure that queries numerous aspects of functioning in the family, community, and work (see Box 7.1). The scale consists of 22 statements describing changes in the soldier's conduct in these areas since the war. In the area of family life, the statements covered such things as the veteran's sexual functioning, the amount of time he spent with his family, how much he talked to family members, and whether new family problems had arisen. Similar phenomena were assessed in the veteran's relations to friends and other people, as well as such issues as trust, dependency, irritability and discomfort in company, quarrels, and ease of talking about personal problems in general and the war in particular. Items about work touched on interpersonal relations with colleagues, interest in the job and worry about it, as well as health-related impediments such as illnesses, doctor's visits, and absenteeism that interfered with job performance. For each item, subjects were asked to indicate whether or not the conduct described applied to them in the previous year. Because examination of their responses indicated that each respondent's level of functioning was usually similar in all three areas, we calculated a single score for each subject.

BOX 7.1

Functioning Questionnaire

Following is a series of statements describing changes that happen to people during their lives. Please indicate next to each statement whether it does or does not describe changes in your life *since the war.*

If the statement is true or generally true for you, circle the letter "t."
If the statement is not true or generally not true, circle the letters "n.t." Remember, the questions relate to the period *since the war.* If you do not understand how to complete the questionnaire, do not hesitate to ask the person in charge.

1. t / n.t.   Since the war I have had occasional difficulties at work that I didn't have before.
2. t / n.t.   Since the war I have been sicker and it interferes with my work.
3. t / n.t.   Since the war I have been absent from work more frequently than before.

(continued)

BOX 7.1 (*Continued*)

4. t / n.t.   Since the war I have spent less time with the family.
5. t / n.t.   Since the war I have had problems with my colleagues at work that did not occur previously.
6. t / n.t.   Since the war I talk with members of my family less than I used to.
7. t / n.t.   Since the war I have been more dependent on others.
8. t / n.t.   Since the war I have had problems with family members that I didn't have before.
9. t / n.t.   Since the war I have been less interested in work.
10. t / n.t.   Since the war I have spent less time with friends.
11. t / n.t.   Since the war I have quarreled more with people.
12. t / n.t.   Since the war I have found it hard to discuss the war with people.
13. t / n.t.   Since the war my sexual functioning has declined.
14. t / n.t.   Since the war I have had less desire to meet with people.
15. t / n.t.   Since the war people annoy me more easily.
16. t / n.t.   Since the war I have been more worried about work matters.
17. t / n.t.   Since the war I have felt uneasy while other people were around.
18. t / n.t.   Since the war I have left all decisions to other people.
19. t / n.t.   Since the war I no longer rely on other people.
20. t / n.t.   Since the war I have felt that people don't understand me.
21. t / n.t.   Since the war I have gone to doctors more often than before.
22. t / n.t.   Since the war it is hard for me to talk about things that troubled me.

First, we assessed the impact of participation in combat per se on the veterans' social functioning. To do this, we compared three groups of subjects: CSR casualties, non-CSR controls, and noncombat controls, who had been drafted for the war but had not been sent to the front. Results showed that (a) CSR subjects had more impairment in their social functioning than both noncombatants and combatants who had fought without a CSR, and (b) the post-Lebanon social functioning of the non-CSR combatants did not differ statistically from that of the noncombatants. In other words, exposure to combat in and of itself did not lead to a significant decline in social functioning; only the sustaining of a CSR in the course of combat did (see Solomon & Mikulincer, 1987a).

Then, to assess more thoroughly the impact of war-induced psychopathology on our veterans' social functioning, we compared the social functioning of PTSD and non-PTSD veterans over 3 years (noncombatants were not included in this comparison, because they did not meet the first DSM-III criterion for PTSD—exposure to "a significant stressor that would evoke significant symptoms of stress in almost everyone"). Results showed that at all three waves of assessment, (a) the PTSD veterans functioned worse than their non-PTSD counterparts; (b) in both groups, the more PTSD symptoms they had, the worse their functioning was; and (c) by far the greatest impairment in social functioning was exhibited by PTSD veterans with antecedent CSR (for further details, see Appendix D).

A comparison between the SFPS scores of the CSR group and those of the non-CSR group revealed that in all the seven areas of functioning, CSR casualties suffered from a greater decline at all three measurements. In general, the level of social functioning among CSR casualties did not change over the 3 years. In the control group, however, there was a decline in social functioning between the first and second years, and an improvement between the second and third years (see Appendix D).

Our findings clearly link postwar problems in social functioning to our veterans' war-induced psychopathology and, furthermore, indicate that the more severe the psychopathology, the greater their difficulty in carrying out the tasks of civilian life. These results in principle parallel the clinical findings presented in the previous chapter, in that there is a gradation of impairment in functioning as well as in symptomatology, with veterans who had both PTSD and CSR showing the worst deterioration, and those with neither showing the least.

As for the veterans who did not develop psychopathology, their combat experience also left residuals on their functioning. Although the difference between their postwar functioning and that of the noncombat controls did not reach statistical significance, our findings show that there was a difference, with the combatants reporting more difficulties. In the previous chapter, I noted that even soldiers without CSR or PTSD thought and dreamt about the war and were somewhat closed, irritable, and depressed at homecoming; their minds were still on the battle and their hearts with the people they had lost. Here, the interviews both with the non-CSR combatants and with subjects who fought successfully in one or more wars before developing a CSR or PTSD inform us that unafflicted combat soldiers may also experience problems in taking up their civilian lives where they had left off.

Soldiers who go to war generally leave behind them a vacuum—in their families, communities, and work—that is filled by the people who stay at home. When they return, they often find that their wives have taken upon themselves both parental roles, that their children have assumed more responsibilities, and that colleagues at work have intruded on their territory (Hill, 1949; Hogancamp & Figley, 1983; McCubbin, Dahl, Lester, Banoon, & Robertson, 1976). This is the case even for Israeli soldiers, who usually serve relatively short stints on the front (only a month or so) before they are discharged and whose jobs are well guaranteed. Whether or not they develop CSR or PTSD, soldiers must reestablish contact and renegotiate their place when they come home. It is for this reason, perhaps, that we found that married soldiers had higher rates of PTSD than unmarried soldiers and that these PTSD rates were associated with levels of family support (Solomon, Mikulincer, Fried, & Wosner, 1987).

The readjustment is often difficult in and of itself, and also because the immensity of the combat experience, the awesome encounter with sudden, brutal, and premature death, and the inevitable acute realization of their own mortality may combine to unsettle former certainties, trivialize former pleasures, dwarf former ambitions and aspirations, and alter priorities. "After all sorts of things in the war, you come home and it's hard to have a normal life, to go on with the agenda," said one veteran. Many veterans thus go through a period of pause and reassessment before resuming their lives at their former capacities.

For PTSD veterans, the readjustment is complicated by their disorder. In their classic *Men under Stress,* which deals largely with the veterans of World War II, Grinker and Spiegel (1945) describe the fragile mental state of the returning soldier who is prone to psychiatric disorder as a consequence of his wartime engagement. As they describe him, he has undergone a draining experience that undermines his ability to assume a responsible, adult role in his home and community. He returns home psychologically exhausted, needy, wanting to receive and enraged when he does not. The psychological energy that would go into constructing or reconstructing his civilian life has been depleted, and he simply does not have the wherewithal to renegotiate the required transition. Hence, although the non-PTSD soldier generally returns to his former self within several months, the PTSD veteran does not. For the soldier with PTSD, the stresses at homecoming are more intense and enduring, and because of the number and frequency of his symptoms, they have a different quality as well.

In the remainder of this chapter, I shall look more closely at the difficulties that PTSD symptoms put in the way of the veteran's readjustment in his family, community, and work.

IN THE FAMILY

When the war ends and the man of the family returns, inevitable tensions arise as the family members renegotiate the redistribution of roles and responsibilities. On the one hand, attempts of the veteran to resume his former role may meet with resistance, or on the other hand there may be pressures on the veteran to resume his former responsibilities quickly, including that of breadwinner, leaving him little time to decompress and digest his war experience. The result is often a certain amount of family conflict.

This can be the case in any family. When the veteran returns home with PTSD, however, these ordinary tensions of homecoming can be vastly compounded. The following description gives some idea of the mental state in which a badly traumatized combat veteran may return to his family. The description is of the homecoming of Michael, whose CSR was recorded at length in Chapter 4. Michael came home looking and acting so bizarrely that he frightened his family. He was dirty, unkempt, and taciturn; burst into tears at the sight of tomatoes on his dinner plate; was too nervous to eat or watch television; and, at night, had a flashback to being shot at in Lebanon. There is no sign whatsoever of his being glad to be back, no pleasure in sex, no sense of security at finally being in the safety of his home:

> At home, my kids got scared when they saw me; my wife, too. I hadn't shaved in a week, or showered. . . . I washed and got dressed, sat down to dinner. And my wife started to ask questions. I didn't want to answer. . . . She put tomatoes on my plate, and when I saw them I started to cry. And how! It was awful. I think my wife gave me a tranquilizer. I couldn't eat, or I ate very little. I couldn't watch television because it made me mad. She said, "Let's watch the news." But as soon as I heard the news, it made me mad. I turned off the radio, the television. I couldn't listen. . . .
>
> I went to bed, but I couldn't fall asleep. And I couldn't even have sex. . . . She tried to calm me down, to encourage me. It could be we did have sex, I don't remember. But without desire. Then at night, she moved a chair, and I jumped out of bed and said, "They're shooting. They're shooting at us." And she said, "It's nothing. No one's shooting at us. Calm down." It calmed me down a bit, but I was still shuddering, and I didn't want to talk.

Most non-PTSD veterans soon take up their former roles and responsibilities, possibly with some readjustments, and achieve a new family balance. From Michael's description, one may glean why it is so much more difficult for the PTSD veteran to do the same.

Of the host of PTSD symptoms, the ones that interfere most with the veteran's reintegration into his family are those that have direct negative effects on social relations (Haley, 1975). These are the symptoms in the second DSM-III category: numbing of responsiveness and reduced involvement in the external world, as seen by diminished interest in significant activities, feelings of detachment or alienation, and constricted affect. The PTSD veteran's elevated level of hostility can also have severe repercussions in his family life, as can his combat-induced depression and phobias. Together or separately, these symptoms make it very difficult for the PTSD veteran to resume the affective and communicative aspects of his roles as husband, father, and son, and in some cases, to shoulder the bread-and-butter responsibilities involved in maintaining a household.

Especially problematic for the PTSD veteran is the resumption of the more demanding and intimate roles of husband and father. Most PTSD casualties are removed and detached from their families. Some casualties withdraw physically: they may stay at work to all hours, go off on trips by themselves, or disappear for hours or days at a time—anything not to be at home. The majority stay at home, but are there little more than in body. Some sit like zombies in front of the television, fending off any interruptions. Some retreat to their rooms. Many neither talk nor listen. Wrapped up in their continued suffering, they describe being unfocused, cut off, or in a world of their own. "My mother is talking to me about dinner, and I'm somewhere else entirely," said one PTSD veteran. "My wife would talk to me, but I wouldn't pay attention. She's talking and my head is somewhere else. As though I'm floating," told another. The more aggressive of them may bully their wives and children into keeping their distance. One such veteran reported:

> I got the family used to not bothering me at all. Simply to let me be, to leave me alone, that I'll do whatever I want, whenever I want, and however I want. That they let me be and don't get near me at all.

Whatever their avenue of retreat, the common denominator is that these PTSD casualties are not emotionally available to their families. Severely handicapped in their capacity for intimacy, many of them cannot touch, caress, or otherwise show affection. Some are so detached that they are unable to pick up or look at a son or daughter born while they were on the front, though they had greeted previous children with the normal fatherly enthusiasm.

In many cases, the hiatus that PTSD symptoms create between the afflicted veteran and his family is exacerbated by his reluctance to talk about the war experiences in which he is so immersed. Shame at his breakdown (if he had a CSR), the wish to spare himself the pain of memory, and the desire to protect his family from the horrors he had gone through may stifle communication altogether or make for partial, truncated revelations that do little to bridge the gap between himself and the wife and children who have been waiting for his return. The family often remains bewildered by the veteran's unusual behavior, whereas the veteran, locked in his silence, becomes even more detached and cut off. He deprives himself of the emotional support his family could potentially give, and deprives his family of the emotional connection and involvement that is their due.

Sexual problems may compound the difficulties that PTSD veterans have in maintaining intimate contact with their wives. Not a few PTSD veterans report a drastic curtailment of sexual activity to the point of complete abstinence. Apathy, depression, constricted affect, and general exhaustion all contribute to a plummeting libido, as the following quotations amply testify:

> My wife doesn't attract me. Nothing interests me.

> Since the Lebanon war, sexual relations have been tired, dull. I have no desire, I'm chronically exhausted. When we have sex, I don't much enjoy it anymore.

> My relationship with my wife became very bad. For about a year I didn't want to lay eyes on her at all. I felt strong disgust. And pain. It's a problem. . . . For about half a year, I didn't touch my wife. After that, when we began to come back together, I had pains. What should have been pleasurable was painful. I would yell, "Who needs it, it hurts." . . .
>
> A few weeks ago, I told her, "I'm not functioning. I don't go out, nothing interests me. I'm tired of everything about you."

The men who made these statements—who find sex boring, burdensome, and even physically painful—reported having had normal sexual interest before their injury.

Some of our PTSD veterans manufacture excuses for their loss of sexual libido, put up obstacles, or if they can, perform to please their wives. One ingenious veteran, for example, suddenly became punctilious about observing the Jewish religious prohibition against intercourse for 7 days after the last menstrual blood: "This gives me an alibi for a sexual rest." When the time ran out and he felt bound to perform his conjugal duty, he would focus on the procreative goal of the act, thinking "let my sperm not be in vain."

However the injured veteran resolves the problem, the lack of sexual interest is confusing and embarrassing, further eroding his already impaired self-confidence and sense of masculinity: "After the war, I was very upset about the subject of sexual relations," said a Ministry of Defense official who had sustained a CSR. "I wanted and didn't want. I wanted and was afraid of not being able to. I felt it wasn't the same as it had been. I didn't know what to do about it. It bothered me a lot." His wife probably shared his confusion. Many wives report feeling rejected, unloved, and frustrated.

Aware of their inability to give emotionally, some PTSD veterans try to compensate their families materially. "I wouldn't relate to them at all, as though I were living by myself," said one of the casualties we interviewed. "Instead I compensated them materially. I didn't feel like anything. I kept thinking that I'd die. So what was it all for? So they might as well have money."

The PTSD veteran's tension, irritation, and hostility further impair his family relationships. Most casualties report increased conflicts with their wives and children. Their children's noise, exuberance, and demands for attention irritate veterans whose minds are on the battlefield, who want to be left alone, who are sensitive to noise, and who are filled with the volcanic rage discussed in the previous chapter.

Batya Fried, project coordinator for a study of the wives of Lebanon war CSR veterans recently conducted by our department, suggests that the underlying source of many of the conflicts that arise in the homes of PTSD veterans is the injury to the afflicted veteran's sense of masculinity. Veterans who had broken down in the masculine role of soldiering and veterans who develop PTSD symptoms that limit their ability to reassume their role as head of the household tend to be very sensitive about all issues that may bear on their masculinity. Thus, minor disobediences in their children, which seem to challenge their paternal authority, can provoke disproportionate rage. Where previously they would have scolded or spanked, they may now beat. One veteran, for example, tells of nearly punching his 2-year-old son when the toddler would not drink his milk.

With their wives, our PTSD veterans tell that frequent causes for quarrels are "trivial" things like the quality of their wives' cooking, neatness in the house, and who does what household chores. These bones of contention all revolve around the traditional definition of masculine and feminine roles. According to Fried, the PTSD veteran is more intent on maintaining traditional male-female differentiation and is more sensitive to infringements.

Most of the veterans we interviewed restricted their aggression to shouting, cursing, and occasionally slapping, breaking things, and throwing things at no one in particular. Where they struck out physically, their children were the most common targets, the right of the father to discipline his children justifying and facilitating the physical aggression. Haley (1975) suggests that fatherhood overtaxes the ability of some veterans to resolve the conflict between the pleasure combat had taught them to take in violence and the guilt it aroused in them. She suggests that the veteran's attempts to control his child may be out of proportion because the natural exuberance and aggressiveness of the growing child reawaken memories of wartime aggression and thus provoke excessive rage and/or guilt over his own sadistic impulses.

In a number of cases, wives were also victims of beatings. One veteran reported beating his mother. The women we interviewed said that the violence seemed to come out of the blue. It was often triggered by jokes or innocent comments that in the past would have made their husbands laugh or shrug their shoulders—for example, a remark to the affect that he does not help her with the dishes. Such things now struck at the PTSD veteran's self-esteem, making him feel that he was being insufferably mocked or criticized. So, in poor control of his impulses, he would hit.

In most of the cases we observed, the violence started after the injury, and without any known background of familial violence. Williams (1980), in a study of wives of Vietnam veterans, found that 50% of the veteran couples who sought her professional help reported wife battering. The battering behavior, however, did not conform to the usual pattern. Ordinarily, battering is a repeated behavior, with each beating leading to another that often is even more violent. In veteran families, in contrast, there were usually one or two extremely violent, frightening episodes that were not repeated and were followed by the couple's seeking professional help. This difference in behavior indicates that wife battering in veterans' families has a motivation and dynamic of its own and links it with the veteran's combat experience.

Fried suggests that the reaction of the veteran's family may aggravate his distress. Frightened by his aggression, by his verbal outbursts as well as physical ones, his wife and children may themselves withdraw. The children often turn to their mother for solace and protection. The mother, in many cases, will shield the children from her husband's rage, sometimes literally placing herself in between and absorbing the blows. These natural reactions make the veteran feel that his authority is being challenged and that he is losing control of his household. It makes him feel even more alienated, misunderstood, rejected, and angry. He may withdraw further and strike out more often.

As noted in the previous chapter, most of the PTSD veterans feel guilty about their aggression. They feel bad about their bad tempers and regret striking out, especially at their wives. Their effort to check the impact of their rage by retreating to their rooms or leaving the house, as many of them do, doubtless averts some serious abuse. It also distances the afflicted veteran even further from his family. Absenting himself from the scene of the quarrel, he cannot resolve the issue in dispute or even communicate why he is angry. Several IDF clinicians have suggested that much of the veteran's distancing himself from his family derives from the guilt he feels about his aggressive urges and from his fear of losing control over them.

In some instances, the veteran's PTSD interferes with not only his emotional functioning in his family, but also his instrumental functioning. Some veterans are too depressed and anxious to do very much of anything. "I don't function," said one such veteran. "I don't go to the bank, I don't go to the supermarket, I don't go anywhere. I don't want to go anywhere. I can't even pick up the bread and milk. I can't stand in line at the store. . . . I can't." Some PTSD veterans are prevented by war-induced phobias from resuming tasks they had previously performed. Driving is one such task. Several of the PTSD veterans we interviewed told that their wives have taken over that chore. Moreover, in some cases, the PTSD veteran's social problems result in the social life of the entire family being curtailed. There are no outings with the children, no visiting for the couple. In the most severe cases, the wives take over the role of major breadwinner.

Many of the difficulties that PTSD creates in the married life of the afflicted veteran can be seen in Micki, one of our most seriously afflicted casualties and one of the few divorcees in our sample. Micki married at age 26, about 7 years after he fainted in his first battle of the Yom Kippur War. The years preceding his marriage were years of struggle during which he desperately tried to escape from his memories of the war on the one hand, and from the inner isolation of the alienated and detached PTSD sufferer on the other.

Soon upon his discharge from compulsory military service in 1976, the first thing he did was to go abroad, where he was spared the sight of uniforms and other reminders of military life. He traveled on several occasions, only to be driven home each time by loneliness—not only by the ordinary loneliness of a person in a foreign country, but by the loneliness suffered by PTSD casualties who cannot get on with others. More will be said on the social problems of PTSD veterans in the upcoming section of this chapter. Here let it suffice to quote Micki's description of the background of avoidance and isolation against which he courted and married the first woman with whom he had a relationship:

> I was abroad for almost a year. I worked at all sorts of odd jobs for the money—then I came back. I had problems there. Problems of loneliness. It was hard for me to form ties with people. In some part of me, I wanted to stay, but I missed my family,

so I came back. Whenever I came back . . . I immediately wanted to leave again. . . .
I went abroad again for 2 months, and when I came back I met her . . . and I said to
myself "Here's my chance," and I stayed with her.

Micki wed immediately after a trip overseas, hoping to find in his
marriage an anchor to stay his desultory indirection and a shield against
his deep inner loneliness. Engaged in his struggle with his war trauma,
he had done nothing to prepare himself for married life, however, and
he became dependent on his wife both materially and emotionally. Having never trained for a trade or profession or held down a steady job, he
was often unemployed and came to see his wife's income as a valued
addition to the national insurance payments he collected. When his
daughter was born, he was overwhelmed by "the excess responsibility,"
and left to his wife the entire responsibility of child care. Above all, he
depended on his wife for the only meaningful social contact he had. She
was virtually the only person to whom he had ever opened up after his
CSR. Other than his mother, she was the only person he felt would not
judge him and whom he ever told about his breakdown: "I have a lot of
things inside me that I don't manage to get out. It's hard for me to communicate with everyone. She's one of the people that I've opened up to."

The problem was that just as Micki's PTSD was a factor in how and
why he wed, it made it most difficult for him to meet the most ordinary
demands of married life. Dissension began soon after the wedding and
became worse after his second breakdown in the Lebanon war. Quarrels
broke out over his irresponsibility, his failure to hold down a steady job,
the drugs he consumed to blunt his recollections of war experiences (see
Chapter 6), his sexual impotence following his second CSR, "and after
that it went to personal matters of what I'm doing and what sort of life is
this." Because of his pent-up rage, the quarrels became vicious and
bitter: "Lots of things I said to her just for the hell of it, because I wanted
to be mean and don't know why." Unable to cope, Micki took to staying
away from home ("I spent as little time as possible at home. I'd come
home only to sleep"). He became an absentee husband in body as well as
spirit.

The inevitable happened; Micki's wife asked for a divorce. At the
time of the interview, about half a year after the event, he was 31 years
old, living with his parents, visiting his 4-year-old daughter only when he
felt up to it, and once again feeling so desperately lonely that he fanta-
sized getting back together with his wife:

It's not easy for me. Lots of times I long for the sharing. I don't think that I've ever
opened myself up, at least in the last years, to anyone as much as I had to her. . . .

The divorce was more a matter of my wife's wanting it. For me it was very good to have a sort of protected place when I was feeling so tense, because I could at least talk about the tensions openly. . . . If she doesn't find someone else she falls in love with . . . I think she'll eventually give me another chance. I very much want her to give me another chance.

There is no saying that Micki or any other PTSD casualty would not have had marital problems without his injury, as many couples certainly do. The push and pull that Micki describes, however—the inordinate need for a trusted person to talk to and for a protected place where it is safe to express and release his tensions on the one hand, coupled with the monumental obstacles to closeness and the assumption of family responsibility on the other—is typical of the marriages of many PTSD casualties we interviewed. Many of these casualties told of good, satisfying marriages prior to their traumatization, and their wives confirmed their assessment. In other families, there were tensions beforehand, and the casualty may have been prone to interpersonal problems. But even where that is the case, it was clear the PTSD vastly exacerbated any marital problems that the casualty might otherwise have had.

In many respects, our findings about the family disturbances of PTSD veterans of the Lebanon war coincide with knowledge about the dynamics in the families of Vietnam War veterans. Polner (1971), in a study based on interviews with families of Vietnam veterans, reports that family members perceived significant impairments in the veteran's emotional stability. In a study of 200 Vietnam veterans who received treatment, Lumry, Cedarleaf, Wright, and Braatz (1970) found that a large proportion of their sample suffered from serious interpersonal problems, especially in their marriages. Haley (1978), Lifton (1973), and Figley (1976) also have observed the veteran's difficulties in maintaining close personal ties.

In some important respects, however, Israeli PTSD casualties of the Lebanon war differ from their Vietnam War counterparts in their family relations. Haley (1978) suggests that for many Vietnam veterans, the transition to the role of husband and father is complicated by their having engaged in guerrilla activities against women and children, making their own wives and children symbolic representations of their wartime aggression. For such veterans, she writes, intimacy with a woman, the birth of a baby, and the more common fatherly chore of comforting a crying child are avoided as evoking wartime associations. We have not found such associations in our interviews.

Fried (in a personal communication) suggests rather that the fact that the deaths of women and children were among the more horrendous scenes that Israeli soldiers witnessed in Lebanon left many of the

PTSD casualties with exaggerated worries about their family's health and security. For example, a scratch on his daughter's hand drove one PTSD veteran into a panic.

Another difference seems to be in the divorce rates of the two groups of veterans. The Center for Policy Research (1979) in the United States reports that the divorce rate among Vietnam veterans is higher than that for the rest of the U.S. population, and the President's Commission on Mental Health (1978) presents figures showing that an estimated 38% of the marriages of Vietnam veterans broke up within 6 months of their return from southeast Asia. Although divorce rates are not available for our sample, our impression is that they are considerably lower, albeit on the rise.

In part, the difference reflects differences in the divorce rates of the general populations of Israel and the United States. At the end of the 1970s, for example, the rate of divorce in the United States was eight times that in Israel (5.2% of all American marriages versus 0.6% in Israel; Muhlbauer & Zemach, 1991). Divorce in Israel is economically more difficult than in the United States and is socially less acceptable. In part, the lower Israeli rate may be attributable to other social factors. One is the scarcity of substance abuse (Micki is an exception) among Israeli veterans; the use of alcohol and drugs for self-medication by Vietnam veterans may well have wreaked more havoc with their family lives than their PTSD symptoms. Another is the sense of obligation borne by the wives of many of our psychiatrically injured veterans, who feel, like much of the rest of the Israeli population, committed to standing by the men who were injured in the defense of their country. It is also notable that, like Micki, quite a number of our casualties married and fathered children in the wake of their CSRs. Many were of marriageable age and probably succumbed, like most of their contemporaries, to the hefty social pressure in Israel to set up house. The impression of my colleagues and I, however, is that among their motives were also the desire to restore meaning to their lives (which their CSR had stripped away) and the desire to reach out of the isolation induced by their disorder.

SOCIAL FUNCTIONING

The obstacles to intimacy, communication, and pleasure that cut so deeply into the PTSD casualty's family ties extend also to his larger social network. With a slightly different emphasis, the symptoms that most interfere with his resumption of social ties are much the same as those that keep him at a far remove from his wife and children, namely, the numbing of responsiveness and reduced involvement with the external world that make up the second DSM-III criteria for PTSD diagnosis.

The impact of these symptoms on the casualty's social life can be seen in the veteran soldier Shlomo. Shlomo, a bus driver by profession, developed PTSD after serving in an infantry unit in the Lebanon war, his second combat engagement. Prior to his CSR, he was a sociable, committed individual. During the Yom Kippur War, he fought with a strong sense of dedication to his buddies and felt himself sustained through heavy fighting both by his responsibility to his crew and the feeling that "we were together." Outside the army, he and his wife had a full, well-organized social life, with Friday night gatherings and group outings with the same people they had known and liked for years. With the onset of his PTSD, however, all this came to an end. Feeling depressed and alienated, Shlomo underwent a change from warm sociability and a normal capacity for pleasure to withdrawal and joylessness:

> I had lots of friends before the war. We were closely knit. We had lots of parties. I felt like everyone else before the war. . . . Me and my wife . . . used to enjoy ourselves in every way. We went to the beach. We ate out. We were active all the time. . . . There was meaning in my life, in everything I did. I enjoyed things. . . . Every Friday night, we had friends over to the house. I had good friends. . . .
>
> [After Lebanon] my desire for company really dwindled. I have none. I feel that everyone is disconnected from me. . . . I have no desire for anything. I want to be alone.

The deterioration of Shlomo's social life encompasses both people and previously enjoyed activities or things. Behind both is the loss of desire—"for company" and "for anything"—and the loss of the sense of meaning that gives simple, everyday events and activities their pleasure and zest, and which, as Titchener (1986) notes, is often eroded in the experience of a catastrophic event. A number of our casualties told of immersing themselves in music; many threw themselves into work. But the aim of these and similar activities is escape from memory, not pleasure, for which the casualties have little capacity.

Depression and grief over fallen friends often make social activity seem vain and pointless (Bleich, Barb, & Kotler, 1986; Glover, 1984). "How can you live it up and have a good time when things like this happen?" said a casualty who had lost a good friend. "I used to like . . . going to a performance, being among friends. I used to do this willingly and with pleasure like a normal person. And here I would say, 'Foolishness. It's not worth it.'"

Continuing absorption in the war keeps some casualties as distant and unfocused with their friends as they are with their families. "When I'm talking to people . . . or when they're talking, I somehow tune out, even though I'm looking straight at them," said a casualty who was plagued by intrusive recollections of the war. "And when they ask me a question, I can't answer because I have no idea what they've been saying."

Anger and hostility are additional factors that work against a satisfying social life. Some casualties keep their distance from others for fear of losing control and striking out. "I was afraid that I could get mad, and who knows what would happen then," said a casualty who broke off relations with all his former friends and went so far as to find work where he could be alone. Many of the casualties we interviewed described relationships ending with fights or arguments. Whereas issues relating to gender roles seem to have sparked the injured veteran's fights with his family, political issues triggered many of the fallings out with friends and acquaintances. Some casualty would blow up at the slightest criticism of the army; others would explode over support for the Lebanon war.

Anxiety, expressed in the various phobias and avoidances discussed in the previous chapter, impedes social life by making it difficult or impossible for the casualty to do things. The not-uncommon war-induced fear of crowds puts moviehouses, theaters, beaches, public picnic grounds, sports stadiums, and many other places of recreation out of bounds for phobic PTSD casualties, as are parties, reunions, and other large gatherings. "Even today [3 years after Lebanon], where there are a lot of people, I don't go. I'm afraid. . . . I'm still anxious," remarked one of our traumatized veterans.

Visiting people or just plain going out for an evening becomes difficult for men who are afraid to drive and impossible for the most seriously disturbed casualties, who fear leaving their homes lest they be bombed or attacked by terrorists. "I feel like a man who crawls into some hole and doesn't want to come out," said one such casualty. Indeed, the entire drive to avoid recollection inhibits sociability. "I didn't want to go out or on any holiday . . . because I felt that if I sat doing nothing I would remember everything that happened," the same veteran reported.

The symptoms named above undermine the casualty's readjustment in both his family and community. Other concomitants of PTSD have less of an effect on the family and more of an impact on the casualty's relations with friends and acquaintances. The guilt and shame casualties feel about their breakdowns in combat, about the posttraumatic symptoms over which they have so little control, and about their difficulties in serving in reserve duty (see Chapter 8) are a major deterrent to the PTSD veteran's reintegration into his community. In Israel, that shame is one of the major motives for the casualties' withdrawal from a society that so values military excellence.

Many PTSD casualties specifically avoid contact with former combat buddies and men in their reserve units. Contact with successful fighters points up their own weakness, emphasizes their feeling of no longer being like everyone else, and intensifies their shame. The problem for the traumatized veteran is that, as a civilian army in which most able-bodied men serve, the IDF is an integral part of the life of most Israeli men. The military ethos, which of necessity imposes on soldiers a discipline of macho pretense that forbids the disclosure of fear, weakness, and certainly of war-induced pathology, applies in Israel not only in the barracks but also in the living room. "I know what it's like to pretend you're not afraid," tells a PTSD veteran of four wars. "At first [after his discharge from service in Lebanon] when I heard a siren, I'd hide. . . . I was scared, but I didn't want to show it."

One is unlikely in Israel to spend an evening with friends where the subject of army service does not come up in one way or another. At the Friday night gatherings that Shlomo and many other PTSD casualties shun, there is almost always mention of the army: who has gone off to reserves, who has gotten back from reserves, what is going on at the borders. Political and policy issues are heatedly discussed by men who will have to implement any decisions that are made. It is difficult for a man to keep his military status a secret in such an atmosphere. There is always the chance that he will be asked what he did in a previous or current war and when he is going to be in the reserves again. To avoid disclosure of his shameful secret, the traumatized veteran may keep his distance not only from his army buddies, but also from his civilian friends.

A related motive for the PTSD casualty's social withdrawal is mistrust. Mistrust has been noted as a factor in the postwar pathology of Vietnam veterans. Glover (1988) names mistrust as one of four subtypes of PTSD that he found among Vietnam veterans and attributes it specifically to an experience of betrayal by a person in authority. Walker and Nash (1981) similarly view mistrust as the outcome of an actual betrayal. They point out that the Vietnam veteran felt used by the U.S. government, which sent him to war but imposed such limitations on the fighting that it was impossible to win; by his peers who dodged the draft; and by society, which recoiled from the things he did. Furthermore, the guerrilla nature of the war, in which it was impossible to distinguish between friend and foe, fostered mistrust that carried over to the soldier's civilian life.

Our impression is that the distrust of our casualties was derived less from specific betrayals than from the nature of combat itself and, more specifically, from their traumatization. This is in keeping with the fact, documented by Glover, that attitudes and feelings of mistrust have been noted in other victim survivor populations, including World War II combat veterans (Lidz, 1946), prisoners of war (Wolf & Ripley, 1947), Jewish concentration camp internees (Krell, 1979), and survivors of floods (Lifton & Olson, 1976). Titchener (1986) notes that people who experience the full force of the threat to their being that is inherent in any catastrophic event lose their basic sense of security and trust in the world.

Soldiers who broke down on the battlefield have particularly good reason not to trust themselves or, by extension, others. They know that their powers failed them in a moment of crisis and that, at some level, they chose their own survival at the expense of their comrades. With that knowledge of their own failings, they are more apprehensive of the weakness and egocentricity of others, and they also have grounds for fearing that others may judge them as adversely as they judge themselves. "I don't trust anyone, including myself," declared Ron, who froze when his friends were calling for help. He had no cause to believe that others would stand by him any more than he stood by his own men.

Soldiers who broke down only after extended exposure to heavy fighting, sometimes over several wars, tend to focus less on how they failed their buddies than on how others failed them, and their mistrust tends to be expressed as anger. Michael, who (as the reader may recall from Chapter 4) held out until the major part of the fighting had ended, bore a lasting grudge against the government and military establishment for the kinds of errors that are almost always committed in the pressure of war. Other casualties complained of supposedly indifferent, callous, or careless commanders.

Some of the more idealistic and perfectionistic casualties (see Chapter 10) maintain that they carried the burden of the dirty work. "I was screwed out there while a lot of guys did nothing," said one such casualty. Such casualties tend to feel a great deal of resentment against people whom they regard as shirkers or slackers. "I have the uncomfortable feeling . . . that I did a great deal and others didn't do anything," said a casualty who had been an exemplary soldier in several wars before he finally succumbed. "I reacted very strongly to people who weren't in the war," said another. They often resent those who had jobs behind lines, men who kept (or seemed to keep) a low profile on the battlefield, and men who were exempted from service for some reason or other. Many of our traumatized veterans perceived such soldiers as self-serving, whereas they (the casualties) were doing all the hard work.

There is probably some truth in at least some of the accusations, though others probably help the casualty to deny or mitigate his own failure. But in all of them there is the casualty's sense that he was betrayed and left alone to his fate. That sense, as discussed earlier, may be instrumental in leading up to a CSR.

These feelings of having been betrayed extend to civilian life. If peers and commanders cannot be trusted, then neither can friends, who are the same people, made of the same stuff. This mistrust may be expressed in feeling that people are out for themselves. "I saw that everyone was out for himself, and if there are friends, it's only out of some personal interest," avows Ami, whose breakdown in the Lebanon war left him isolated and detached from family and friends alike.

Mistrust is behind the conviction, widely held among PTSD casualties, that others do not quite understand what they have been through. The description by Yitzhak, who broke down after several weeks of sustained fighting with the ground forces, of an argument he had with a friend in the air force conveys the strength of this feeling:

> I said to him, "In your life, you've never felt a shell land next to you; you've never felt an RPG hit you inside an armored personnel carrier. I've felt it in the flesh. I've felt it. You don't know what it is to have a friend die. You don't know what it is to have a friend wounded. You don't know how much a wounded man wants to live. You've never seen blood." I said to him, "You've never unloaded the bodies of twenty young soldiers from tanks. I have." I said to him, "That's why I hate the war."

Ostensibly, the argument was about the Lebanon war. But what gave it its force was Yitzhak's sense that he alone knew how terrible the war was.

The devastating impact of shame and mistrust on the PTSD casualty's social life may be seen in Micki, whose social isolation, as was noted, helped drive him into a marriage for which he was not prepared. As Micki told it, he was a sociable high school student, with plenty of friends and an active participant in social activities, including a rock-and-roll band and a youth movement. After his CSR in the Yom Kippur War, Micki promptly cut off ties with virtually all his high school and army buddies. "I simply didn't want to see any of them any more," he reported.

> It's often hard for me to look people in the eyes. It gives me a feeling that they're prying into my soul, that they know exactly what's happening inside me, what I feel, and it usually puts me off. . . . I'm simply not strong enough. I don't have enough strength to cope. And I don't want other people to see that. Usually when I feel bad,

all that I think when someone looks at me is that everyone knows the state I'm in. . . . People right away ask you . . . right away, probe . . . so I think 4 or 5 times before I begin to talk to anyone. I think 10 times over whether he's a person I can trust. . . . I don't want people to know my problems. . . . It's a matter of judging you.

Micki was ashamed both of his breakdown and the problems it created in his life. Ever since his CSR, he had regarded himself as weak and unable to cope. The breakup of his marriage, hastened by his severe PTSD; his failure to establish himself economically (discussed in the following section of this chapter); and the incapacitating anxiety attacks he suffered every time he received a summons to reserve duty confirmed his failure in his own eyes and made him feel ashamed in front of others.

Deeply ashamed of himself, Micki feared and distrusted people. He saw them as prying, probing, and judgmental. Still feeling himself as vulnerable, exposed, and helpless as the CSR casualty, he perceived society in much the same way as the wartime enemy: inimicable and threatening to the remaining integrity of his ego.

The intensity of his shame and concomitant fear of exposure made it easier for Micki to be alone than in company. The only friend he had, aside from his divorced wife, was another CSR veteran and drug addict like himself, whom he could trust not to judge him because "he went through more or less the same things." For the rest, Micki stayed clear of meaningful social contact. He got into fierce political arguments with his former in-laws, participated in Peace Now (an Israeli activist group) demonstrations to express his disaffection with the Israeli government, and when he got so lonely that he could no longer bear it, overcame his phobia of crowds and forced himself to go to an occasional party where he would "act like I'm there" and feel as lonely as when he was by himself.

I noted in previous chapters that the general public, as well as the casualty, tends to regard a CSR as a failure and betrayal, and PTSD as a sign of weakness. What must be made clear in this context, however, is that at least in Israel, the PTSD casualty's social alienation is largely his own doing. The soldier who is evacuated from the front on account of a CSR does not wear a sign around his neck, and most people with whom he comes into social contact need not have any idea of the circumstances of his discharge. Then, even if they do, it is unlikely that long-standing friends would reject the casualty on that account, or on account of his subsequent withdrawal or hostility. Casualties told us that they felt different from former friends, and that they no longer felt that they belonged. But none told us that he had actually been rejected. On the contrary, it is they who stopped going to Friday night gatherings to which they were still invited, they who stopped speaking to erstwhile friends, and they who perceived society as hostile and dangerous.

AT WORK

Like reintegration into family and social life, the almost immediate return to work after a war is difficult for most veterans, and more difficult for the traumatized ones. For many veterans, interest in the job may wane; achievement, money, and status—the end rewards of work—may come to seem irrelevant. In non-PTSD veterans, the disengagement usually soon gives way to a return to the bread-and-butter banalities that sustain us and, sometimes, also to an energetic spurt of building and reconstruction, man's age-old answer to death. In PTSD veterans, the disengagement tends to be deeper and to reflect less a search for meaning than the impact of their symptoms.

The difference in the processes can be seen in a single veteran of both the Yom Kippur and Lebanon wars: Avi, who lives on a moshav (communal settlement) and manages a grocery store. In the Yom Kippur War, Avi lost a cousin with whom he had grown up and been very close, but he himself did not sustain any psychiatric injury. After the war, he went through a period of mourning and grief that expressed itself, among other ways, in a general disinterest in work. This, however, gave way within a few months to a renewed spurt of energy, drive, and ambition:

> [After being discharged] I went back to the moshav. First I did an inventory at the store, because someone else had worked there for 6 months. And I began to work on the farm. At the beginning, I told myself I wouldn't work hard. I didn't have a mind for work. I said, "People are dying. Money isn't worth anything." But you know how it is. Little by little you begin to get into the routine. I had to support my family. I started with vegetables. I put a lot of energy into the store, and I worked hard on the farm. . . . I built a house. We moved there. . . . When I got married, my wife didn't bring anything . . . I got everything by myself. I came back from the war and began to build.
>
> During the war, the guys would talk. I'd tell them, "My cousin worked hard. Days and nights. He had tractors. He bought a new car only a month before the war. He didn't get to enjoy it. So what good did all the work do him?" I'd say, "We'll get back from the war. God will give us bread to eat. That's enough. What more do you need?" But afterwards you want more and more and more.

After the Lebanon war, Avi did develop PTSD. He had the same feelings of "What's it all for?" as he had after the Yom Kippur War and felt similarly apathetic, disinterested, and depressed. Only now, his

PTSD undermined his control of his physiological and emotional responses, and his behavior on the job reflected less a philosophy of life and reassessment of values than the sheer impact of his disorder:

> I continued to work . . . [but] I came every other day. I'd be at work, have attacks [of hyperventilation]. Sometimes when I got an attack, I'd drive to the beach and burst into tears. I wasn't in control of it. When I calmed down, I'd go back. . . . I had trouble concentrating. . . . I wasn't interested in anything.

Avi's unremitting anxiety made it impossible for him to perform his duties properly. The high absenteeism, sudden running out on the job, inability to concentrate, global disinterest, and general loss of control he recounted are typical of the behavior of many PTSD casualties at work.

As with family and social relations, certain PTSD symptoms interfere with functioning at work more than others. Among the most widely mentioned interferences are memory and concentration problems, hostility, and sleep difficulties. Casualties tell of staring into space and their minds wandering. Some dwell on wartime incidents, on their breakdowns, or on their general sense of failure. Many of them tell of starting a task, being interrupted, and forgetting what they were doing. The following is only one of many examples: "I often forget things. For example, I take measurements for something, the telephone rings, I talk, and when I hang up I don't remember what I was doing. . . . I begin something else, then suddenly, maybe after 10 minutes or half an hour, I remember what I'd been doing earlier."

Heightened irritability and uncontrolled outbursts of rage cause business losses and interpersonal conflicts. I noted in the previous chapter casualties who broke expensive equipment and who attacked their employees or coworkers. Men constantly on the verge of bursting out would have special difficulty in working with others, especially in positions where tact and patience are called for.

The difficulties that PTSD casualties have in falling and staying asleep may compound the problems of poor concentration and hostility. More directly, men who cannot sleep at night begin their workday tired, nervous, and anxious. They have trouble pulling themselves out of bed in the morning, getting dressed on time, making their way through rush-hour traffic, facing their boss and colleagues, settling down at the job, and dealing efficiently with the problems that arise in a working day.

In certain cases, it is not symptoms as such that impair job performance but rather the generalization of emotions involved in traumatic wartime incidents to other areas of life. A doctor in our sample, for example, found it difficult to be around a particular piece of hospital machinery whose sound reminded him of the rattle of ammunition and flying gravel.

The impact of generalization on job performance can be seen very directly in Jacob, a bus driver before his breakdown who found it impossible to sit behind the wheel after a series of mishaps on a large truck during the Lebanon war. As a driver and medic, he was exposed both to the close sight of many dead and wounded and to real personal danger. At one point, he jumped out of his moving vehicle while it was being bombed only to be hit in the eye by splinters from an exploding shell and to lose consciousness. When he came to, he crawled back into the vehicle, deciding that if he was going to be shelled, it might as well be inside as on open terrain. As the shelling continued, the vehicle in whose enclosure he had sought at least a symbolic sense of safety became a trap. He wanted to jump out again, but he was "frozen . . . as if there were heavy weights on my hands and feet." Finally, just as he managed to put his hands out to make the leap, the truck fell into a ravine.

After the war, he generalized the threat associated with the truck to other vehicles. He stopped driving his car and could not bring himself to work behind the wheel of his bus:

> I came home and began to have symptoms. The bus that I had driven became a monster. It suddenly became very big. I was afraid to go inside. I was afraid to look at it. . . . They tried to get me back on the job. There's a bridge going up to the central bus station in Haifa. When I drove onto the bridge, I lost consciousness.

He had to give up the job as a bus driver that he had held for 19 years.

The problems created by PTSD thus often reduce the casualty's efficiency at work and restrict the type of jobs he can perform.

Some casualties are virtually incapacitated by their PTSD. Again one can take Micki as an example. Micki was injured shortly after he had matriculated from high school with good grades and completed a highly selective IDF officer's course. After the war, the promise he had shown dissipated. He went from one odd job to another, none of them commensurate with his abilities or offering the possibility of advancement. He would quit jobs to go abroad or be fired either for staring off into space or for disappearing without notice when a summons to reserve duty threw him into a panic. Whatever ambitions he may have had prior to combat, his PTSD annihilated them. To prove to himself that "I'm not one big zero," he applied to a top-ranking Israeli art institute but lost interest once he was accepted; he repeated the ego-boosting exercise with Tel Aviv University, but again he lacked the drive to follow through. At one point, his father sent him to Italy to study goldsmithing so he could join in a family business. Driven by loneliness, though, he came back after a brief stay and got married.

At the time of the interview, 12 years after his first CSR in the Yom

Kippur War and 3 years after his breakdown in Lebanon, Micki was working part-time in a record shop. The job had the dubious advantages of allowing him to start at noon after frequently sleepless nights and of not overtaxing his impaired capacity for concentrating. It had the disadvantages of providing neither challenge nor a living wage, so that at age 31, after his divorce, he was forced to move back with his parents and was unable to pay child support for his 4-year-old daughter.

Unlike Micki, however, the vast majority of casualties accommodate to their injury and manage to maneuver around it. Quite a number switch jobs. One of our sample found a job as a driver because he had become too tense and restless to sit in an office. Another, who could not cope with company, went from job to job until he found one where he could work in a room all by himself. Jacob was initially transferred by the bus company where he was employed to a clerical job; then, when that was unsatisfactory, he was made a first-aid instructor to drivers in training, which he enjoyed because it enabled him to play out the ego-enhancing role of army medic in a nonthreatening situation.

Other casualties keep their jobs and make enormous efforts to adapt to their PTSD. They function acceptably despite headaches and heart palpitations, rein in their irritability, and somehow maneuver around other symptoms. A teacher, for example, who prior to his injury taught without notes, told how his posttraumatic memory and concentration problems made him resort to writing out elaborate notes: "It's terrible for me, I have to write everything on slips of paper like an 80-year-old, and sometimes I have to search for the slip. I used to remember everything." He remained an effective teacher and retained the respect of his students by spending hours on class preparation.

The incentive for PTSD casualties to make such efforts may be that work provides benefits that are particularly relevant to them. For some casualties, the workplace serves as a nexus of support. It is a world of men, many of whom know the reality of soldiering. This, of course, can threaten the PTSD veteran who compares his failure to cope with their success. But practiced soldiers can offer a nonverbal understanding that wives and children cannot provide. Several of our casualties describe bosses who were extraordinarily tolerant of their lateness and absenteeism; who put up with their apathy, bad tempers, and poor output; and who refrained from asking questions when they were not wanted and provided a listening ear when it was. These were bosses for whom the casualties would do the world when they were able, and who were thus instrumental in their recovery.

For many PTSD casualties work offers escape—both from the emotional demands of their wives and children and, more often, from memory. Work was synonymous with health for Itzhak in the last chapter, because it helped to ward off the pain and frustration he felt when he was unoccupied. Other casualties seconded this feeling. "I almost stopped thinking about it [the war] altogether," said a PTSD veteran who made a point of working two shifts a day. "You don't have much time to think about anything else." Another confessed that "my only relaxation was escaping reality. . . . I wouldn't come home. I'd stay at work till I dropped from exhaustion." Yet another put it this way: "I felt a need to work hard, hard, so that I could find myself some place. . . . I was very distressed internally. . . . Driving the bus is the only thing that calms me down. . . . That's what saves me." Working overtime is thus perhaps as common among PTSD casualties as lateness and absenteeism. Repetitive physical labor, which provides a direct outlet for tension and aggression without taxing the casualty's impaired concentration or social abilities, is particularly useful. Casualties variously describe engaging in gardening, carpentry, and other physical hobbies for relief.

This immersion in work occurs at the expense of family and social life. It can also be argued that by diverting the casualty from his problems, it prevents him coming to grips with them. On the other hand, to the extent that it provides the casualty with an outlet for his tension and a means of controlling his pain, it may serve a therapeutic purpose. A Ministry of Defense official described the process by which his immersion in his work helped him to overcome the posttraumatic problems of alienation, detachment, apathy, and inability to concentrate that plagued him on his return from the front:

> For the first 6 months or so after the war, I was an astronaut. I was floating, couldn't get myself together. I went back to work, but I simply couldn't get into it. . . . I didn't feel like I belonged. My ties with the guys in the battalion were much stronger than with the people at work. . . .
> It was only about a year later that I began to get back to my former self. I reached the conclusion that I had to try harder at work and forget the things I'd gone through. I began to invest a great deal at work, including overtime . . . simply to busy myself more with day to day matters so that I shouldn't have so much free time to myself.

Another casualty told how his work in computers served as a means of coping with the guilt he felt after having been discharged from the army on account of his PTSD:

> As soon as I was discharged, I went back to work. Most of the guys were still in the army, so I had to work very hard because a lot of them weren't there. Maybe it was also a kind of compensation for my being civilian while they were in Lebanon.

Yet another benefit of work for some CSR casualties is that it helps restore some of their undermined self-esteem and sense of vitality. This is what Micki was trying to do when he applied to schools. Ron is very clear about these motives in his own activity: "In spite of everything, I put a lot of pressure on myself and had to prove to myself that I was capable of succeeding, that I'm not worthless, that the war hadn't finished me, that I'm not dead, that I exist." Similarly, Michael's shame and humiliation drove him to prodigal efforts to prove himself a mensch—a decent and able human being, recognized as such by his fellows. Work and school were the proving grounds:

> I was listed as a casualty, as crazy, and I wanted to do something . . . I got promoted at work. I took courses. . . . There were people who said, "Someone who was injured like that will never be a mensch," so I wanted to prove that I could be.

Their compulsive, often frenetic immersion in work brings the PTSD casualties who adopt this means of coping obvious benefits, including the not inconsiderable advantage of material success. It counters the downward pull of apathy and depression, it compensates somewhat for the damage done by bad temper and poor memory and concentration, and it is a more productive means of coping than absenteeism and nonperformance.

Nor should the improvement in the mental status of casualties who throw themselves into their work after an initial phase of not functioning be scorned. Indeed, many of the casualties quoted in the above pages, including the doctor who would not bear the noise of a machine he had to work with and the teacher who had to write out detailed notes for every class he taught, advanced in their jobs. Some amassed considerable wealth, and others gained status.

Nonetheless, the casualties' frenetic activity aimed at warding off memories, avoiding thought, releasing tension, compensating for guilt feelings, and proving themselves cannot be considered an adequate substitute for the pleasure of doing a job one enjoys for its own sake or for focused, purposeful efforts to achieve a goal outside of oneself. Although casualties who function poorly at work subsequent to their injury generally feel bad on that account, those who function well (in the technical sense of the word) by virtue of their escapism, nervous energy, or compensatory zeal thus rebuild their damaged self-esteem only partially and do little to affect their PTSD symptoms. As Ron put it, "Materially I'm very rich . . . but emotionally I'm still very poor." We can say that their compensatory functioning at work is the lesser of two evils.

8

If at First You Don't Succeed
Military Functioning after CSR

Israel has the dubious distinction of probably being the only democratic country in the world where men serve in the army for 6 long years: 3 in regular service between the ages of 18 and 21, then about 3 more parcelled out in annual reserve duty periods of 1 to 2 months until they are 55. The legal requirement to serve has been imposed to enable the country to meet the unceasing (thus far) threat to its security with the extremely limited manpower at its disposal. There are almost no exemptions. Students can be called up in midsemester, dentists summoned from their private practices, and clerks called out of government offices.

They are called as needed, for drills, guard duty, the provision of routine maintenance or services, or special operations. Often enough reserve duty is uneventful, and there are men who welcome it as a respite from work and family. At other times, it can pose a real danger, especially for the men in combat units. Retaliatory raids are sometimes carried out by reservists. Some of the soldiers who flew to Uganda in the 1975 Entebbe operation to rescue kidnapped Israeli hostages were also reservists, and so were the soldiers who crossed into Lebanon in the 1977 Litani operation. Reservists have formed the bulk of the manpower in Israel's unfortunate succession of declared and undeclared wars. In the 3 years that the IDF spent in Lebanon, as in previous conflicts, reservists were generally called up for a 30-day tour of duty, discharged, and then called up once or twice again.

The ability of the traumatized war veteran to function in the military is thus a crucial issue in Israel. It is vital for the IDF to know how such soldiers can be expected to function, so that it can place them to best advantage. Manpower needs and considerations of morale—both of the army unit and of the casualties—make it imperative not to forgo the service of men who could contribute valuable labor or skill. On the other hand, no one benefits from the exposure of vulnerable men to situations with which they cannot cope or that may worsen their disorder.

The most direct test of military functioning, obviously, is in war. What happens to traumatized veterans when they are reexposed to combat? Chapters 12 and 13 will answer this question with respect to soldiers who were inadvertently redeployed in Lebanon following unidentified psychiatric disorders (mostly in the Yom Kippur War). But just as obviously, psychiatrically injured men cannot be returned to combat simply for the purpose of methodical assessment. Fortunately, we have two other means at our disposal. One consists of our subjects' perceived self-efficacy in future combat, as assessed by our self-report questionnaire. The other consists of their attitudes and feelings toward and behavior in reserve duty, as gleaned from their interviews.

PERCEIVED SELF-EFFICACY IN COMBAT

The concept of perceived self-efficacy in combat was adopted as a mediating variable that could predict the future combat functioning of traumatized veterans. As defined by Bandura (1977, 1982), *perceived self-efficacy* is the judgment a person makes about how well he or she would execute a variety of behaviors in a prospective situation. Bandura contends that people constantly assess their range of capabilities and that these assessments guide and influence their behavior. When people consider activities to be within their capacity, Bandura suggests, they are willing to invest effort and energy and to persevere in the face of obstacles or aversive circumstances. When they regard an activity as exceeding their ability, however, they tend to minimize their efforts, perform less effectively, or avoid the activity altogether. Other researchers have also consistently found perceived self-efficacy to be a valid predictor of behavior in a variety of circumstances, including the cessation of smoking following intervention (Condiott & Lichtenstein, 1981; McIntyre, Lichtenstein, & Mermelstein, 1983), use of analgesis in childbirth (Manning & Wright, 1983), and reactions to fear-producing situations (Bandura, Hess, & Adams, 1982).

Bandura makes a convincing case for the idea that past experience in a given area is a major determinant of perceived self-efficacy in that field. It thus seemed to my colleagues and me that CSR casualties, who failed to function adequately in combat, would suffer (in addition to their other personal and social problems) an impairment of their perceived self-efficacy in combat. It also seemed reasonable that PTSD veterans without an antecedent CSR would report a similar impairment, for although they weathered the immediate stress of battle, their disorder reflects their ultimate inability to absorb and integrate the calamity.

To assess these hypotheses, we constructed our own questionnaire (see Box 8.1), which presents 17 specific battle events chosen on the basis of a thorough review of the literature and interviews with combat-experienced IDF psychologists. The items include incidents such as "A shell explodes nearby," "You see the body of a dead soldier," and "It looks like the battle is lost." Respondents were asked to indicate on a 5-point scale (ranging from "Very well" to "Not at all") how well they believed they would be able to function in each situation were they to confront it that day. Following Bandura's methods, two scores were computed for each respondent: (a) *Strength* of perceived self-efficacy was the average rating for all 17 items, and (b) *breadth* of perceived self-efficacy was the number of situations with which the respondent indicated he believed he would be able to cope at least to some extent. In both measures, the higher the score, the higher the perceived self-efficacy.

The results (Weisenberg, Schwarzwald, & Solomon, 1991) sup-

BOX 8.1

Perceived Self-Efficacy Questionnaire

Now we will present different situations that occur in combat. Please indicate next to each one to what extent you think that you would be able to function as required *today* should such situations happen to you.

	To a very great extent	To a great extent	Somewhat	Not much	Not at all
1. The first shell lands near you	1	2	3	4	5
2. Seeing the first fatality	1	2	3	4	5

(continued)

BOX 8.1 (*Continued*)

	To a very great extent	To a great extent	Somewhat	Not much	Not at all
3. Many bullets whistling past you	1	2	3	4	5
4. A good friend is injured in combat	1	2	3	4	5
5. The battle seems lost	1	2	3	4	5
6. You think the commander is mistaken in his calculations	1	2	3	4	5
7. You have been wounded	1	2	3	4	5
8. The commander has been wounded severely or killed	1	2	3	4	5
9. Running forward under fire	1	2	3	4	5
10. Our soldiers are firing on you in error	1	2	3	4	5
11. A good friend has been killed in combat	1	2	3	4	5
12. Extended fighting without sleep	1	2	3	4	5
13. Seeing the first casualty	1	2	3	4	5
14. The enemy is attacking and response is impossible	1	2	3	4	5
15. You're not sure the battle is necessary	1	2	3	4	5
16. Many shells are falling near you	1	2	3	4	5
17. You feel detached from your unit	1	2	3	4	5

ported only our first hypothesis. During all 3 years of the study, soldiers who had been diagnosed with CSR during the Lebanon war reported lower perceived self-efficacy in combat, with a lower average strength of endorsement (see Figures 8.1 and 8.2). Among PTSD casualties, how-

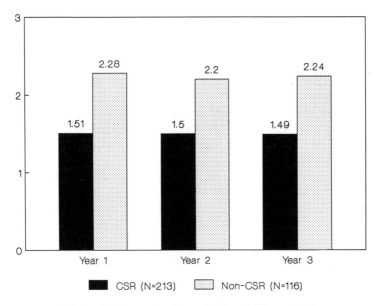

Figure 8.1. Strength of perceived self-efficacy (PSE).

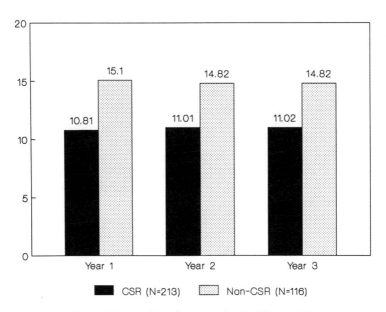

Figure 8.2. Breadth of perceived self-efficacy (PSE).

ever, as can be seen from Figures 8.3 and 8.4, a drop in perceived self-efficacy in combat was apparent primarily among those with an antecedent CSR. PTSD casualties without a diagnosed CSR did not show a corresponding drop; their perceived self-efficacy was similar to that of the rest of the non-CSR controls (see Figures 8.3 and 8.4). These results were stable over all 3 years of the study. Despite the passage of time, which had a healing effect on other outcomes, the perceived self-efficacy of CSR veterans remained as poor at the end of 3 years as it was in the first year of the study. They did not regain their self-confidence or improve their injured self-images.

As in many of our measures, the question once again arises as to whether this finding is an antecedent or an outcome of CSR. It might be argued that CSR soldiers had less confidence in their combat ability than their non-CSR counterparts even before they went into battle, and that their poor opinion of their capacities augmented their anxiety and thereby made them more susceptible to a breakdown. This line of reasoning is not inconsistent with Bandura's (1982) view that self-efficacy is determined by past experience, and because the data were all gathered after the war, the possibility cannot be ruled out. Nonetheless, the careful matching (discussed in Chapter 2) of CSR and non-CSR subjects for premilitary motivation, adjustment, and personality, including the ability to deal with physical and psychological hardships, makes this train of development unlikely. So do the soldiers' interview accounts of how they went into battle. Like the two CSR veterans discussed at length in Chapter 4, many of our casualties went off to war with abundant self-assurance, gained from the high morale of the IDF and from its succession of victorious contests.

It seems far more likely that the decline in perceived self-efficacy among CSR veterans is a consequence of the breakdown itself. This view accords with Bandura's contention that failure in a task lowers a person's perceived self-efficacy in that specific area. As will be discussed further in Chapter 10, CSR soldiers generally regard their combat breakdown as a failure and an indication of their inability to cope with the stress of battle. Their low endorsements on the perceived self-efficacy questionnaire are corroborated by their free-form assertions, in which "I don't know how I'd cope if I had to fight another war" was a frequently voiced sentiment. Danny, a computer analyst who suffered a CSR in the Yom Kippur War after his tank drove over a land mine and he had to run by foot through a minefield under heavy enemy fire, stated that "the one fear I have is of having to fight in a war again, because I don't know how I'd function in a real combat situation."

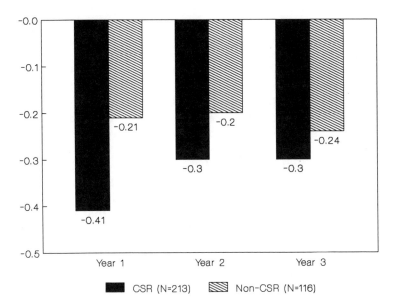

Figure 8.3. Correlations between strength of PSE and PTSD intensity.

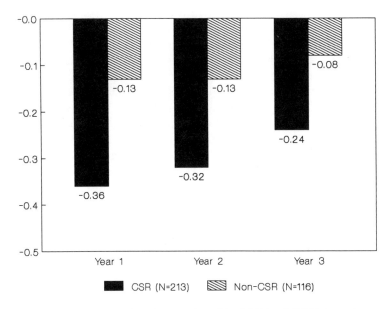

Figure 8.4. Correlations between breadth of PSE and PTSD intensity.

One of the most interesting and surprising findings of this study is that PTSD casualties who did not suffer an antecedent CSR did not report a loss of self-confidence in their soldierly abilities. The perceived self-efficacy results accentuated the distinction between the two types of PTSD—with and without a prior CSR—more than any of our previous measures. This was initially surprising, especially because (as the reader will see in Chapters 12 and 14) many of these veterans in fact showed problems in reserve duty, where their symptoms were exacerbated. The possibility that their self-confidence may be a product of denial thus comes to mind. As may be recalled, the CSR and non-CSR study groups were defined by the fact that the former all sought psychiatric intervention, whereas the latter did not. Although the motives for coming or not coming to therapy are complex, one of the things that keeps suffering veterans from seeking help is the desire to ignore or deny their distress. The same denial might have kept them from admitting to a blow to their self-confidence in the all-important military domain.

In retrospect, however, the finding is consistent with our knowledge (see Chapter 5) that PTSD without antecedent CSR is a distinct clinical entity, differing in scope and intensity from PTSD with antecedent CSR. The unimpaired perceived self-efficacy among casualties who developed their PTSD after successful combat may simply be another indication of the lesser severity of the disorder in this group.

The finding is also consistent with Bandura's view of perceived self-efficacy as based on past experience. The fact is that, unlike their counterparts with CSR, most of these soldiers did withstand the rigors of the battlefield, and so had reason to believe that they would be able to do so again. If some of them had unidentified breakdowns, the fact that they were not referred for therapy may also have contributed to maintaining their original estimation of their ability to function in combat. The need for therapy, among CSR casualties as well as others, tends to force a person to recognize his inabilities, and psychodynamic therapy in particular tends to reinforce that recognition. Identified CSR casualties who were referred for treatment, and in many cases persisted in it, may thus have become more aware of their vulnerabilities than PTSD sufferers without antecedent CSR. Thus, although in some non-CSR PTSD veterans the report of relatively high perceived self-efficacy is probably a sign of denial, in others it is probably an honest indication of the sound view they have of themselves. At least some of these soldiers are probably less likely than identified CSR casualties to see themselves as inadequate either in general or in the military sphere.

RESERVE DUTY

The Israeli called up for reserve duty—usually once a year in periods of lull, more often in wartime—is required to make a rapid transition from civilian to military life. He bids farewell to his family and friends, receives paid leave from his job or business and enters a radically different environment. Instead of choosing his clothes in the morning, he dons a uniform; instead of making decisions, he obeys orders. The army appropriates his time, his privacy, his freedom; it forces him to forgo familiar sources of affection and support, an abundance of creature comforts, and the security derived from familiar patterns and routines. The transition tends to be sharp and quick. Unlike in regular service, there is no adjustment ritual upon entry or decompression time on discharge. The citizen becomes a soldier within a day, and within a day the soldier is thrown back into his civilian roles as son, father, husband, and breadwinner.

For many men, the periodic metamorphosis allows a respite from the tensions of daily life; they leave home almost as if for a vacation and return feeling refreshed and ready for renewed efforts. But for many others, the forced change is disrupting and unsettling, especially as they get older. They may find their duties physically strenuous, the forced compliance of military life irritating, and the arbitrary sweeping away of habits and routines jarring.

Moreover, reserve duty constitutes a powerful threat that is both symbolic and real. It is a living reminder of what everyone knows but tries not to think about: that the army is an instrument of war and that they, its soldiers, can be the victims of war. As soon as they don the uniform and walk onto a military base, they know that their chances of being engaged in some form of fighting are more than theoretical. This is true even in periods of relative lull, such as between the Yom Kippur and Lebanon wars, and is all the more so after the Lebanon war. For nearly 3 years after the formal cease-fire in August 1982, the IDF was still stationed beyond Israel's northern border, and reservists were sent in large numbers to the front. Since the pullout, the IDF has made occasional incursions into Lebanese territory, and terrorists coming from Lebanon, Jordan, Egypt, or the Mediterranean Sea have penetrated or tried to penetrate Israel's borders. Reservists have born the brunt of many of both the defensive and offensive operations.

The numerous psychological burdens of reserve duty make it a kind of crucible wherein the soldier's potential in combat can be tested. Although not every man who functions successfully in the reserves will necessarily fare as well in the greater heat of more protracted and intense warfare, those who have trouble in the reserves are obviously unlikely to withstand the stress of war.

Interviews with our subjects show that whether or not any given stint of reserve duty is actually dangerous, the summons to serve frequently brings on anticipatory anxiety and augmentation of symptoms. Call-up orders are the bane of the CSR casualty's life. Said Ron, speaking for many: "Every time a summons comes in the mail, I feel that my world is falling into shambles." Headaches, heart palpitations, and digestive problems such as diarrhea and vomiting are among the common somatic responses. Not a few CSR veterans report shaking and trembling with fear upon receiving the call-up notice. Depression, loss of appetite, and an upsurge in war-related thoughts and nightmares are also reported.

In some cases, the period before going to reserve duty is marked by heightened family tensions, with even more than the usual fights that PTSD veterans tend to get into with their wives and children, and increased work problems stemming from nervousness, lack of concentration, and absenteeism. Several of our chronic PTSD veterans reported that the only time they were symptom free was when they were abroad, when the threat of being called up to reserves was temporarily inactivated.

Many of the emotionally wounded veterans were bothered not only by the prospect of having to fight again, but by symbolic threats associated with the reserves. The sight of uniforms evokes strong fear and aversion, as do weapons and military vehicles, even when they are quietly packed and parked. Thus, for many such veterans, even walking onto an army base in the relatively safe center of Israel was extremely anxiety provoking, and they avoided doing so. Even such routine matters as an army request for an address update would throw some veterans into a panic, making them feel as if they were being called up to war again.

Usually the veterans were frightened by the threat of injury or death implied in military accoutrements. Among CSR veterans, there was also often the fear of being put to the test and failing again. Weapons practice in the reserves arouses both types of fears. Veterans who have trouble controlling their rage tend to be most frightened by the thought of running amok and hurting someone with the weapons.

In an article in the Hebrew medical journal *HaRefuah,* Neuman and Phenig (1986) relate that ever since the 1973 Yom Kippur War, an increasing number of soldiers have been approaching IDF mental health facilities with requests for psychiatric discharges from reserve duty. Among the various groups enumerated are both CSR veterans (who, despite their treatment, remained fearful of serving) and non-CSR veterans with either clinical or subclinical PTSD. Even for the veteran without an antecedent CSR,

> the reserves call-up is an additional irritant that brings up threatening associations and memories that are generally suppressed. They see the return to reserve duty, even in peacetime or in behind-line units, as a threat to the psychological balance they achieved with a great deal of emotional effort. (p. 204)

The authors label the phenomenon "traumataphobia"—an aversion to and fear of returning to the traumatic situation or to any situation reminiscent of it.

Among our sample, some veterans solved the problem of reserve duty by obtaining discharges on physical grounds. Some requested psychiatric discharges, frankly declaring their inability to cope in a military setting of any sort. For many injured veterans, however, the problem was more complex because of the high premium placed on military service in Israel. On the one hand, there is an almost universal sigh of relief on the part of CSR veterans upon receiving a discharge, a widely expressed sense that an onerous weight has been lifted. On the other hand, the discharge often brings with it feelings of exclusion from the comraderie of Israeli men and of failure in one's civic duty and masculine responsibility.

So, Neuman and Phenig's observations notwithstanding, many emotionally injured veterans do make formidable efforts to remain in the army or to be reinstated after a temporary discharge. As one of many examples, we may cite Joseph, the senior physician at a major Israeli hospital. Joseph fought in three wars and sustained two CRSs before he finally accepted his inability to function in the combat reserves.

After his CSR in the 1973 Yom Kippur War, he was offered a discharge from reserve duty but declined it. Instead, he specifically asked to be assigned to areas where there was unrest, using the argument that he wanted to be placed where a heavy work load would keep him too busy to get upset. His request was granted, and he was stationed in the Jordan Valley, treating soldiers injured by mines or in the numerous conflicts with terrorists coming from Jordan. Throughout his service there, he was caught in the throes of his major dilemma. Every time he was summoned, his PTSD symptoms (which were under control in civilian settings) rose to the surface, and soon enough he would be forced to ask "not to be placed in situations I couldn't deal with." At the same time, he consistently refused to request a discharge. Having been brought up on the ideal of sacrifice for his country and having internalized the image of the Israeli soldier as an "invulnerable James Bond," he felt that making such a request "was not very honorable" and adamantly refused to give in to his weakness.

In the 9 years between the Yom Kippur and Lebanon wars, the only time he did not suffer from PTSD symptoms at all was during a 3-year stay in the United States, where geographic distance mercifully prevented him from serving. Yet back in Israel, when his profile—his combat fitness rating—was lowered on physical grounds, he struggled with the authorities to have it raised to full combat capacity; then, when it was raised, he fought to be assigned to a crack unit in the armored corps. "Between '73 and '82 my motivation was very high," he explained. "I never asked to be discharged from the reserves because of emotional problems, even though the service was very difficult for me psychologically." It was only following a reactivation of his CSR in the Lebanon war (as discussed in Chapter 12) that he resigned himself to doing his reserve duty in a hospital in the center of Israel. "This is the first time in my entire service that I saw that I couldn't do as much as I wanted."

For Joseph, and others like him, reserve duty, especially in combat units, recreates the original conflict that brought on their CSR. As we recall, the CSR soldier is caught in a conflict between the desire to do his duty to his country and comrades and the desire to save his life by fleeing. Every time the CSR veteran goes into the reserves, the conflict is renewed. Joseph dealt with the conflict using counterphobic defenses, demanding strenuous and dangerous assignments to prove to himself and others that he was not afraid. Other CSR veterans in our sample used different techniques for coping with the dilemma.

For example, Ron, whose CSR in the Yom Kippur War went undetected, put his considerable manipulative skills to use in order to remain in the highly valued parachutists while consistently avoiding the military drill that is an integral part of reserve duty in a combat unit. Every call-up notice he received made him shake and tremble, "as though I were being called up to war again." He was afraid of armored personnel carriers—he had sustained his CSR while riding in one—and of weapons. Yet, unaware that he had sustained a psychiatric injury, he never asked for a discharge.

Instead, he consistently evaded every live-weapons exercise in the 9 years between the Yom Kippur and Lebanon wars. Exploiting the elitist esprit de corps in the parachutists, he won his commander's trust by going out of his way to be helpful and cooperative, willingly taking on extra duties and filling in for other squad commanders. "But when the crunch came and there were live-weapons exercises, anything having to do with fire and combat, I systematically improvised a solution," he confessed. Once he claimed that his grandmother had died, another time that his wife had hurt herself and was in the hospital. What frightened him most, he says in retrospect, is "the thought that I might make some drastic mistake, that I could kill someone because of my nerves." It was only when he was drafted to the Lebanon war that he asked for a discharge. His request was denied, and, like Joseph, he had a second CSR, which finally won him a temporary release from service.

At the other end of the spectrum, Aaron, a high-ranking official in the Ministry of Defense, employed an elaborate system of monitoring to cope with his anxiety. After sustaining a CSR in the Yom Kippur War, he suffered from chronic PTSD right up through the Lebanon war 9 years later, but he continued to serve regularly in a patrol unit. His fear of reserve duty focused on the not-unfounded possibility of being taken prisoner and tortured to disclose the security information he had by virtue of his position in the defense ministry.

He handled his apprehensions by making elaborate mental preparations. Unlike most PTSD veterans, who are upset by security-related news, Aaron made such news an obsession. "Beginning with the Yom Kippur War," he reported, "I had the feeling that I had to be at the center of things, to know what was going on." He listened to the news compulsively, every hour on the hour. He read newspapers, straining for every possible hint of another war. He analyzed the minutest details, checked them against maps, and gathered information from friends who had come from the field. He brought a transistor to work. If he happened to be at a meeting, he would stop on the hour, ask for a few minutes of quiet, listen to the news briefs, check that everything was all right, and only then go back to the discussion. At night, he assiduously watched the 9 o'clock news on television and would not go to bed before hearing the final radio news broadcast at midnight.

> If I know the news, I might at least be able to prepare myself emotionally if another war breaks out. Every time I went into the reserves, I analyzed the situation, and my behavior accorded with the analysis. If I knew that the situation was relatively calm, so was I. I knew what I was getting into, what sort of things I'd be doing, and I went without undue worry.

The other side of the equation is that when the signs pointed to danger, he was much less calm.

In Lebanon, he served as an administrative officer in an armored battalion. When the order to open fire arrived, he was suddenly flooded with memories of the Yom Kippur War. Although he was supposed to stay behind the lines, he wanted to be with the rest of the men, so that if something should happen to him they would be there to rescue him. He jumped into a truck and drove up to the front. After Lebanon, he was transferred to a unit behind the lines, to his great satisfaction.

Technically speaking, all of these CSR veterans—and many like them—functioned in the combat reserves. None of them asked for a discharge; none behaved so badly as to provoke even disciplinary action, to say nothing of a dismissal. It is quite clear, however, that men who go to reserve duty with the anxiety that these injured veterans brought to it are unlikely to make effective combat soldiers. Many of the mechanisms they used to enable themselves to continue to serve in the reserves would alone undermine their effective coping with battle. Indeed, many of them broke down again in the next war they fought, and as we shall see in Chapters 12 and 13, the strains of reserve duty generally worsened their condition and made them more vulnerable.

Our interview data thus support the conclusion drawn from the responses on the perceived self-efficacy questionnaire (Box 8.1) and even strengthen them. On the questionnaire, CSR veterans with PTSD revealed their conscious doubts of their ability to function in combat. The interview data point to their intense fears of a much lesser military challenge, and moreover suggest that although many CSR veterans recognize their limitations as soldiers, quite a few do not. The veterans who persist in serving in combat reserves despite considerable apprehensions and augmentation of PTSD symptoms imply by doing so that they regard themselves as capable of performing on the battlefield. For such soldiers, true awareness comes slowly, sometimes after repeated stints of combat reserves, sometimes only after a second reaction. As Joseph put it after his reactivation in Lebanon:

> The thought of serving in another war frightens me very much. I don't know how I'd deal with it. Between periods of reserve duty, I feel quite well, but as soon as there are [call-ups for] reserves, my response is much stronger than I thought it would be, so it's very hard for me to predict.

One wonders how many of our subjects similarly hid their fear from themselves.

For both the army and the individual CSR veteran with PTSD, the most viable alternative would seem to be noncombat reserve duty following a period of therapy. In fact, the IDF currently channels many CSR veterans—both those who ask to serve and those whom it thinks are able to serve—into noncombat units, sometimes on the front (as in the case of Michael, discussed in Chapter 4) but more often within the relative safety of Israel's borders. Some casualties are not ready for that solution, and most require somewhat special accommodations (e.g., they may not be able to handle weapons or do guard duty). But when the various factors are taken into consideration, both the IDF and the casualty may benefit from the arrangement.

Avi, discussed in Chapters 3 and 6, was given a temporary discharge from reserve duty after his CSR in the Lebanon war. For about a year after his breakdown, this previously active and resourceful man was afraid to drive, avoided crowds, consumed several packs of cigarettes a day, and was deeply depressed. He had no illusions about his inability to cope with reserve duty. Shortly after his breakdown, there was a sudden vehicles draft, and an army representative knocked at his door. He refused to open up; when his wife did open the door, he refused to go out.

Nonetheless, "it's a lousy feeling in front of your children," he reported. "Everyone says, 'my father went to reserves.' And 'my father doesn't go to reserves' is an unpleasant feeling." So, after 2 years of not serving, Avi asked to be reinstated in a noncombat unit. This was not so easy to find, because the commander at the draft station was concerned about Avi's limitations—his inability to do guard duty or handle weapons and his general nervousness. But Avi persisted, and finally the officer in charge of telephone communications agreed to take him on.

Eager to serve, Avi plunged into his new assignment with the same energy and vigor he brought to the running of his small farm and to the management of the grocery store where he was employed. He promised the commander that the latter would not regret taking him on, and he was true to his word. When work had to be done until 2 in the morning, he stayed on. When there was a weeklong exercise, he worked days at the store and nights at his reserve job.

To be sure, he never entirely shook off the anxiety that reserve duty provokes in CSR casualties, and the ongoing inner need to prove himself added to his tension. Nonetheless, the army gained a highly motivated worker with considerable energy and organizing skill. And Avi was able to live down the ignominy of his CSR and regain his sense of belonging, usefulness, and mastery. As he told the interviewer: "I serve. I'm a citizen like everyone else. I'm all right. I'm not a fighter, but I contribute."

There are many Avis among our CSR casualties. Some will probably serve in limited but useful capacity for many years to come. Others may go on to recover enough to rejoin the fighting forces.

In summary, it may be stated that the army serves a crucial and unquestioned role in ensuring the continued existence of the state of Israel. The social cost of a psychiatric breakdown during war is thus far greater here than in many countries. For many men, though, the army also serves as an arena in which their masculinity is put to the test, and there is thus a great deal of added anxiety connected with success or failure in this context. The price that our casualties pay for failure is therefore not only a social one, but also (and to a greater degree) a personal one in terms of self-esteem.

9

Body and Soul

A mental health clinic is not usually the first station for soldiers with somatic problems. More often they turn to a medical doctor, even though the underlying problem is psychiatric. Being unaware of and/or reluctant to admit their emotional distress, they seek help from their general practitioner or IDF doctor, presenting somatic problems. This situation has led a longtime IDF physician to joke that lower back pains are the major medical problem in the Israeli army. He called them the soldiers' fig leaf—a discrete cover for emotional distress, more acceptable both to the army and the men themselves than the pain of the mind.

After the Lebanon war, many of the traumatized soldiers who reached our clinics, either directly or referred by their physicians, reported (along with their PTSD symptoms) a slew of physical complaints running the gamut from the proverbial back pains to nausea and diarrhea, headaches and chest pains, muscle spasms, and general exhaustion.

Their reports accord with the large body of research linking stress to a wide range of illnesses in the general population (see Bourne, 1969; Cannon, 1953; Selye, 1956; Wolff, 1953) and particularly with research that has found increased ailments in survivors of various forms of traumatic stress, including the Nazi Holocaust (Eitinger, 1964), natural disasters (see Baum, Gatchel, & Schaeffer, 1983; Davidson & Baum, 1986; Titchener & Kapp, 1976), and combat (Card, 1983; Stauffer et al., 1949).

Yet, suggestive as these findings are, they leave open the question of whether our patients' somatic complaints were related to their psychiatric injury or simply an outcome of their combat experience. After all, war may be considered sufficiently traumatic in and of itself, even without a stress reaction, to induce illness. Several studies have linked participation in combat directly to an increase in nonsurgical illness. Rubin, Gunderson, and Arthur (1972) found that the rate of somatic illness among pilots flying combat missions in a 6-month deployment in Vietnam was twice as high during the combat period as in the same amount of time before or after combat. In a similar study, Rahe, Gunderson, and Arthur (1970) found that the frequency of acute illness reported among navy and marine personnel reached its peak when their ships approached the combat zone and took part in combat operations. Similarly, Rubin, Gunderson, and Doll (1969) reported that somatic illness among the crew of an attack carrier consistently increased during periods of combat as compared to periods of lull, and that the rate of somatic illness was highest among men who had performed physically demanding or hazardous tasks or worked in a hostile environment. These studies have all consistently shown that somatic problems among military personnel increase as pressures, dangers, and demands accrue.

None of these studies had follow-ups, however, and there has been little research on the long-term health aftereffects of combat, so the precise link between combat and somatic complaints is undefined. The somatic problems may be short-lived; alternatively, they could impair health for long periods. Also, these studies would seem to suggest that combat itself is responsible for our patients' physical complaints. Thus, the many veterans who did not have CSR or PTSD and who never reached our clinics might have suffered from no fewer physical disturbances, or even more.

The latter possibility is suggested by much of the combat stress literature that came out of World War II, which regarded psychological and somatic manifestations of combat stress as mutually exclusive. The claim was that the expression of distress served as a ticket out of the battlefield and that some soldiers chose a somatic ticket, whereas others chose a psychological one; soldiers who evinced physical problems did not show emotional ones, and vice versa. In keeping with the fig-leaf view of somatic complaints, some of that literature suggested that people who expressed their distress physically were not always aware that they were suffering emotional distress.

On the other hand, the more recent literature linking somatic illness to combat does not rule out the possibility that the pathogenic effects of combat are differential, with psychiatric casualties at a higher risk than others for somatic disturbances. In fact, several studies have linked somatic disturbances specifically to PTSD. McFarlane (1988) reports that physical symptoms were the main reason that 5 out of 9 chronic PTSD subjects consulted their general practitioner after an intense Australian bush fire, and shows how in a number of cases the presenting headaches, hypertension, bodily aches, and so forth distracted attention from the underlying psychiatric disorder and delayed diagnosis. Davidson and Baum (1986) found that following the Three Mile Island nuclear scare, residents of the area with PTSD-like symptoms exhibited significantly higher rates of urinary norepinephrine and higher blood pressure (physiological measures of stress) than controls who lived farther away. In a study comparing veterans who served in the Vietnam War with Vietnam-era veterans who did not serve on the front, Stretch (1986) found that "the veterans with the greatest amounts of PTSD symptomatology also had the greatest number of physical health problems" (p. 164).

COMBAT STRESS AND SOMATIC ILLNESS AMONG ISRAELI SOLDIERS

To obtain a clearer view of the relationship between combat and illness, my colleagues and I assessed the health status of various groups of IDF soldiers 1, 2, and 3 years after their participation in combat in the summer of 1982 (Solomon, 1988; Solomon & Mikulincer, 1987b; Solomon, Mikulincer, & Kotler, 1987). The assessment was carried out by way of a self-report questionnaire designed by our research team to evaluate their physical health in terms of somatic disorders, somatic complaints, and health-related behavior.

The first part of the questionnaire (see Box 9.1) dealt with the subjects' medical history. Its purpose was to control for possible prewar differences, because a history of medical problems has been shown to increase the risk of both somatic and psychiatric illness (Solomon, Mikulincer, & Kotler, 1987). It asked whether any of them or their close relatives had ever been hospitalized on account of a physical or psychiatric disorder, and it presented them with a list of illnesses (including cancer, heart disease, diabetes, hypertension, and mental disorder) and asked them to indicate whether or not they or any of their close relatives had had these conditions. These particular illnesses were questioned because the literature indicates that stress is implicated in their genesis. No prewar differences were found in the health status of our CSR and control subjects in any of the areas examined (personal or familial history of somatic or psychiatric problems, and previous psychiatric treatment or hospitalization).

BOX 9.1

Health Questionnaire (Part 1)

1. Have you ever been hospitalized?

                          1. Yes   2. No

    If so, for which illness? _____

2. Does anyone in your family (parents, brothers, sisters) suffer from the following diseases?

                    Cancer   1. Yes   2. No
                    Heart disease   1. Yes   2. No
                    Diabetes   1. Yes   2. No
                    Hypertension   1. Yes   2. No
                    Mental illness 1. Yes   2. No

3. Have you ever suffered from emotional or mental problems?

                          1. Yes   2. No

    If so, describe: _____

    _____

4. How old were you when you had an emotional problem?   Age: __

5. Did you seek professional help (physician, psychologist, etc.) due to a nervous or emotional problem?

                          1. Yes   2. No

6. Have you ever been hospitalized in a psychiatric facility?

                          1. Yes   2. No

The second part of the questionnaire was intended to evaluate the health consequences of the war. Subjects were asked three groups of questions pertaining to their health in the previous year. The first group (see Box 9.2) queried major stress-related physical ailments—allergy, hypertension, ulcers, digestive problems, heart disease, chest pains, diabetes, stroke, and back pains—asking whether the subjects had developed any of these in the previous year.

BOX 9.2

Health Questionnaire (Part 2)

7. How would you define your general current health status?

    1. Very good   4. Poor
    2. Good   5. Very poor
    3. Not so good

8. If your health status is not good, indicate from which problems you suffer: _____

    _____

9. Have there been any changes in your health status in the past 10 months (approximately since the Lebanon war, excluding war injury)?

    1. My health status remains unchanged.
    2. My health status is better than it was.
    3. I have health problems that I didn't have previously (details):

    _____

    _____

10. During the past 10 months, did you begin to have a problem in any of the following areas?

1. Allergy	1. Yes	2. No
2. Hypertension	1. Yes	2. No
3. Ulcer	1. Yes	2. No
4. Other digestive problems	1. Yes	2. No
5. Heart disease	1. Yes	2. No
6. Chest pain	1. Yes	2. No
7. Diabetes	1. Yes	2. No
8. Stroke	1. Yes	2. No
9. Back pains	1. Yes	2. No
10. Pains or other illness	1. Yes	2. No

    Detail other pains or illness: _____

The second and third groups (see Box 9.3) addressed health-related behavior. The second group queried possible outcomes of either physical or psychiatric wartime injuries; one question asked whether the subject had begun taking any new medication on a regular basis, the other whether he was absent from work for medical (somatic, psychiatric, or psychosomatic) reasons. The third group focused on changes in health habits, asking whether the subject had made any changes in the amount of cigarettes, alcohol, or drugs he consumed. These three habits were chosen as possible responses to the stress of combat that might mediate the relationship between stress and illness.

BOX 9.3

Health Questionnaire (Part 3)

11. Have you been absent from work due to illness for more than 7 days during the past 10 months?

    1. No   2. Yes (details): _____

12. Have you begun to take medicine regularly during the past 10 months?

    1. No   2. Yes (details): _____

13. During the past 10 months, has there been any change in the amount of hard liquor you drink?

    1. I didn't drink previously and don't drink now.
    2. No change, I drink the same amount.
    3. I drink less alcohol than before.
    4. I drink much more than before.

14. During the past 10 months, has there been any change in the amount of cigarettes you smoke?

    1. I didn't smoke previously and don't smoke now.
    2. No change, I smoke the same number of cigarettes.
    3. I smoke less than before.
    4. I smoke a bit more than previously.
    5. I smoke a lot more than before.

(*continued*)

BOX 9.3 (*Continued*)

15. In the past 10 months, has there been any change in the amount of drugs you take?

    1. I did not take drugs before, and don't now.
    2. No change, I take the same amount of drugs.
    3. I take less than before.
    4. I take a bit more than before.
    5. I take much more than before.

The questionnaire was administered 1, 2, and 3 years after the war to various groups of IDF soldiers. The first issue we focused on was whether participation in combat as such had detrimental nonsurgical health consequences. This question was dealt with in the first year of our study (Solomon & Mikulincer, 1987b), in which health assessments were made on five groups of veterans: two groups of CSR veterans, 225 with PTSD (CSR/PTSD) and 157 without (CSR/NPTSD); two groups of matched non-CSR combat controls who participated in combat but did not sustain a CSR, 53 with PTSD (NCSR/PTSD) and 281 without (NCSR/NPTSD); and one group of 88 noncombat controls (NCC) who were combat ready but, for logistical reasons, had not been sent to the front.

Percentages of somatic complaints in these five groups are presented in Figure 9.1. Statistical analyses showed that soldiers who had participated in the war without either sustaining a CSR during the fighting or contracting PTSD afterward did not differ significantly from the soldiers who had not participated in battle in the number of physical complaints they reported. That is, participation in combat alone, without any psychiatric impairment, did not lead to negative health sequelae.

Thus far, our findings parallel the results of some earlier studies of the health consequences of catastrophes that raise doubts about a direct stress-illness diathesis. Particularly pertinent are several controlled studies of survivors of the Nazi Holocaust, acknowledged to be among the more horrendous catastrophes of this century. An investigation of 77 female survivors of Nazi concentration camps and other Israeli women by Antonovsky, Maor, and Downy (1971) found that although the survivors were emotionally less well adjusted than their nonsurvivor counterparts, there was no difference in the physical health of the two groups 25 years after the liberation. Similarly, more recent controlled studies of

Holocaust survivors by Eaton, Sigal, and Weinfeld (1982) and Levav and Abramson (1984) find little evidence of long-term physical conse-quences.

But the parallel is only partial. None of the above cited studies make any distinction between survivors who had PTSD and those who did not or who had regained emotional integration. Our investigation does. As can be seen from Figure 9.1, significantly more PTSD veterans (both with and without a prior CSR) than noncombat controls reported in-creased work absenteeism, starting the use of new medication, raising their alcohol and cigarette consumption, and the onset of chest and back pains and digestive problems. In other words, our findings suggest that health deterioration following a catastrophe is associated with the emo-tional disorder suffered therein.

These results coincide with Stretch's (1986) findings with regard to the health sequelae of the Vietnam War. Stretch, too, failed to note any difference in the self-reported postwar physical health status of combat and noncombat veterans (i.e., between his Vietnam and Vietnam-era

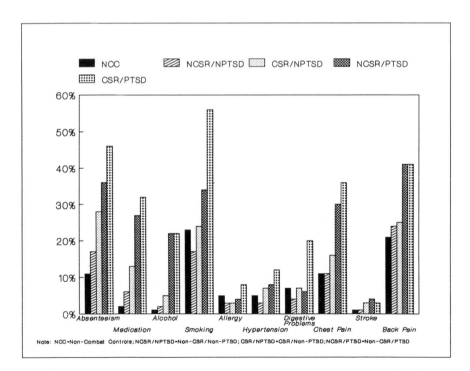

Figure 9.1. Percentages of subjects who reported somatic problems 1 year after the war.

veterans as a whole). He did find significant differences, however, between Vietnam veterans who sustained PTSD at any time after their tour of duty and remaining Vietnam veterans:

> PTSD-classified veterans currently have significantly more respiratory and overall health problems than do the non-PTSD classified Vietnam veterans. PTSD-classified veterans have also had significantly more past problems across all categories of health, including overall health, than have the non-PTSD classified veterans. (p. 164)

Having answered in the negative the question of whether participation in combat itself led to increased somatic complaints among our subjects, my colleagues and I turned to look more specifically at the consequences of psychiatric injury in combat. Here we assessed the relationship between CSR and PTSD on the one hand, and the veteran's somatic health and health-related behavior on the other. Here, we focused our analyses exclusively on our combat veteran subjects, comparing first the somatic complaints of our CSR subjects and matched non-CSR controls, and second the complaints of current PTSD and non-PTSD subjects in the two groups.

To begin with, we found that 1, 2, and 3 years after the outbreak of the Lebanon war, our CSR casualties reported significantly more somatic complaints than non-CSR subjects. As can be seen from Table 9.1, they endorsed more increases in work absenteeism and in alcohol and cigarette consumption and higher rates of onset of digestive problems and of chest and back pains than soldiers who had not sustained a CSR. In the course of the 3 years, their level of endorsement declined slightly, but the only significant changes were a decrease in back pains set off by an increase in work absences, which paralleled the trends in the control group. The statistical analysis did not disclose any significant interaction between study group and time of measurement. That is, the differences

Table 9.1. Percentage Rate of Endorsement of Somatic Problems in Each Study Group at Each Point of Time

Somatic complaints	CSR			Non-CSR		
	Year 1	Year 2	Year 3	Year 1	Year 2	Year 3
Absenteeism	5.8	41.1	46.4	5.1	16.7	22.1
Alcohol	15.6	15.9	21.2	3.4	7.8	6.9
Smoking	44.4	39.8	40.9	21.1	16.5	20.9
Hypertension	8.9	13.1	6.6	6.0	7.8	4.3
Digestive problems	15.9	12.7	13.1	6.0	8.6	1.7
Chest pains	29.1	29.6	20.7	12.1	8.6	7.8
Back pains	32.9	36.1	23.0	24.1	33.6	18.1

in the somatic complaints of the CSR and control groups remained stable over the 3 years of the study.

Similarly, at all three points of time, soldiers with current PTSD endorsed a higher rate of somatic complaints than soldiers not so diagnosed. As can be seen from Figure 9.2, the relationship between PTSD and somatic complaints was generally stronger in the CSR group than in the non-CSR group. The relationship between PTSD and somatic complaints was fairly stable over the 3 years in the CSR group, but in the non-CSR group the relationship strengthened as time passed: in the third year, the connection was three times as strong as it was in the first year.

Taken all together, our data show that our subjects' somatic complaints and the deterioration of their health-related behavior following the Lebanon war went hand in hand with their psychological disorder. Psychological and somatic manifestations of distress are not mutually exclusive in our subjects. In some of our casualties, physiological symptoms may serve to mask the emotional illness, making it difficult for the unsuspecting doctor to diagnose. But it is clear that the aches and pains of the body in our subjects add to rather than substitute for the distress of their hearts and minds.

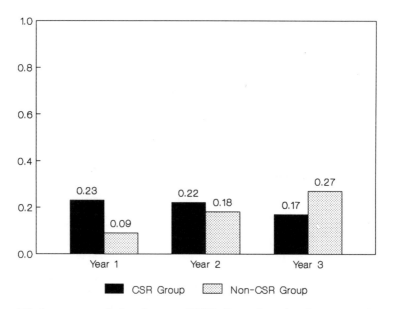

Figure 9.2. Average correlations between PTSD diagnosis and endorsement of somatic complaints.

To some extent, the physical complaints may be part and parcel of the psychological traumatization. CSR often includes physical manifestations, such as diarrhea, vomiting, nausea, enuresis, chest pains, and other physical symptoms (Kardiner, 1947); and PTSD, according to DSM-III (APA, 1980), is marked by an increase in somatization. In this respect, psychological trauma is similar to mental disorders such as anxiety, depression, and panic disorders, in which somatic manifestations are often observed (Kardiner, 1947). The studies cited above showing an increase in somatic illness during battle suggest that just as our veterans' psychological difficulties derive from their war experience, so do their physical ones, and in the case of PTSD casualties, the two linger on together. Although combat itself is insufficient to bring about negative health effects, the same factors that are involved in the genesis of our subjects' CSR and PTSD may be implicated in their subsequent physical discomforts. In making huge demands on their coping resources and draining their energies, the stress of combat would make the more vulnerable soldiers susceptible to both somatic and psychiatric illness.

Our subjects' somatic complaints may also be an outcome of their psychiatric disorder. Engel (1968) suggests that illness is commonly preceded by a period of psychological distress in which the individual feels unable to cope, a situation Engel terms "the giving-in—given-up complex." According to Engel, this complex is characterized by five psychological features:

> a feeling of giving up, experienced as helplessness or hopelessness; a depreciated image of the self; a sense of loss of gratification from relationships or roles in life; a feeling of disruption of the sense of continuity between past, present and future; and a reactivation of memories of earlier periods of giving up. (p. 293)

These are much the same features that are prominent in CSR (see Chapter 4) and/or PTSD (Chapter 6). Though they are neither necessary nor sufficient conditions for illness, Engel argues that the temporary breakdown of the psychological coping mechanism leads to the activation of a biological, neurally regulated emergency pattern that undermines the organism's ability to deal with concurrent pathogenic agents, and thus promotes the development of illness.

In a complementary vein, Titchener (1986) proposes that following psychological trauma, a growing hypochondriasis takes over in certain victims, and somatic symptoms become the focus of their lives. In his view, the avoidance, withdrawal, and psychic numbing with which traumatized individuals attempt to control and regulate the onslaught of traumatic memories may usher in a process of posttraumatic decline characterized, among other things, by increasing isolation and preoccupation with the physical self. In one patient he describes, "walling off his despair over the loss . . . was made possible by substituting the more acceptable pain and spasms in the head, neck, and back" (p. 10).

CONVERSION REACTIONS

Yet another type of association between emotional disturbance and somatic functioning can be observed in casualties suffering from *conversion reactions,* in which there is dysfunction in some part of the body (e.g., paralysis or blindness) with no actual organic impairment. In these cases, it is thought that psychological factors interfere with bodily functions in a way that conveys symbolic meaning to the symptoms.

The process of a conversion reaction can be seen in Avraham, whose symptoms go back to the Yom Kippur War, when, as a 26-year-old reservist, he served in a unit that forded the Suez Canal. Exposed to heavy shelling, he witnessed his fill of crushed and fragmented corpses. His most horrible experience was a direct phosphorus hit on the raft bridge he was manning, which left many wounded and about 10 soldiers "burnt and shrunken to a stick."

Highly motivated, Avraham was like many good soldiers who, at least on the surface, take the barbarities of war in their stride. "I didn't feel any special stress," he reported, beyond what he considered "natural" to a situation in which one sees one's friends maimed and killed. His concern was with doing his duty: preventing others from being killed and, after the phosphorus attack, wrapping the charred corpses.

The attack must have been fearsome, because none of the other men in the unit were willing to tend to the dead, as is required by the regulations of the IDF and the precepts of Judaism. Being a responsible soldier and a religious Jew, Avraham felt it incumbent to take upon himself the burial rites. Volunteering to shroud the corpses, he came into intimate contact with their burnt and mutilated forms. Even here, he "did the work without any special shock."

He continued to serve on the front for another 6 months or so, remaining an exceptionally cool and efficient soldier. After he was discharged, he resumed his life with no apparent aftereffects, except for a 6-month mourning spell during which he had little interest in going out or seeing friends. In the ensuing years, he fathered three children and advanced in his career, becoming assistant principal in the school where he taught. He also volunteered to take a course and join the army's rabbinic corps, knowing that it entailed caring for the dead and wounded.

When the Lebanon war broke out, Avraham went without any more than the usual trepidation. He told of an easy time, in contrast to what he had during the Yom Kippur War. He cared directly for only two wounded soldiers and, for the rest, spent his time keeping up the flagging morale of some of the men in his charge.

The first sign of combat stress came only on his home leave, when he felt "pain in every part of my body," which soon gave way to a distinct burning sensation. Notably, he had not the slightest inkling of its origin and made no connection whatsoever between it and the charred bodies he had tended in the long-past Yom Kippur War. "Suddenly, I felt my whole side burning," he reported "'What,' I said to myself, 'am I burnt? Nothing happened to me. Why is my side suddenly burning?'"

Seeking relief, Avraham went to his general practitioner, who prescribed tranquilizers that he refused to take. "I said, 'I'm going to start taking tranquilizers? I never took any in my life. What do I need tranquilizers for?'" When the burning sensation persisted, Avraham tried to allay it with sleep, to no avail, and took his temperature to check whether he had a fever, which he did not. As the end of his leave neared, he turned to his army physician, simply because he was in too much physical pain to return to duty. Failing to find any medical disorders, the physician asked Avraham to relate his war experiences and, upon hearing them, referred him to our mental health clinic. Avraham came reluctantly, wondering, "How do you connect this up?"

It was only after a period of therapy, during which he was encouraged to discuss his war experiences in greater detail than ever before, that Avraham began to have the dreams and nightmares that disturb most PTSD casualties and to make the connection between his burning sensations and his experience wrapping phosphorus-charred bodies in the Yom Kippur War.

That the veterans who endorsed the highest rates of somatic complaints and changes in health-related behavior were the PTSD casualties with antecedent CSR is consistent with this group's higher endorsement of distress on the other measures we have used. As with those endorsements, the cumulative impact of the stress of an unresolved CSR adding to the stress of combat and the stress of a posttraumatic reaction would seem to contribute to this group's higher rate of somatic complaints.

In keeping with Titchener's (1986) view that PTSD casualties who do not succeed in working through the psychological conflicts engendered by the trauma shift their attention to bodily problems, it may also be suggested that the PTSD casualties with antecedent CSR may find in their physical symptoms a welcome *ex post facto* rationale for their breakdowns in combat: their bodies, not they themselves, are responsible. This is not merely an alibi, for CSR casualties who go on to develop PTSD remain plagued by the overwhelming helplessness embodied in their breakdown and continue to regard themselves as weak and unable to cope (see Chapter 8). Such a rationale would perhaps free them from some of the terrible shame of their failure in one of the most valued masculine roles in Israeli society. It would serve to hide their shame and enable them to maintain a modicum of self-esteem.

HEALTH-RELATED HABITS: CIGARETTE, ALCOHOL, AND DRUG CONSUMPTION

As noted above, changes in health practices—namely, the increased use of prescribed medication and increased cigarette, alcohol, and drug consumption—were assessed both as possible health-related outcomes of participation in combat and as mediators in the stress-illness diathesis.

The increased use of medication and of cigarette and alcohol consumption endorsed by our CSR and PTSD casualties is consistent with earlier findings. Increased risk for drug and alcohol abuse was found among PTSD casualties in the general population (Helzer, Robins, & McEvoy, 1987), and increased use of prescription drugs, alcohol, and cigarettes was noted in survivors of the Buffalo Creek flood (Gleser, Green, & Winget, 1981). Numerous studies have demonstrated the greater incidence of drug and alcohol abuse and of resort to prescription medication among Vietnam veterans than among comparable controls (Card, 1987; Egendorf et al., 1981).

The increased use of medication is often a direct outcome of CSR and PTSD, in that minor tranquilizers, analgesics, antidepressants, and other drugs are commonly prescribed in the treatment of these disorders. As for the increase in smoking and drinking, CSR and PTSD soldiers may be employing alcohol and tobacco as tranquilizing substances to assuage distress.

The use of illegal drugs was acknowledged by only a minuscule portion of our subjects. In part, this reflects the relatively low drug use among Israeli combat soldiers, who are chosen from among the more highly motivated and psychologically fit recruits, and who tend to be from strata of the Israeli population where drug use is frowned upon and rare. It also reflects the naïveté of the question. The use of illegal drugs in the IDF is considered a serious offense and dealt with severely. In a country where army service is practically a lifelong commitment and military performance has wide-ranging repercussions on a man's civilian life (see Chapter 8), there were possibly some veterans who chose not to admit to their drug use on a questionnaire filled out at a military base and administered by men and women in uniform.

Micki, who had a CSR in the Yom Kippur War and again in Lebanon, was one of our only interviewees to discuss his drug use freely. An extremely lonely and isolated veteran who felt that "everything ended after my army service," he told how alcohol and drugs help him to maintain a tenuous hold on his emotions, reduce tension, suppress intrusive thoughts, and blunt the pain of his injury:

> Today I use mainly a lot of alcohol. I was told that the alcohol won't let me break down. I know it's what keeps me going. . . . It blunts my senses. I simply don't have the thoughts all the time. . . . The one thing that helps me when I'm tense is to drink. . . . I drink when I need it, and I don't drink all the time. But there was a long period when I was on cocaine all day . . . and there were also periods when I took a lot of uppers. . . . I don't know if it's a good solution, but the feelings they give me help me to be calm, so they're important to me.

Alcohol and cigarettes, to say nothing of drugs, are pathogenic substances. When they become important in the life of the traumatized veteran, they have all too well-known health consequences. Excess drinking often brings about cirrhosis of the liver; smoking increases the risk for cancer and heart disease. These changes in health practices also have ramifications in the veteran's personal and social lives (see Chapter 7). One of them is the increase in work absenteeism that our CSR and PTSD subjects reported.

ASSESSING SOMATIC PROBLEMS: SELF-REPORT AND MEDICAL EXAMINATION

It is unfortunate that the health data in this study were collected without concomitant medical examinations. This leaves open the possibility that our psychiatric casualties may have overreported their health problems. Most people have aches and pains of some kind or other, and subjective judgment has a good deal to do with when we define them as painful or disturbing. It is not implausible that the propensity of CSR and PTSD casualties to regard themselves as sick or weak in light of their psychological problems might make them more prone to interpreting their physical sensations or discomforts as more problematic than their emotionally uninjured counterparts. This possibility receives some support from our finding of primarily increased somatic expressiveness without increased physical morbidity: chest pains but no heart disease, digestive problems but no ulcers.

Medically based research conducted by former IDF chief psychiatrists Shalev, Bleich, and Ursano (1990) points in the same direction. They used a subsample of our subjects to compare Lebanon war CSR casualties with chronic PTSD and matched non-CSR/non-PTSD combatants. The comprehensive evaluation, which was carried out in the summer of 1985, included a self-report medical questionnaire, a physiological workup with physical and medical examinations, a multiple-stage incremental-load ergometric test, and a number of biological examinations. Results showed (a) increased symptom reporting in CSR subjects unmatched with findings in the routine medical examination; (b) deterioration in health practices (increased cigarette smoking, alcohol use, taking of prescribed medication, and obesity) among the CSR group; and (c) significantly less effort tolerance in the CSR group.

The absence of physiological confirmation, however, by no means obviates the negative health consequences of CSR and PTSD. Many stress-related disorders, including heart disease and ulcers, take a much longer time to develop than the span of our study; so do the disorders linked to smoking and drinking. Others do not show up readily in the physical examinations that are conducted for research purposes. For example, one of the CSR subjects in the Shalev et al. study died of cancer 3 months after the medical workup, in which his illness was not detected. Moreover, the rates of the disorders we did not find (heart disease, ulcers, stroke, allergy, and diabetes) in a healthy population of males in the age group of our subjects are very, very low. So even if there was an increase in these disorders, it may well not have shown up in a sample of several hundred.

My personal impression is that there was in fact an increase in illness in our psychiatric casualties. During the three waves of measurements, there were always veterans who came up to me to ask for assistance in navigating the bureaucracy of the medical corps. Some came with psychological problems, others with physical ones. Of the latter, more than a few came bearing letters and other documentation from their family doctors, who had diagnosed hypertension and, I recall, four new cases of diabetes in the CSR group.

Be this as it may, whether our PTSD and CSR subjects have diagnosable diseases or are "only" somaticizing is perhaps more important in scientific than in human terms. The burning sensation from which Avraham suffered and the headaches, backaches, chest pains, and assortment of other ills that our psychiatric casualties reported may not have mortal consequences, but like their DSM-III-defined PTSD symptoms and their heightened psychiatric symptomatology, their somatic complaints impair their functioning and affect the quality of their lives.

10

The Imprint of Trauma

In this chapter I will try to suggest some of the factors that render the aftermath of CSR so deep and enduring in our casualties. Focusing on the Israeli context in which the disorder occurs, I will discuss the imprint of vulnerability left by the breakdown; the casualties' feelings of shame and weakness at having "failed" in the masculine task of national defense; and the salience of war in this country, indicating how each contributes to prolonging our casualties' suffering long after they have been removed from the stress of the battlefield and are safe and sound at home.

THE IMPRINT OF VULNERABILITY

The wide, deep, and enduring wounds of war incurred by our CSR casualties were evidenced in their PTSD and general psychiatric symptomatology, impaired social functioning, and somatic problems. The CSR casualties' all-encompassing distress suggests that the psychological breakdown on the battlefield represents a major rupture in their psychological structure.

The persistent and intense distress may stem from the nature of the breakdown itself—what the CSR is and what it does to the psyches of the men who sustain it. As pointed out in Chapter 4, a combat stress reaction is the culmination and epitome of a process in which the individual is stripped of his sense of safety and mastery and experiences the full thrust of his vulnerability and existential helplessness. The CSR casualty is overwhelmed both by the external threat and by his own feelings of impotence.

A CSR is a painful and incontrovertible demonstration of how little control the casualty has over himself. Most of the major components of CSR, as revealed by the analyses presented in Chapter 3 and observed by others, testify to the casualty's loss of command over his behavior, thought processes, and physical and emotional reactions. The CSR casualty is unable to handle his anxiety; his efforts to block it by physical and emotional distancing are essentially compulsive and involuntary; the loss of self-control (i.e., weeping, vomiting, diarrhea) that expresses it provides most graphic evidence of his lack of mastery; and the disorientation and cognitive disturbances to which it gives rise deprive him of the ability to make the judgments and decisions necessary to choice and self-direction.

Like Ron and Michael, whose breakdowns were described in Chapter 4, one after another of the CSR casualties we interviewed told us, "I couldn't move," "I couldn't do a thing," or "I couldn't go on." This sense of utter helplessness, coming as it does under life-and-death circumstances, leaves an indelible *imprint,* analogous to the "death imprint" noted by Robert J. Lifton (1968). Like the imprint of death, the imprint of utter helplessness and vulnerability is not readily erased.

Brutally stripped of the psychological defenses that sustained him earlier, the traumatized soldier is exposed—naked and utterly unprotected. He emerges out of his ordeal without the basic psychological equipment that in the past enabled him to block, screen, and evaluate noxious stimuli (thus allowing for his adequate functioning). Reacquiring and redeveloping a shattered sense of safety is not an easy task. Listening to our traumatized CSR casualties, we often heard them say "I'm not the same person I was before—something broke inside of me" or "I'm finished; the war broke me." Both the casualties and their families recognize that something fundamental has changed inside of them, and that a transformation has occurred. The traumatic event marks a radical break and subsequent change in personality and behavior. Casualties regularly speak of "before" and "after" the war as two separate entities.

One may attempt to explain why the sense of mastery should be so difficult to recover once it is lost in a CSR on the basis of the classic work of Titchener and Ross (1974). Elaborating on Freud's concepts, Titchener and Ross assert that the mind is equipped with a "stimulus barrier" that filters out sudden or excessive outside excitation that could upset ego integration and personality organization. They hold that "psychic trauma occurs when the level of outside excitation or stimuli exceeds the capacity of the stimulus barrier to resist its intrusion, with the result of a breakthrough, disturbing integration, upsetting equilibrium, and leading to degrees of disorganization and imbalance of mental function" (p. 42).

They describe a multistaged process that transforms the external stress into inner trauma. The process begins with an external event that the individual perceives as a threatening stimulus requiring a response. This is followed by a stage of intrapsychic information processing in which the person must cope not only with the overt pressures but also with the internal covert stresses aroused by the traumatic experience. An emotional trauma occurs when the individual feels that he cannot keep out the stimuli with which he is being flooded. He feels helpless and believes that he cannot find the resources needed to cope effectively with the external stress. According to the authors, this flooding creates structural personality changes that lead to psychological symptoms or changes in behavior patterns.

In the dynamics it attempts to capture, Titchener and Ross's description of psychic trauma applies to all of our traumatized veterans, both those who developed PTSD after withstanding the stress of the battlefield and those whose PTSD followed a CSR. The dynamic is that the external chaos and threat of the war shatter or flood the mind's protective stimulus barrier (i.e., the psychological mechanism that filters external stimuli), which allows them to penetrate inside (hence the intrusive imagery) and to upset the mind's ability to process thoughts and feelings with its former efficiency. Recovery, the theory implies, involves the reconstruction of the stimulus barrier separating inside and outside, enabling the mind to process information in an orderly fashion.

Titchener and Ross caution that identifying this process does not help in predicting which individuals will recover from psychic trauma and which ones will undergo enduring character changes (i.e., in which casualties the psychological damage will be slight and soon remedied, and in which it will be deep and persistent). But it stands to reason that one of the factors involved is the nature and force of the trauma, and another is the person's capacity to resist it.

All traumatized veterans have been overwhelmed by an excess of wartime stimuli and the concomitant anxiety. But the CSR casualty, in contrast to veterans whose PTSD is not preceded by a battlefield breakdown, is also overwhelmed by his total helplessness in a life and death situation. Both the war and his utter helplessness have crossed the barrier and become internal realities.

Titchener and Ross's description parallels Shaw's (1987) view that CSR occurs when the soldier is stripped of the psychological defenses that keep out full awareness of his mortal danger. This is the dynamic suggested in our casualties' sense of walking naked down Dizengoff and of being without a roof—images of missing essential clothing or shelter that would protect them from the elements (their bodies from the physical exposure to enemy fire, their minds from grasping the extent of their mortal danger and the totality of their helplessness to avert it).

With the collapse of the psychological defenses that ward off awareness of death and help soldiers to cope, the helplessness that characterized the soldier's CSR remains a permanent feature of generalized vulnerability in his mind. It persists in the anxiety that CSR casualties continue to feel for years after the end of the war in their view of the world as a dangerous place, and in a permanent legacy of wariness, caution, and insecurity.

The PTSD, preponderance of intrusion and avoidance responses, and high levels of psychiatric symptomatology of CSR casualties represent their failure to rebuild and remobilize their shattered defenses or to regain the comforting feeling of personal security and mastery. The lost sense of mastery in trauma victims is painfully replaced by "pessimism, emptiness, and hopelessness" (Titchener & Kapp, 1976). Their psychic structure has been transformed in such a way that in some cases it can never be reconstructed, and in others only with great effort.

THE SHAME OF IT ALL

Both the casualty and the society at large tend to perceive a combat stress reaction as a failure and betrayal. In a time of crisis, when other people's lives depended on him in a most direct, immediate, and basic way, the CSR casualty let down his comrades on the front and his friends and family back home. This is true, though perhaps to different degrees, whether the CSR occurred right in the middle of the fighting (as in Ron's case) or after the immediate danger had abated (as in Michael's case).

All combat soldiers face the formidable task of dealing with the reality of injury, mutilation, and violent death they encounter on the battlefield. Dreams, nightmares, and waking contemplation of the slaughter they have witnessed are common among even unafflicted combat veterans. So is grief for fallen friends, often expressed in temporary moodiness and withdrawal.

But CSR casualties must also come to terms with the fact that they failed in a time of crisis. The consequences of their failure at a critical juncture include low self-esteem, shame, and fear of social rejection. "I'm not a hero," one casualty put it succinctly. "They evacuated me . . . and I felt humiliated. The guys are still in it and I'm not," said another. And yet another noted, "There were times I didn't want to leave the house. I didn't want to be seen in public . . . I was ashamed."

Although the imprint of vulnerability is a direct outcome of the combat stress reaction, the radical loss of self-esteem is a secondary effect that contributes to the prolongation of the casualty's distress. In Israel, well-ingrained social norms intensify the shame (and concomitant sense of nonbelonging) with which these casualties must contend, precisely when the imprint of vulnerability makes it difficult for them to contend with very much at all.

THE SABRA ETHOS

Israeli men are under intense cultural pressure to be strong, writes psychologist Amia Lieblich (1978) in her penetrating book *Tin Soldiers on Jerusalem Beach*, based on 10 years of work leading Gestalt therapy groups for Israeli men and women in the helping professions. "Strength is of tremendous importance to Israelis and their identity as individuals," she concludes. "Moreover, the need for power is so central that any signs of weakness are regarded as threats to the identity-as-a-whole and are, therefore, concealed from view" (p. 40).

The centuries of Jewish persecution culminating in the Nazi Holocaust and the day-to-day reality of the opposition of Israel's Arab neighbors to its existence, Lieblich argues, have made strength a prerequisite to survival in Israel and created a "pressure toward heroism," especially in the military realm. Israelis are educated to dedicate their lives to national goals and this education is accompanied by the message to "be strong," with strength being defined as both physical and emotional. It includes ideals of competence, responsibility, efficiency, and the ability to solve problems and to get out of tight spots. In many cases, the message is internalized and generalized, leading to the formation of a "tough" facade that prevents access to the weaker parts of the self.

The stereotype Lieblich delineates is accepted in large part by Israelis themselves, so much so that it is incorporated into the language. In Hebrew, the native-born Israeli is called a *Sabra*, after the indigenous cactus that is proverbially hard and prickly on the outside and soft and sweet within. The image of the Sabra is meant to convey the humanity beneath the Israeli's tough surface, and also the conviction that the better, softer parts must be concealed beneath a protective and threatening covering. Perhaps inadvertently, it also discloses the fear of how vulnerable the soft inner life is, should one's defenses be punctured.

   Lieblich's observations are based on a healthy population. Applied to CSR, her analysis suggests that the casualty's sense of helplessness on the battlefield constitutes a fundamental threat to his identity. Conceivably, a CSR would leave less of a searing imprint on men who were less identified with mainstream Israeli values and more ready and able to accept their frailty and the frailty of the human condition. Lieblich's view of the Israeli character implies that the duration and severity of the posttrauma in so many of our CSR casualties are, among other things, functions of their sense of acute shame—their difficulty in accepting the weakness that their breakdown so mercilessly demonstrated. "It could be that there were tougher guys," said Michael, an immigrant to Israel who had invested a good deal of effort in adapting to the social demands of his new country, "that I'm a softer type . . . I like art a bit. I'm a bit weak."

   The idea that the CSR casualties who are firmly implanted in the mainstream of Israeli society and have a high level of group identity and a strong need to conform to conventional social norms have a particularly hard time recovering is suggested by several IDF clinicians who have worked extensively with chronic PTSD casualties. Former IDF clinicians Nachi Alon and Haim Omer (Omer & Alon, 1983) report that

> most of the men suffering from the syndrome have an extreme need to perform well and succeed in competitive situations and a tendency to assume responsibility very early in life. These traits . . . are . . . a superficial facade covering a basic problem with masculine identity. The trauma [CSR], which is, objectively, sometimes only a slight injury or accident, receives this tremendous impact because of the inability of this sort of personality to face feelings of helplessness or lack of control.

Naomi Gilboa, former chief IDF clinical psychologist, has said that many of the PTSD casualties she saw struck her as individuals who "make high conformist, perfectionist demands on themselves."

   Our observations also suggest that CSR casualties who go on to develop chronic PTSD have the same need to be, and show themselves to be, strong. It is not mainly the shirkers, the soldiers who keep a low profile, the ones who might be considered weak and inept, who seem to succumb to the stress of combat. Our interviews leave the strong impression that among our hardest-hit CSR casualties are many soldiers who stand out for their bravery under fire, spirited dedication, and driving sense of responsibility.

   Joseph, for example, who broke down after his tour of duty in the Yom Kippur War, located the seeds of his reaction in his convictions and conduct during the war of attrition that preceded it, in which he functioned in exemplary fashion as a young medic:

I was convinced that one lived in the sort of tradition in which . . . one sacrifices his life for the other. I would go to retrieve corpses under fire, even though I thought it was altogether stupid. Soldiers would beg that their friend was lying outside. They couldn't bring themselves to touch the corpse. And they would ask me to go and pull the body under cover. And I would do it. I would go on foot from bunker to bunker with a knapsack on my back for anyone who didn't feel well, because that was the teaching we grew up with. . . . Possibly, if I had been taught differently, that the Israeli soldier is a person like any other, . . . not an invulnerable James Bond, then maybe it would have been different.

Joseph's idealism, strong sense of duty, and (as he adds) a "need for control" that made it difficult for him to tolerate the bungling, inefficiencies, and uncertainties that are inherent in any war were not the immediate causes of his CSR. But they hampered his ability to accept his failure of heroism and to come to terms with his behavior under stress, which Titchener (1986) considers a prerequisite of recovery.

Other of our CSR casualties exhibited similar values and behavior. "It's important for me to be all right," said Avi (who broke down when he was recalled to Lebanon after completing a tour of duty there), explaining why he was always ready to take on more than his share of the work in his unit. Jacob, who served as a combat medic in the Yom Kippur and Lebanon wars and felt that his CSR in the latter "paralyzed me," recounted loading the dead onto trucks and treating the wounded "between one Katyusha and the next," with inadequate supplies and no rest ("because I felt that I was obligated . . . to give better treatment than everyone"), until he finally collapsed after 3½ days without sleep.

There is doubtless a certain amount of self-idealization in the presentations that Joseph, Avi, and Jacob gave of themselves that helped them to justify their breakdowns and to live with the deep shame of their collapse. Nonetheless, their descriptions of their idealistic, dedicated, and responsible behavior in combat was corroborated by others and impressed our clinicians as essentially accurate. Even the choice of this type of rationalization (as opposed, for example, to blaming the CSR on their buddies or the army establishment) tells of the value they placed on the ideals they named. For men like these, the sense of helplessness and loss of control involved in a CSR were more devastating than for less demanding personalities, who were more ready and able to accept their weakness and the weakness of the human condition.

UNMANNED IN THE MILITARY

The fact that the collapse, with all of its inherent helplessness, occurred precisely in a military situation makes it especially hard to bear.

Marked by a cessation in military functioning, CSR is a breakdown in an area of life that is highly respected and even admired in Israel. The IDF is widely regarded as the only body that will and can protect the lives of the Jewish people and the Jewish state. The consensus that the army is the only safeguard of our individual and national survival is deeply rooted and cuts across almost all political and ideological differences.

The importance of the army in Israel derives from the precarious situation of the Jews in both the past and the present. Ever since the expulsion of the Jews from Palestine by the Romans in 70 A.D., Jewish history has been punctuated by periodic persecutions and expulsions, culminating in the Nazi Holocaust. Being both unarmed and stateless, Jews could neither defend themselves nor flee to a sure and permanent haven. During the Holocaust, the inability of the Jews to fight and the refusal of most countries to admit Jewish refugees resulted in the destruction of one-third of the Jewish people. Virtually every Israeli, including those of Eastern origin, carries within him the memory of the 6 million Jews exterminated by the Nazis. The power of the state of Israel, the only sovereign home for the Jews, is seen as the only protection against persistent persecution and the only assurance that Jews will never again go defenseless to the slaughter. The IDF is perceived as the only force capable of maintaining that power.

The current threat to Israel's physical existence reinforces and strengthens that perception. Israel may be the only country in the world whose territory is the object of irredentist claims and whose very right to exist is openly and vociferously denied by its neighbors.

The threat to personal and national survival is ever present and very real. With an area of only 21,500 sq km—44 km at its broadest, and a mere 6 km at its narrowest—Israel is vulnerable to being overrun. The burden of defense is carried by a population of 4 million people, as opposed to Egypt's 36 million, Jordan's 1.7 million, and Syria's 6.6 million, to name only the border countries who in the past have joined forces against us. In the first days of the 1973 Yom Kippur War, as the Syrians attacked from the Golan Heights in the north and the Egyptians crossed the Suez Canal in the south, there were so many casualties that people were genuinely afraid that Israel would be wiped out. This fear has never really abated.

The knowledge of what he is fighting for is thus embedded in the consciousness of every Israeli soldier. The underlying theme is *ein breira* (there is no alternative). Fighting for home and country is not just a patriotic slogan, but the motivating force behind military service in Israel. The conviction that we are forced to defend ourselves, rather than hatred for the enemy, is what spurs our soldiers and gives meaning to their sacrifice.

As already noted, military service is literally seen as the protection of home and family, so there is absolutely no tolerance for evasion of any kind. The IDF is a broadly based civilian army recruited from men and women of all walks of life. To make up for the extremely limited manpower, men serve in active reserve duty, for which they can be called up as required for between several weeks and several months a year until they are 55. There are no exemptions for students or professionals, either in regular or reserve service.

Attempts to dodge the draft are seen as deviant. In most circles of Israeli society, any youngster between the ages of 18 and 21 who is not in uniform is looked upon with suspicion. The social consensus is that the burden of defense is everyone's and, as such, should be equally divided. The pressure to serve is so pervasive that it is not uncommon for young men who receive medical exemptions to volunteer for noncombat units. Members of the Knesset (Israel's parliament), one of the very few groups who are exempt from reserve duty, often volunteer and appear at sessions in uniform. Service in the military is regarded as so vital that it is often a requirement for employment.

Given the profound and extensive role of the army in national life, it is natural that military performance is held in high esteem, and opposition to it scorned. Rolbant, an American sociologist who interviewed soldiers and published a book entitled *The Israeli Soldier: Profile of an Army* (Rolbant, 1971), noted the considerable social pressure applied, and internalized, to promote dedication among the ranks:

> Men said that what worried them was what others would think of them or what their friends and families would feel about them when they came home. The vague fear of shame, of possible ostracism or disapproval they might experience on getting home alive, unscathed, featured prominently in the boys' worries about their behavior on the battlefield. Everybody knew where you were, or what outfit you served, what you did or failed to do, so that it was imperative to return with a clean bill of moral health, morality in this case being judged by standards of selflessness.

These observations were made in 1970, before the army's lack of preparedness in the Yom Kippur War and the divided public opinion on the Lebanon war somewhat moderated Israelis' uncritical faith in the military establishment. The basic feeling, however, remains strong, and "unselfish" military service—where the soldier places the well-being of the group before his own life and safety—is still regarded by the individual and society as a whole as a prerequisite for manhood.

The strong influence that this expectation has on the behavior and sense of identity of Israeli men may be illustrated by a personal story told by a psychiatrist on reserves with the IDF, Ilan Kutz (1987), at the Van Leer Institute conference on stress held in Jerusalem:

> I was one of the few reservist physicians who were called up to the Entebbe opera-
> tion [to rescue Israeli hostages kidnaped by Uganda's Idi Amin in 1975]. On Satur-
> day morning at six o'clock, I got this call: "Come to the Headquarters of the Sur-
> geon General." I never go there . . . it isn't my unit, so it already sounded
> suspicious. . . . I told the family and a friend of mine who was staying with me, "The
> crazy guys are going to Entebbe. They must be out of their minds . . ." I mean, I was
> only guessing, it was top secret.
>
> I got into my car and drove there, and once we got there, the first thing they
> told us is that nobody is allowed to leave the room. So this of course strengthened
> the suspicion. And then Dani Michaeli [then Surgeon General] came and told us:
> "This in fact is what we are going to do. I won't tell you any more right now . . . until
> we go to the airport and board the planes. . . . But anyone who's afraid and fears
> that it's too much, he can get up and go."
>
> Now I can tell you that I was very afraid. But why didn't I leave? Because
> walking out of the room meant not only losing my pants, but what's under them.
>
> OK, there is a conflict here, and the conflict is that you want to save your life,
> but you have all the invested emotional identity.

Unlike Kutz, who never had a breakdown in combat, the CSR casualty "walked out of the room" to save his life. The price he pays is the "emotional identity" invested in and linked to faithful army service. That identity includes his sense of masculinity, his sense of competence, and his sense of social belonging.

Many CSR casualties thus spend inordinate amounts of time and energy pondering why it happened to them and contemplating the consequences. They ask themselves, could the breakdown have been averted? How many men lost their lives on account of my fear? If my legs hadn't locked, could I have reached the men who were calling for help? Said Ron: "This feeling pursues me to this very day—that I don't know if I could have helped or not." Some casualties blamed army inefficiencies or government policy for their breakdown. Others attributed it to the circumstances of war. Most, harsh judges of themselves, were wracked by guilt-provoking and ultimately unanswerable and self-defeating questions about what their CSR implied about their characters and the damage it might have done to others.

Ashamed and afraid to provoke pity or contempt, many casualties went to great lengths to hide their stress reactions and subsequent PTSD from their colleagues and friends, and some even kept them secret from their wives. In CSR casualties who go on to develop PTSD, this tangled web of bad self-feelings, the loss of face and of self-respect, and the struggle to maintain a facade of strength and competence at odds with one's inner reality keep the casualty involved with the trauma, add to the difficulty of working through the losses and the horrors of the battle-field, and increase his isolation. They add to the already considerable discomfort of posttraumatic symptoms and can only exacerbate them.

Conceivably, the consequences of a CSR would be less devastating were other arenas in Israel endowed with the high social value of the army. If there were, successful performance in other areas (the love of work, for example) might help restore the CSR casualty's lost self-esteem, compensate for his failure, and allow him to demonstrate his worth. Performance in combat, however, is the ultimate male proving ground in Israel. For the CSR casualty whose self-image rests to a great extent on his ability to meet social expectations, there is no socially recognized area in which he can counter or overcome the shame of his failure in the military.

THE SALIENCE OF WAR IN ISRAEL

The third factor that I would like to suggest contributes to the prolonged suffering of our CSR casualties is an external one—the sa-lience of war in Israel in general, and in the case of the Lebanon war in particular, the intense media coverage and public controversy that ac-companied it.

Even when there is no formally declared war, Israel is never really at peace. There have always been border incidents and terrorist attacks. Between the brief, intense wars that make international headlines, there have been less well-publicized, undeclared wars of attrition that dragged on for months and years. Men are constantly leaving work and home to go off to reserve duty, and when one does not go oneself, there are friends, acquaintances, or family members to see off and then to receive back, sometimes with news of the front.

The perpetual threat to Israel's existence permeates every area of life in this country, from the tension on the streets to the intimacies of the family. The precarious security situation is always on people's minds, always a topic of conversation, and always in the media. No one in Israel is unaffected by or indifferent to it. CSR casualties, highly sensitized to anything that recalls their war experiences, are inevitably distressed by the constant undercurrent of threat in Israel.

For the CSR casualties of the Lebanon war, the problem was inten-sified. Lebanon was Israel's longest uninterrupted military engagement. Although the formal cease-fire was signed in August 1982, Israel did not withdraw its forces until the spring of 1985. Until then there were peri-

odic, and widely broadcast, flare-ups. The protracted fighting emphasized the tenuousness of Israel's security situation, to which everyone in
Israel is sensitive, but to which CSR casualties (who experienced first-
hand their helplessness in face of the life threat) are especially sensitized.

For some casualties, the ongoing fighting posed the genuine danger
of being called up to the front again. Soldiers were routinely called up to
Lebanon in short stints. They would serve for 30 days or so, be discharged, then be called up again several weeks or months later. IDF
policy is to return as many CSR casualties to the front as possible. This
policy is militarily expedient and justified medically by apparently helping to prevent chronicization (Solomon & Benbenishty, 1986). The
thought of returning to combat within a few months after a CSR, however, is understandably frightening. It is not impossible that in some
casualties, recovery was impeded by the anxiety of having to fight again,
and in other casualties by the desire to avoid doing so. Whether they
were recalled to the front or not, the ongoing fighting constantly reminded the casualties of their inadequacies as their friends and neighbors continued to be sent to Lebanon.

Moreover, the continuation of the war also kept in sharp focus the
conflict between duty and self-preservation that the CSR resolved, but
only temporarily. Though he was off the battlefield, the continued fighting reminded the casualty that he had chosen flight over fight. In this
context, his symptoms served to say, "I'm really ill; even though I wasn't
wounded physically, I was no more fit to remain on the battlefield than
soldiers who were injured, and I'm no more fit to go back there." But the
continued fighting also meant that the dilemma that the CSR had tried
to resolve was not fully resolved. As long as the war was going on, the
casualty continued to be confronted with the necessity of a choice that he
had not been able to make in the first place. The need to make that
choice would be a continual source of stress augmenting the CSR casualty's suffering.

The issues raised by the ongoing fighting were brought home for
the CSR casualty (as well as for everyone else in Israel) by the extensive
media coverage of the war. The Lebanon war was Israel's most thoroughly covered war. Throughout the entire period of Israel's involvement in Lebanon, millions of TV watchers—among them CSR
casualties—were treated every evening to live, color reports of events on
the front. Journalists went out on patrols with the units and photo-
graphed confrontations with terrorists, which were then broadcast. Because Israel had only one TV station, virtually everyone watched the
ongoing fighting.

Moreover, casualties were duly and publicly counted. The nightly news unfailingly began with the names of the day's casualties and the announcement of the hour and location of funerals. Sometimes coverage from the funerals was televised. Usually the age of the casualties was given; sometimes there were descriptions of the casualty's personality, background, and accomplishments, reinforcing the painful perception of a life having been cut off before its time. These nightly television broadcasts were supplemented by hourly updates on Israeli radio, and Israeli newspapers of those days were amply sprinkled with black-bordered announcements of the deaths of men in their young and middle years. Many of the CSR casualties we interviewed reported that their symptoms always became more severe after they watched a vivid television broadcast of the war. In short, the entire situation prevented CSR veterans from relaxing, fixated their trauma, and retarded their recovery.

The national debate over the necessity of the war may also have played a part in prolonging the distress of CSR casualties. The Lebanon war, in the opinion of a not insignificant part of Israel's population, was Israel's first (and thus far only) war of choice. It was undertaken on Israel's initiative to remove the threat of well-armed and determined Palestinian forces on the northern border. In the view of many people, however, the threat was more long-term than immediate. Moreover, the government exceeded its declared aims of ousting the Palestinian terrorist organizations from a depth of 40 kilometers. From almost the first days of the war, then, there was a national debate as to its wisdom and legitimacy that became sharper as the fighting dragged on and the fatalities mounted. The debate was conducted in the media, in the workplace, in many homes, and in many army units.

For CSR casualties who were still caught up in the dilemma of fight or flight—duty versus self-preservation—the debate might have served to justify their having saved their skin through their breakdowns and to legitimize the prolongation of symptoms that might keep them off the front. If there are enough people, ranging from friends, colleagues, and army buddies to figures in high positions in the political and military establishments, who question the wisdom and justification of the war, then why stick one's neck out to fight it? One might just as well continue to have symptoms that keep one safe and sound at home.

In trying to answer the question of why our CSR casualties have fared so badly in the long run, both individually and as a group, I have concentrated on the Israeli context of their breakdowns. But although the factors discussed are special to Israel, with its hostile neighbors and all-important army, they are not unique to this country.

Notwithstanding the changes wrought by the women's movement, I think it safe to say that most societies (or at least large parts of them) still associate military performance with manhood, and not a few still regard the military as the proving ground for masculinity. Similarly, the Sabra ethos finds plenty of echoes in a slew of other cultural values, including the Protestant work ethic with its emphasis on mastery and performance, the British "stiff upper lip" with its denigration of both expressiveness and weakness, and the strutting *machismo* (in all its variations) that is still all too familiar in many parts of the world.

In Israel, the various factors presented as contributing to the long-term impact of CSR tend to be exacerbated and to exist in an extreme. I would be surprised, though, if they were absent in other settings and did not play a part in CSR in other armies as well.

11

Yet Once More
The Effect of Repeated Wars

Shortly after the Lebanon war, I held a series of meetings with Dr. Dan Enoch, the IDF's chief psychiatrist. Dr. Enoch, a man in his late 30s at the time, had extensive battle experience, both as a combatant and as a physician. He served in the Six-Day War, the Yom Kippur War, and in Lebanon. Shortly before the Yom Kippur War broke out, the platoon in which he was the medical officer entered a mine field. At great personal risk, he helped rescue and treat many of his comrades, for which he was later redecorated with the Gallantry Medal.

Speaking about his experience in Lebanon, he said:

> I've been in a lot of wars, but with every one of them, I become more and more frightened. It's as if whatever protective skin I had when I started out was rubbed and chafed so much that it got thinner and thinner. I had survived so many times that in Lebanon I was afraid I was tempting death.

This man had never had a combat stress reaction, in Lebanon or in any other war. In Lebanon he served in Damoor, where his mental health unit, the closest one to the front, was under constant fire. Few mental health professionals in the IDF were so close to so much shooting. As chief psychiatrist, he led his men with outstanding courage and composure and with remarkable success, often administering frontline therapy in the midst of heavy shelling.

His sobering admission made me think of the old Jewish saying, "If cedars go up in smoke, what happens to the little lichen?" (Mishna, Tractate Moed Katan). After all, most soldiers in the IDF, as in every

177

army, are not heroes, but ordinary men—some more resilient, some less. Dr. Enoch's statement made me wonder: If a man like this feels that he has reached the limit of his powers, what of the others who have to fight in multiple wars? How many wars does it take to wear them down? And what of the CSR casualties who are drafted for yet another war? As indicated in Chapter 8, many of the Israeli soldiers who participated in the Yom Kippur War and sustained psychiatric injuries actually fought again in Lebanon. How do men who broke down in combat fare when they have to face a similar ordeal yet once more?

The question of what a soldier's chances are of coming through multiple wars psychologically unscathed is obviously vital to the military planners in Israel, who have to decide on the placement of personnel and if and when to release soldiers from service. It is also important in purely human terms. Because most countries are fortunate enough not to have to confront that question, it is not surprising that there are no direct studies of the issue. Our first step was thus to look at the literature on stress in general. This offered several somewhat contradictory views.

The first, the *vulnerability perspective,* considers repeated exposure to stressful events a risk factor. It holds that every stressful life event depletes available coping resources and thereby increases vulnerability to future physical and emotional disturbances (Coleman, Butcher, & Carson, 1980; McGrath, 1970; Selye, 1956; Vinokur & Selzer, 1975). Applied to combat, this theory would predict that every war a soldier fights requires the expenditure of a high level of energy for readjustment, depletes the combatant's energy reserves, weakens his resilience, and renders him more vulnerable to subsequent combat stress. Thus, according to this perspective, with every war a soldier fights, his chances of sustaining a combat stress reaction increase.

The second view, the *immunizing perspective,* considers repeated stress beneficial because it contributes to the development of useful coping strategies. Each similar hardship increases familiarity, leading to a decrease in the amount of perceived stress and enabling more successful adaptation (S. Epstein, 1983; Janis, 1971; Keinan, 1979). All military training, for example, is based on the assumption that the more experience soldiers have in handling simulated combat situations, the better they will perform on the battlefield. The soldier, like the immune system, becomes sensitized. He is thus permanently altered, harboring the potential for a future enhanced response on reexposure to a similar threatening stimulus. This view implies that with every war a soldier fights, his resilience increases and his chances of suffering a CSR decrease.

The third view, the *stress resolution perspective,* suggests that it is the outcome of the earlier experience and not the simple exposure to stressful events that determines their impact on subsequent health (Block & Zautra, 1981). The idea here is that successful resolution of a stressful episode leads to a feeling of well-being and enriches coping resources, whereas an unsuccessful coping experience leads to increased distress and impoverished coping resources. Extrapolating from this perspective, the crucial factor in the impact of repeated combat exposure would be how well the soldier fared in dealing with the stress of his previous war. If he carried out his duties satisfactorily and without psychiatric mishap, he would have a good chance of doing so again in a subsequent war; but if he had a CSR he would, by the same reasoning, be likely to also suffer a second reaction.

With these three perspectives in mind, we set out to investigate the effects of prior war experience and CSR on the combatants in Lebanon (Solomon, Mikulincer, & Jacob, 1987). For this purpose, our subjects were presented with a list of the seven Israel-Arab wars to date and asked to indicate whether or not they had fought in each, and if so, whether they had suffered a CSR episode. To ensure accuracy, their replies were checked against computerized IDF records.

THE IMPACT OF PRIOR WAR EXPERIENCE WITH AND WITHOUT CSR

Our first step in assessing the impact of prior war experience was to divide each of our two study groups, the CSR casualties and non-CSR controls, into three categories in accordance with their past combat experience: (a) soldiers with no combat experience prior to the Lebanon war, (b) soldiers with past war experience who had *not* previously sustained a CSR, and (c) soldiers with prior war experience who had suffered a CSR in a war before Lebanon.

Analysis of their answers shows a significant relationship between prior war experience and CSR in Lebanon. As can be seen from Figure 11.1, the soldiers who had the highest CSR rates in the Lebanon war were the ones who had experienced a previous CSR episode. Sixty-six percent of the subjects who had broken down under the stress of an earlier war broke down again in Lebanon. The soldiers who had the lowest CSR rates were those who had previously fought without incident; only 44% of these soldiers had breakdowns in Lebanon. In the middle were the novices, who had never been tested on the battlefield and derived neither the possible advantages nor disadvantages of an earlier trial by fire; their CSR rate was 57%.

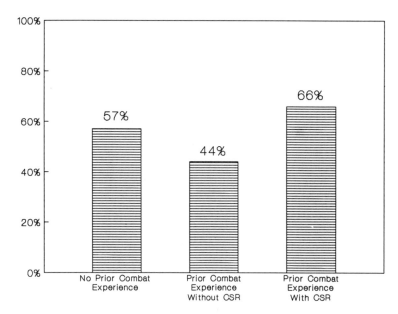

Figure 11.1. CSR rates in the Lebanon war according to prior combat experience.

Albert Bandura (1977), whose view of the impact of prior experience on subsequent self-assessment helped earlier in this book to formulate and explain the deleterious effects of CSR on the casualty's subsequent perceived self-efficacy, is instructive also in explaining the prominence of stress resolution in these findings. As mentioned in Chapter 8, Bandura contends that the way in which people cope with adversity conditions both their self-expectations in and actual coping with subsequent difficulties. People with a history of successful problem solving develop a sense of mastery that encourages them to persevere when the going gets rough. People with a history of unsuccessful coping come to see themselves as incompetent and put less effort into meeting subsequent challenges. These ongoing self-perpetuating processes have been repeatedly documented in a variety of situations (Maier & Seligman, 1976; Mikulincer, 1986).

Our findings suggest that they also hold for combat. In Chapter 8, it was shown that soldiers who had CSRs had lower perceived self-efficacy in combat than other veterans, and noted the numerous fears of handling weapons, of losing control of their rage, and, above all, of failing again, that they bring to military situations. The current findings on their actual performance in Lebanon indeed confirm the predictive accuracy of their apprehensions and low self-expectations.

NUMBER OF PRIOR WARS

To assess further the effect of repeated exposure to combat, my colleagues and I asked ourselves whether the *number* of prior combat experiences in and of itself was a determinant of breakdown. In other words, do warriors become stronger and more resilient with increasing combat experience, or do their skins become thinner (as Dr. Enoch said of himself) and their powers to withstand the stress decline with every war they fight?

To investigate this question, we compared the CSR rates in Lebanon of combat veterans with and without a previous CSR, according to the number of wars in which they had fought prior to Lebanon. As can be seen from Figure 11.2, repeated combat exposure takes its toll on both the comparatively vulnerable soldier who had experienced a CSR prior to Lebanon and on the relatively resilient fighter who had not. Among previous CSR casualties, CSR rates increased linearly with the number

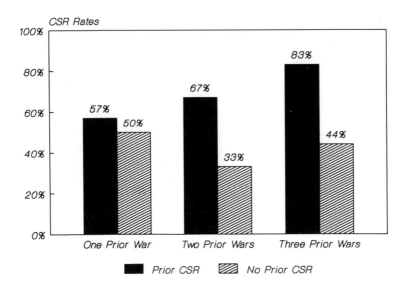

Figure 11.2. CSR rates in Lebanon according to type and number of prior combat experiences.

of previous war experiences. The more wars CSR soldiers had fought in before Lebanon, the higher their CSR rates in Lebanon: 57% following one war, 67% following two, and 83% following three or more.

But the experience of previous wars also affected veterans who had no record of an earlier CSR. Although their overall CSR rates were lower than those of former CSR casualties, 50% of the veterans in our sample who had withstood the stress of one war succumbed to a CSR in Lebanon, whereas 33% of those who had come through two previous wars without a CSR and 44% of those who fought successfully in three wars also had combat stress reactions. These figures, with the non-CSR veterans of two and three wars showing lower CSR rates in Lebanon than the non-CSR veterans of one war, indicate that soldiers who are more resilient to begin with tend to stay more resilient, and they suggest something of the remarkable stamina of many veterans of multiple wars. But the figures, with the upward turn of the CSR rate following three wars, also suggest that given repeated battery, the boldest and bravest, the most balanced, and the most thick-skinned may all be psychologically undone by the onslaught of war. With the accumulated stress of successive wars, the lessons and positive experience of the past (i.e., the benefits of successful stress resolution) offer less and less protection. When multiple wars are the norm, the question becomes not whether a soldier will sustain a CSR, but when.

The differential impacts of multiple combat experiences in our subjects are described by two models of the impact of stressful life events on people's subsequent coping with adversity. The *life change model* postulates that the greater the magnitude of earlier stresses, the more vulnerable the individual is to the adverse affects of subsequent stress. This model describes the linear relationship between the number of prior wars and CSRs in Lebanon found in the CSR casualties of earlier wars. The *modified life change model* suggests that only low and high levels of prior stress lead to subsequent vulnerability, whereas moderate levels do not. The reasoning behind this model is that whereas high levels of prior stress undermine the person's coping resources, low levels of stress leave him unprepared to cope with adversity in the future, and moderate levels of stress allow for successful learning experience that can prove useful in the future and also boost self-confidence. If one prior war can be considered a relatively low level of stress, three prior wars a high level of stress, and two wars a moderate level of stress, this model describes the curvilinear relationship found in subjects without a prior CSR. Our findings suggest that the factor that determines whether the relation is linear or curvilinear is the manner by which the previous stresses were resolved, that is, whether the soldier did or did not have a CSR in former wars.

BATTLE INTENSITY IN LEBANON, FORMER WAR EXPERIENCE, AND CSR

When we were planning this particular phase of our study, we had good reason to believe that however prior battle experience affected soldiers' performance in Lebanon, its impact would be related not only to past events (e.g., the number of previous wars and their psychological outcome) but also to the nature of the current battle experience. Studies on the relationship between stress and illness have consistently recognized the important role of *stressor intensity* in determining subsequent health outcomes (Janis, 1971; Murrel & Norris, 1984; Selye, 1956). In combat, where the amount of stress is related to battle intensity, a very large number of studies have shown battle intensity to be the most consistent predictor of CSR; the more intense the fight, the more dead and wounded, the more CSR casualties (Mullins & Glass, 1973). It thus appeared to us that current battle intensity could mediate the impact of prior war experience and prior CSR(s) on the mental health outcomes in Lebanon.

But how? Might really tough battle in Lebanon moderate or even obliterate the effects of previous battle experience, with and without CSR? Such an outcome is suggested by what Ruch, Chandler, and Harter (1980) have termed the *suppressor model* of stress, whereby life-threatening situations that require the individual's undivided attention for survival leave little room for the influence of past experience. If this model is in fact applicable to combat, it would predict that under intense battle conditions, novices and seasoned warriors—former CSR casualties and non-CSR veterans alike—would all have similar chances of sustaining a CSR. What a soldier may have learned in past wars will not help him; nor will any prior depletion of his coping resources substantially hinder him relative to other soldiers. According to this model, the strengths or weaknesses created by prior exposure would have a significant bearing on a soldier's coping powers and mental health only when combat conditions are of relatively low intensity.

Or might the scenario read the other way around, in line with the *amplifier model*? This model holds that intense current stress amplifies both the beneficial and deleterious effects of past experience with stress. Applied to battle, it would mean that the skills and self-esteem a successful soldier may have acquired in previous wars would serve him in coping with the massive demands of intense combat. On the other hand, a soldier whose emotional strength has been undermined by a prior CSR would not have the emotional wherewithal to meet the demands of intense battle, though he might have enough to deal with combat that is less intense. Extrapolating from this model, one would expect CSR rates to vary according to prior combat experience only under intense battle conditions, not when the battle was of low intensity.

In order to assess the role of current battle intensity in shaping the impact of prior combat experience on CSR risk in Lebanon, we asked our subjects about their perception of battle intensity in the Lebanon war and divided them into two groups—those who rated their experiences as high intensity, and those who rated them as low intensity. These groups then were subdivided in accordance with whether they had fought in a war before Lebanon, and if so, with or without a CSR (Solomon, Mikulincer, & Jacob, 1987).

We found an interesting pattern. As can be seen from Figure 11.3, in conditions of high battle intensity, all three groups had substantially higher CSR rates than in conditions of low battle intensity. Furthermore, experienced soldiers who had not suffered a previous CSR were the least likely to sustain a CSR in Lebanon, whether they perceived the intensity of current battles as high or low.

Among soldiers who perceived the current war to be of low intensity, those with a prior CSR were more vulnerable to a Lebanon CSR

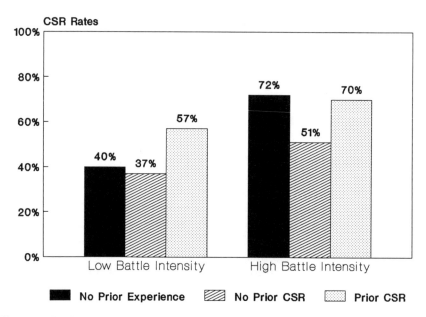

Figure 11.3. CSR rates in Lebanon according to prior combat experience and battle intensity.

episode (57%) than non-CSR soldiers with and without prior war experiences (37% and 40%, respectively). Among the soldiers who perceived the current battles to be of high intensity, however, soldiers with prior CSR and soldiers without prior war experiences had higher CSR rates (70% and 72%, respectively) than veterans of past wars without prior CSR (51%).

These findings support both the suppressor and amplifier models, and they are instructive in demonstrating the complex effects of recurrent stress exposure on the risk for subsequent CSR. The comparison of soldiers with prior CSR to those without combat experience supports the suppressor model, because the two groups have very similar CSR rates in conditions of high battle intensity. Only when battle intensity was perceived as low were the detrimental effects of prior CSR noted. High-intensity battles thus seem to suppress the effects of prior experience. The battle itself becomes the primary determinant of a current CSR, and the added vulnerability of previous CSR casualties over novices vanishes.

In contrast, the comparison of soldiers without prior CSR to those without combat experience supports the amplifier model. The fact that soldiers did or did not participate in previous wars made a significant impact on CSR rates only under conditions of high battle intensity, where a stress inoculation effect of prior combat experiences was noted. Under conditions of low battle intensity, CSR rates for novices and experienced veterans without prior CSR were virtually the same (40% vs. 37%, respectively).

One possible explanation for this last finding is that a soldier's successful past experience can provide him with a repertoire of effective coping responses for dealing with the exhaustion, pain, and confusion of intense battle. In such circumstances, the ability to evaluate adequately the bombardment of incoming stimuli and to make decisions substantially deteriorates. Soldiers with prior success in coping with war can draw on their past experience better than either soldiers without prior experience or those with unsuccessful experience.

CAN A "SUCCESSFUL" WAR REPAIR
THE DAMAGE OF CSR?

In the previous section, I looked at CSR rates in Lebanon as a function of type and number of prior combat experiences, on the one hand, and of battle intensity in the current war, on the other. The positive influence of a "successful" combat experience on subsequent vulnerability to CSR was clearly and consistently demonstrated in even the most high-risk situations (i.e., following repeated wars and under conditions of high battle intensity). The finding that the ability to withstand the stress of combat in one war had a powerful positive impact on veterans' coping in subsequent wars led my colleague and I to wonder, however, whether a "successful" combat experience might not also serve to undo or alleviate the damage of a previous CSR. In other words, once we saw that successful coping in one war could *prevent* a CSR in the next, we asked whether it might not also serve to *heal* the impairment brought on by a CSR in the past.

This idea was also voiced in an article published in the daily newspaper *Ma'ariv* in September 1982 that bore the enthusiastic headline, "In Beirut, Uri Overcomes Battle Shock from the Yom Kippur War." The piece recounts the reporter's meeting with a friend who had broken down in the Yom Kippur War and then fought in Lebanon without succumbing to a CSR. As the former casualty told it:

> When the firing started, I had the feeling that I was going crazy again, like in a space ride backward. A fast, crazy ride, where you're ranging distances. All you have to do is close your eyes and you're in the canvas tent [where CSR and other casualties were treated] again. . . . It frightened me. This backward journey gave me the feeling that everything was falling apart again. Then I came back to myself. This isn't CSR now. Believe me, it's something else. . . . No, I swore to myself that I wouldn't break down again. I swore that I'd never go into battle shock again. And I didn't. After all that I saw in Beirut, after the shellings, after the bombings . . . maybe I lost my sensitivity. . . . [It] toughens you.

The optimistic tone of the passage, the laying to rest of anticipatory anxiety, and the boost to self-esteem implicit in newly successful coping all ring an encouraging note. The sequence, starting with apprehension and ending with triumph, describes what might be considered a corrective emotional experience, whereby a later success reverses the psychological damage of an earlier failure.

But how true to life is this rendition? Is there not perhaps a certain idealization or wishful thinking in the notion that a successful combat experience can undo the negative impact of an earlier unsuccessful one? And even if it can in some cases, how often? How representative is the case reported here?

Because the issue has important practical implications in Israel bearing on the placement and redeployment of CSR veterans, we decided to assess it empirically. In order to do so, we compared the post-Lebanon health and adjustment of two groups of soldiers, all of whom had actively participated in both the Yom Kippur War and the Lebanon war: soldiers who had experienced a CSR in the Yom Kippur War but not in Lebanon (the Yom Kippur group) and soldiers who did not sustain a

CSR in either war (the control group). If a "successful" combat experience does indeed repair the damage of a previous breakdown in combat, one would expect to find the health and adjustment of the Yom Kippur CSR group to be no different from that of the control group.

Our data indicate that on the whole, the men who once sustained a CSR are unlikely ever to regain completely their former equilibrium. In comparison to the non-CSR controls, the Yom Kippur casualties showed more PTSD-related symptomatology and more general psychiatric symptomatology (see Solomon, Oppenheimer, Elizur, & Waysman, 1990a). Although these differences do not mean that the 1973 casualties were still ill in 1985, they do show that 12 years after the soldiers' combat breakdown they still bore its lingering impact, which affected many areas of their lives. Their having managed to cope with the stresses of a latter war did not reverse or undo the damage of their earlier breakdown.

CSR changes something fundamental in a person's psychological makeup. According to Jon Shaw (1987; see Chapter 4), who did extensive work on psychic trauma in war, a CSR occurs when the soldier can no longer sustain the illusion of immortality with which most men enter battle. Irrational though it may be, this "magical conviction that they are mysteriously impervious to spattering bullets and exploding shells" (Shaw, 1987) is an essential defense that enables soldiers to continue fighting and keep their fear at bay. When this basic illusion of invulnerability is unmasked by a CSR, the soldier is overwhelmed by the reality of his helplessness and isolation. The brutal awakening is bound to have long-ranging consequences, for the cherished illusion is also the basis for his feelings of comfort, safety, and well-being. These findings clearly support Shaw's thesis and indicate that the damage created by a breakdown on the battlefield is still evident 12 years later and is not undone even by a subsequent successful experience in a later war.

PRIOR VULNERABILITY

Before I close this chapter, I would like to address an issue that raises its head with every new finding as to the detrimental consequences of CSR: the issue of prior vulnerability. One may argue that the severity and endurance of postwar distress among these psychiatric casualties might simply be a result of their greater initial vulnerability. On the surface, it is not implausible that men who broke down in battle were more vulnerable to begin with than men who were able to contain their distress. In its specific application to the findings of the heightened CSR risk of former casualties in subsequent combat, the argument would be that both the soldier's former and subsequent CSRs are the outcome of his inherent vulnerability to stress. This view holds that soldiers differ in vulnerability prior to their first battle, and that the more vulnerable soldiers break down once and then again, whereas the more resilient warriors hold out from war to war. In addition, the enduring impairments found among CSR casualties who have weathered a subsequent war without breaking down may also be seen to reflect their basic inherent vulnerability.

Although it is generally agreed, following Kardiner (1947), that the fundamental cause of combat-related pathology is the massive encounter with violent death, a number of professionals have indeed proposed that prior personality plays a role in when and how the pathology develops. Horowitz and Solomon (1978) suggest that Vietnam veterans who fought effectively on the field but broke down later had greater coping powers. Hockings (1970), a staunch proponent of the view that the roots of posttrauma are in the traumatic experience, concedes that pretrauma personality conflicts may have an impact on how soon psychopathology develops in a catastrophic event. Hendin and Pollinger-Haas (1984) show the role of the soldier's prewar personality in the specific contents and foci of his PTSD.

Empirical studies have yet, however, to uncover individual personality traits or characteristics that may function as risk factors for the development of CSR. But because some veterans *do* in fact sustain a CSR more than once, whereas others prove consistently resilient, the possibility still cannot be totally ruled out. As pointed out in Chapter 2, however, our CSR and control groups were carefully matched for age, rank, and military assignment. IDF placement procedures result in units being highly homogeneous, with soldiers in the same units inordinately similar in preconscription character and personality. In addition, soldiers who are selected for combat units must all pass rigorous physical and psychological screening procedures, so all our subjects are, in a sense, a group selected for health.

Moreover, the soldiers who fought in Lebanon after a prior combat stress reaction are an even more select group. Most of them could have received an honorable discharge, had they so desired, and saved themselves the throttling of another war. Clearly, they are not cowards, weaklings, or shirkers. Furthermore, our finding of increased CSR rates in the Lebanon war among heretofore non-CSR soldiers—men who, by this reasoning, were not inherently so vulnerable—after three wars and when battle threat was perceived as high points squarely at the negative effects both of recurrent exposure to the same stressor and of current battle stress on all men.

12

Reactivation
Trauma Deepens Trauma

The Lebanon war brought to the IDF mental health clinics numerous second-time CSR casualties, the human embodiments of the statistics in the previous chapter. As I was going through their files, I found myself reading more and more about their experiences in the Yom Kippur War, which was fought in October and November of 1973. Most of them had their first diagnosed CSRs in that year; in some cases, the earlier reaction went undiagnosed but became apparent in the psychiatric intake following the breakdown in the Lebanon war.

It struck me that these soldiers' Lebanon CSRs were not fresh episodes, but reactivations or exacerbations of earlier ones. In telling about their Lebanon reactions, second-time casualties constantly referred back to incidents in the Yom Kippur War, and the content and context of the latter breakdowns echoed to a greater or lesser degree the earlier trauma. There were even soldiers who said outright that their Lebanon breakdowns were triggered by associations with and recollections of Yom Kippur War experiences.

Reactivation of stress disorders is a well-known phenomenon that may occur following a large range of aversive events. In a thorough review of the literature, Silver and Wortman (1980) wrote that "Even when individuals appear to recover from an aversive life event, there is . . . evidence to suggest that feelings of severe distress and disorganization may emerge at a later date" (p. 308). They note that reactivations of an initial stress disorder have been found by various researchers among both rape victims and the bereaved.

Most reactivations that have been observed occurred after a long interval unmarked by any abnormal distress and could be precipitated by any of a large range of occurrences that recalled the original trauma. Lindeman (1944) reported the reactivation of unresolved grief reactions that were brought about either by "deliberate recall of circumstances surrounding the death or spontaneous occurrences in the person's life" (p. 144). Bornstein and Clayton (1972) reported anniversary grief reactions in more than two-thirds of the widows and widowers they interviewed. Weiner, Gerber, Batlin, and Ark (1975) reported the recurrence of bereavement symptoms precipitated by "anniversaries, memories, meetings, geographical locale, etc." (p. 64). With the reactivation of their initial grief reactions, the men and women cited in these articles were suddenly reimmersed in the mourning process, with all its attendant feelings of sadness, pining, and depression. Among rape victims, Burgess and Holmstrom (1974) and Notman and Nadelson (1976) report unresolved feelings reemerging many years after the assault, giving rise to acute depression, anxiety, and phobic behaviors much like those commonly experienced in the period immediately following a rape.

Reactivation of stress disorders has also been found among combat veterans. In their 20-year follow up of World War II veterans, Archibald and Tuddenham (1965) found that symptoms of traumatic stress that had been latent in their patients since World War II became evident during the aging process. Christenson, Walker, Ross, and Maltbie (1981) report experience consistent with these findings. Over the years, they found increasing numbers of World War II veterans who "showed exacerbation of symptoms of a traumatic stress disorder." Presenting a case that illustrated a reactivation "precipitated by an event that simulated the original trauma," they went on to suggest that "losses associated with involutional age, including parental loss, children leaving home, pending retirement and increasing medical disability all serve as stressors that may reactivate a latent traumatic stress disorder" (p. 985). More recently, Faltus, Sirota, Parsons, Daamen, and Schare (1986) reported on Vietnam War veterans who responded with reactivated symptomatology when they attended war memorials and other public ceremonies that reminded them of their combat experience.

On the whole, however, little is known about reactivation, and even less about reactivation of war-induced disorders following reexposure to combat. DSM-III, which names acute, chronic, and delayed PTSD, makes no mention of reactivated PTSD. Empirical study is difficult because few people are exposed to similar stressors (to say nothing of catastrophic events like war) more than once. Moreover, those who are and who do sustain reactivations are not always aware of the original source of their second stress reaction.

Thus, although there is ample evidence of reactivation of stress disorders of both military and civilian origin, we know little about either its course and precipitating factors or its clinical picture.

COURSE AND PRECIPITATING FACTORS

To find out more about the course of reactivation and the factors precipitating it, I reviewed, along with three experienced psychiatrists, the medical files of all the Israeli soldiers diagnosed with CSR or PTSD during or immediately after the Lebanon war for cases that showed indications of previous war-related traumatization. The files included thorough psychiatric evaluations that the soldiers underwent for diagnostic purposes preliminary to receiving psychiatric treatment at the IDF central mental health clinic, as well as assessments and summaries of therapy sessions made by the treating clinicians. Indications of a recurrency could be either a previously diagnosed disorder or information in the intake history or therapy sessions suggesting previous traumatization on the battlefield or PTSD symptoms between the wars.

A total of 35 cases were singled out by all four reviewers as suffering from recurrent traumatization. As the reader will recall from the previous chapter, these represent only a small portion of the second-, third-, or fourth-time combatants who developed CSR or PTSD in Lebanon. Each of us on the research team then reviewed each of these files independently, checking the intake clinicians' diagnoses of PTSD against DSM-III criteria and noting whether each was (a) a first-time occurrence, (b) a reactivation of a dormant or resolved CSR from the 1973 Yom Kippur War, or (c) an exacerbation of residual PTSD symptoms present between the wars.

Then we met to discuss the cases in depth and formulated a taxonomy of recurrent CSRs consisting of four broad categories. These drawn up, we read the files once again and classified each. The few cases where there was initial disagreement were discussed until they were categorized to everyone's satisfaction. To weed out fictitious or erroneous reports, the soldiers' accounts were checked against computerized military records containing their combat, somatic, and psychiatric histories.

The information reported here is based on the 35 cases of reactivated or exacerbated trauma that were in our files by 1985. Since then, more have come to our attention as veterans have continued to seek help. What all of them have in common is that the content of the second episode is related less to the *immediate* circumstances than to those of the original breakdown. The cases differ, however, in several important respects: the scope and severity of the symptoms between the two wars, the similarity of the events that precipitated the first and second stress reactions, and the objective severity of the stress required to bring on the second reaction.

The cases we found run along a continuum. At one end are the *uncomplicated reactivations* of soldiers who seemed to have completely recovered from their Yom Kippur War traumas and whose stress reactions in Lebanon were precipitated by incidents directly reminiscent of those that had brought on the original ones. In the middle are soldiers who showed symptoms between the wars but continued to function at least partially. Some reacted with *specific sensitivity* only to military stimuli, which proved especially disturbing during reserve duty; others showed *moderate generalized sensitivity* that affected their civilian functioning as well. At the far end of the spectrum are veterans whose Yom Kippur reactions left such *severe generalized sensitivity* that it virtually ruled out normal functioning in the between-war period, and who were so vulnerable that they had full-blown stress reactions in response to stimuli that were only remotely threatening. The following four cases illustrate the spectrum. The percentage of veterans falling into each of the four categories is presented in Figure 12.1.

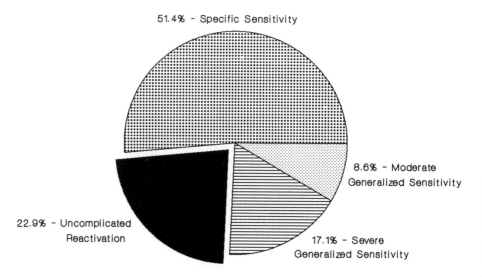

Figure 12.1. Types of reactivated PTSD.

UNCOMPLICATED REACTIVATION

Twenty-three percent of our subjects had classical reactivations, which are characterized by a symptom-free period between the original and reactivated traumas and a triggering incident directly reminiscent of the first stressor. Some of them had a diagnosed CSR or PTSD during or immediately after the Yom Kippur War; in other cases, the signs of their distress were not diagnosed. In all of the cases, whatever residuals might have lingered on between the wars were completely submerged. The veterans who had classical reactivations picked up the pieces and resumed their daily business, including reserve duty, untroubled by any of the standard PTSD symptoms or associated features. The first indication that not all was well came with their combat stress reactions in the Lebanon war.

When the Yom Kippur War broke out, Reuven was a 19-year-old kibbutz member doing his compulsory military service as a tank driver with the armored forces in the Sinai. He told us that in his first battle, he was called upon to defend his battalion's stronghold in an area swarming with Egyptian infantry; the orders were to run them over. It was a gruesome episode. Reuven drove over dozens of Egyptian soldiers intent on mounting the tanks. Out of the entire company, not a single vehicle remained intact with all its men. In the end, an Egyptian soldier managed to climb up onto Reuven's tank and throw in a grenade. Reuven was the only one of the crew not to be killed. He jumped out of the tank and continued to bail out the injured (under direct artillery fire) until he, too, was finally hit. He was taken to the hospital, with splinters throughout his body, for the first of several operations and did not return to service until 7 months later as a tank instructor.

In the hospital, Reuven felt lucky to be alive and got on with the business of physical rehabilitation, overcoming a limp and the paralysis of one of his arms. Once back on the kibbutz, though, he had trouble sleeping and felt anxious, especially about going back into the army, and he was bothered by the scenes he had witnessed. His distress was serious enough for the kibbutz doctor to refer him to the IDF mental health clinic and to require that he receive short-term ambulatory treatment.

For all practical purposes, he soon took up his life and went on quite well. He finished up his regular service in 1975 and went back to the kibbutz, where he worked and, in 1979, married a woman with whom he had a warm and close relationship. Not long before the Lebanon war broke out, he went back to college to study practical engineering with a major in electronics. His wife gave birth to a baby boy.

Reuven's reserve service also went smoothly. His Yom Kippur War injury had left him with motor difficulties that would have made it possible for him to ask to remain in a noncombat unit, but he refused this option. Once his regular service was over, he went back to the battalion he had fought with in the war. He engaged in all the regular exercises and formed good relations with the other men, with whom he remained in contact even after he left the unit following the Lebanon invasion.

The first ominous sign came only when he was drafted for Lebanon: a slight unease that could still be pushed aside as long as nothing stirred it up. But something did. On his second day in Lebanon, Reuven, once again a tank driver, was in a three-vehicle convoy that was attacked by Syrian troops. The first tank was hit directly, resulting in many dead and wounded. Neither Reuven nor his crew were injured, but right from the beginning of the battle, Reuven felt that he could not manage. He felt paralyzed, that his reactions were slow, and that he wouldn't be able to respond quickly enough if he were needed.

The resemblance between this incident and the one in the Yom Kippur War is too close to require elaboration. As Reuven put it, "it aroused what lay dormant inside of me for 9 long years." The next day, the third day of his Lebanon tour, Reuven approached his company commander and received a 2-day home leave. When he got back, he went to see an IDF mental health professional stationed in the area and received a transfer. For about 10 months after that incident, he had nightmares and sleep problems, difficulties concentrating, poor appetite, and sexual difficulties. According to the therapist who treated him:

> During the Lebanon war, it seems that Reuven had begun to react right from the beginning because his exposure to military stimuli reactivated extremely difficult experiences of the Yom Kippur War, which had never been worked out since they did not interfere with his functioning.

SPECIFIC SENSITIVITY

This type of reactivation, occurring in 51% of our subjects, is similar to classical reactivation in that the veteran in this category also resumed his work, family, and social life without undue problems. To himself and to others, he seemed to have resolved any traumatogenic experiences he may have had in the 1973 Yom Kippur War.

It differs from classical reactivation in that throughout the interwar period the veteran feels noticeable anxiety in the presence of military stimuli: the summons to reserve duty most strongly, but also such symbolic threats as the sight of uniforms and war films. These can lead to nightmares, diarrhea, loss of appetite, depression, sleeplessness, hyper-sensitivity to noise (especially that of weapons), or any of the other standard PTSD symptoms or associated features. Despite their heightened tension, however, the veterans in this group usually performed their interwar reserve duty well. They invested a great deal of effort in coping, denying, or repressing their fears so as to carry out their tasks.

When the Lebanon war broke out, they could no longer contain their heightened sensitivity to military stimuli. Most of the soldiers in this group reacted with high anticipatory anxiety to the order to report for active service. Once they were mobilized and crossed into Lebanon, their stress residuals were further exacerbated. As in the cases of classic reactivation, most of them suffered a full-blown CSR or PTSD in response to events that reminded them of their Yom Kippur War combat. Sometimes the precipitating event occurred in heavy fighting; in other instances, being in a battle zone and hearing shooting from afar was sufficient provocation.

Zohar, a 27-year-old reservist and father of two at the time of the Yom Kippur War, conducted himself with extraordinary courage, initiative, and composure in very heavy fighting. On the sixth day of his combat tour, in the course of a chase that took him into an Egyptian-controlled area of the Sinai, Zohar's armored personnel carrier (APC) came under massive attack. Determined not to let himself be passively "splattered against the walls," Zohar jumped out of the vehicle, grabbed his MAG submachine gun, and "started shooting like crazy" at 20 to 30 Egyptians, who were near enough for him to see their death throes. Suddenly, the APC was hit by a missile. Six out of the nine crew members, including the commanding officer, were killed; the driver lost one eye and was wounded in the other; and the medic, in what was apparently a CSR, sat on the sidelines "as though he were watching a play." Zohar himself was struck in the chest, his muscle torn away from the rib cage and blood pouring out of a cut vein. Yet, realizing that flight was their only hope, he grabbed the barely seeing driver and the stupefied medic and ran them through a barrage of Egyptian missiles toward a retreating Israeli APC, which at first mistook them for the enemy and also shot at them. By the time they climbed onto the moving Israeli vehicle, Zohar was wounded also in the foot and abdominal area.

Zohar soon closed off thoughts of the fearful attack. In the hospital where he was operated on, he politely but firmly repulsed the social worker sent by the IDF. He ignored his depressive feelings and sensations of heaviness on the chest. At home, he said nothing on the subject to his wife, not wanting her to feel sorry for him. At the end of 2 months, he was back at his bank job, despite the pain of his stitches. Taking in-service training courses, he steadily rose from the lower ranks up to the position of branch manager. His relations with his friends and immediate and extended family remained warm. He fathered a third child. About 2 years before the outbreak of the Lebanon war, he moved to another town, where he was elected to serve on the municipal council. He described the major change that came over him as a result of his war experience as a mellowing of the intolerance of youth, brought about by his newly gained awareness of the absoluteness of death.

Only in the military sphere was he unable to fully seal off his traumatic experience. Whenever he received the brown IDF envelope calling reservists to duty, and in other situations that reminded him of the Yom Kippur War, he suffered from terrible nightmares. One recurrent dream was of his last sight of his commanding officer: the upper half of the dead man's severed trunk face up in the sand, his blue eyes wide open as though they were looking out. Before the Yom Kippur War, Zohar had enjoyed his reserve duty and even taken pleasure in the challenge of catching infiltrators. Now, when a call-up order came, he would become anxious and depressed and nervously count down the days until the beginning of his service. Nonetheless, it never occurred to him to request a transfer out of combat service, to which his physical injuries may have entitled him. After a few days back in service, the tension he felt subsided, and he took part in maneuvers without feeling much pressure.

The outbreak of the Lebanon war shook up the equilibrium he had managed to maintain throughout 9 years of combat reserve duty. Even before he was called up, he became extremely anxious. He dreamt that he was standing with his unit at a crossing point of Israel's border with Lebanon and had to urinate. The dream woke him, and to his horror he realized that in fact he had almost urinated in bed. The near, though averted, loss of bladder control symbolized for him the more general loss of control he felt over his impending summons to war.

The first thing he did when he received the summons was to tell his commanding officer, "I'm willing to do anything, but I can't look at an APC." The commander agreed to assign him to a jeep, but none was on hand when the time came to move into Lebanon, and he was placed with the crew of a vehicle of the type he feared and hated. "I saw black the minute I had to get into the APC, and I had the terrible feeling that I'm about to get into trouble again." Once inside, he felt pressure on the chest and depressive feelings similar to those he had immediately after the Yom Kippur War. To relieve tension, he began to gripe with the other men about why they were in Lebanon and other such matters. Eventually he was evacuated on account of a shrapnel wound through the cheek that required surgery. Although he realized that the wound was not serious, it confirmed his feeling that he was "playing with fate."

A second stint of reserves in Lebanon a year later finally brought matters to a head. Tense and depressed, he was constantly afraid of being fired at. Driving a jeep now, whenever he passed a group of Arabs, he would floor the accelerator so hard that the crew would ask him whether he had gone crazy. He was unable to sleep at night and felt on the verge of exploding. When his unit was to do maneuvers in an APC, he hid and, when he was found out, told his commander, "Listen, I went through something that makes it hard for me to function on an APC, and I'm asking you to take that into consideration." The commander refused to release him from maneuvers. On his first home leave, Zohar wrote a detailed letter of his Yom Kippur War experience to the divisional commander and brought it to him personally. The divisional commander read the account, released him from the remainder of his reserve stint, and referred him to an IDF mental health clinic.

MODERATE GENERALIZED SENSITIVITY

The third category, to which 9% of our subjects belonged, marks a significant deterioration in the casualty's entire interwar experience. From here on, the first CSR impinges on the casualty's entire life, not only on his relatively self-contained periods of reserve duty. The casualties in this group demonstrated a generalized sensitivity to stimuli only remotely related to war. They reported anxiety, sleep disturbances, nightmares, restlessness, irritability, and uncontrollable outbursts of anger and other PTSD symptoms in civilian settings and intensifications of these symptoms in the reserves.

Most of the soldiers who suffered from such generalized sensitivity went to great lengths to avoid situations that aroused their strong anxiety. Some resorted to alcohol or drugs, usually to little avail. Their PTSD symptoms thus impaired their functioning in both civilian and military life, though most of them made strong efforts to continue their reserve duty despite their difficulties.

These soldiers had experienced chronic PTSD ever since the Yom Kippur War. With keen intuition of their limitations, they became extremely anxious when they were called up for Lebanon. Most of them reacted with a full-blown CSR following exposure to relatively minor military stimuli.

Yossi was 21 and nearing the end of his regular service in an elite parachute unit when the Yom Kippur War broke out. A platoon sergeant by then, he fought with the commandos and then in the "Chinese farm" battle, notorious among Israeli soldiers for its slaughter. He remembered little of the course of the battle, but feelingly recounted a gruesome incident in which the head of a soldier, still bearing its helmet, came flying from an adjacent trench into his own. "It's impossible just to let something like that pass," he said. In the course of the battle, 8 out of his 30 men were killed. Except for himself and another platoon commander, all the commanders in his company were killed; not a single squad commander survived. Yossi's position of responsibility made the bloodshed even worse for him. As he explained it, it was he who had to urge reluctant soldiers to fight; then, when he tried to save the situation, his request for permission to retreat was turned down.

Yossi was finally evacuated to a hospital in Israel, riddled with shrapnel in his hands and legs. In addition, he suffered from amnesia—remembering almost nothing, not even how to read. When he recovered from his physical injuries, he was sent to a psychiatric hospital. At the end of his treatment there, his therapist recommended that he be sent back to his unit.

On the day he was to leave the psychiatric hospital for his unit, he telephoned his platoon commander's home and learned that the man had been killed in a car crash while dozing at the wheel. Enraged at the senseless death after all they had done to survive on the battlefield, he threw the phone across the room so hard that it shattered against the wall. Then he ran into his room, repulsing the people who ran after him, and huddled up on his bed "like a baby." He postponed his return to his unit for 2 days by telling the psychologist that he had to go to the dentist, but was finally driven back, much against his will, by his father. On the front again, he developed all sorts of tics, and he requested and received his battalion commander's permission to go home.

Despite his stay in the psychiatric hospital, Yossi was unaware that he had sustained a CSR. Intent on resuming his military service, he pressured the psychologist to eradicate all mention of his treatment. Aside from his return to reserve duty, however, most of his life was seriously affected by PTSD symptoms after the Yom Kippur War. Socially, he felt he did not fit in and was easily irritated by people. Unable to control his anger, he beat his girlfriend and even his mother. He had trouble falling asleep and frequently woke up once he did. He felt heavy and depressed. His memory loss persisted and he had to learn to read again. In the reserves, he felt tense.

After 2½ years, his condition improved somewhat, but with definite qualifications. He married his girlfriend but continued to beat her. He went from working at odd jobs to full-time employment at the company where his father, a longtime employee, had pulled strings to get him a job. Yossi reported that he put very long hours into work. In addition to working overtime at his regular job, he delivered newspapers in the early morning hours and picked fruit in the evenings. The reason he gives for his frenetic pace was to earn the money to pay for fertility treatments for his wife; however, the use of work as an escape from both memory and intimacy cannot be ruled out. A similarly ambiguous pattern marked Yossi's conduct in reserve duty. He performed his tasks faithfully, but he was so tense and anxious that he got into repeated conflicts with his commanders and comrades. Here, too, Yossi attributed his difficulties to his wife's fertility treatments, in that he was stationed too far from home to return in the event that she ovulated. Here, too, we may assume that at most the fertility problem compounded and masked the true origin of his anxiety.

In the Lebanon war, Yossi did not function from the very beginning. While his unit was being shelled, he told, "I just kept out of the way and didn't do a thing." Later on, when they came under heavy Katushya bombardment, he felt "on the verge of exploding." Eventually, he was "saved" by a routine home leave, from which he refused to return to duty.

For a month, he stayed at home, just lying around, smoking cigarettes, and drinking coffee. He did not bathe or shave, talk to his wife, or look at the son who had been born the year before (following the protracted and expensive fertility treatments in which he had invested so much effort). Constantly enraged, he would scratch the walls with his nails. He had terrible dreams in which his Yom Kippur War experiences "all came back in a huge onslaught." He was finally referred to an IDF mental health clinic after he cursed out and threatened to shoot the army representative who had been sent to bring him his military recall order.

SEVERE GENERALIZED SENSITIVITY

At the furthest end of the spectrum, encompassing 17% of our sample, are men whose entire lives between the wars were dominated by their PTSD. Some married, went to school, and kept down jobs, but their behavior was so bizarre and phobic that their still being listed on the IDF's active roster could be regarded only as an oversight. The "imprint of vulnerability" left by their first stress disorder remained very close to the surface in them. In contrast to the others, their anxiety was global. The arrival of the call-up order to Lebanon brought on such an immediate and severe stress reaction that they were never even sent across the border.

Eitan was a 21-year-old tank mechanic doing his 3-year mandatory service when the Yom Kippur War broke out. He had his first CSR 2 weeks later when he sustained a slight neck wound near his ear: "There was an Egyptian air attack. I was in danger. I began to feel afraid. I was afraid something might happen to me. When I was wounded, guys were killed right next to me. It scared me."

That fear never left him. After 2 weeks in the hospital (where only his physical injuries were treated) and 2 weeks convalescing, he was sent back to his unit. Although his unit had been moved to a noncombat zone, a base south of Tel Aviv, he noted, "It was hard for me to go back to the army. Ever since I was wounded, I was afraid of everything. I was very careful. For example, I would walk in the street and think a bomb was going to fall on me."

Between the wars, he took endless precautions. He stayed off buses because they were occasionally terrorist targets, and he tried to dissuade his parents from riding them as well. When he walked the streets, he was always on the lookout for potential hiding spots. Afraid of unknown places, especially in the dark, he inevitably stayed home a lot and had no friends.

His main contacts were his family: his parents, to whom he felt very close, and his brother and sister. Like most psychiatric casualties, however, he didn't tell them of his distress or of his all-consuming fears. Nor did he tell them of his recurrent nightmares of fighting. When he married, he felt that it was important to keep his terrors from his wife; but as ashamed and secretive as he was, he slept with a rifle under his bed.

The distance that Eitan maintained in relationships that he defined as close extended to his work. In a superficial sense, he did well. He took a course in production engineering and worked in his profession in a number of jobs until he found one to his liking. What pleased him most about his most recent job, though, was the isolation it allowed him. In contrast to the job he had held before that one, the laborers did not have access to his office, and he could immure himself there.

In reserve duty, his miseries were compounded. He did not sleep very well. "I'd plan where to sleep in case terrorists came in. I had all sorts of thoughts: Would it be better for me to be on the left or on the right of the door, where they wouldn't see me? Would it be safer to sleep on the upper bunk or on the bottom one?" He preferred doing menial kitchen work to going out with a crew "because I'd be afraid that something might happen." When the guys talked about their war experiences, it got on his nerves and he would steer the conversation toward a neutral topic, such as sports.

Eitan's stress reaction in the Lebanon war occurred inside of Israel when he was sent with his unit to the Golan Heights. Rumors of an impending Syrian attack caused his immediate collapse before a single shot was fired. The extreme panic that Eitan described feeling was so out of proportion to the situation that it is clear his previous CSR was behind it:

> I felt that something was happening to me. I had a feeling that something would happen, maybe I'd be killed. Fear. My lips dried up. It was hard for me to breathe. I was afraid to go to the dining room to eat because there were so many people, in case a bomb fell. I was even afraid to go to the showers. The guys would go shower at night. I wouldn't. I was afraid that there'd suddenly be a bombing in the middle of the shower. . . . I couldn't do anything. I sat in one place, too scared to move.

One of the other soldiers brought him to the medic, who referred him to the IDF mental health installation at Carmiel, near the northern border, where he spent 2 weeks receiving simulated frontline treatment. The examining clinician noted Eitan's anxieties up to the time of the war and concluded: "During Lebanon when he went to the Golan Heights, he reached a climax of anxiety that was expressed through trembling, excessive perspiration, and shortness of breath. He was withdrawn, immersed in himself, cried, didn't want to make contact." Two days later, another clinician noted: "A case of reactivation."

Our analysis shows that reactivation is a multiform phenomenon. The four groups presented above represent various points of the pathology/recovery spectrum that is part of the natural course of PTSD (Solomon, Garb, Bleich, & Grupper, 1987). These points do not necessarily imply a stepwise course of recovery or deterioration; few if any casualties progress in orderly fashion from one stage to another. The points do, however, serve as an index of the extent to which the initial trauma had or had not been contained and adapted to. As one moves along the spectrum, the casualties are less and less able to cope with their Yom Kippur traumatization and more and more vulnerable to retraumatization in Lebanon, in that it took progressively less dangerous situations to provoke their collapse.

Contrary to expectation, classical reactivation, salient in the literature, was not the major form. Less than one-fourth of our subjects actually seemed to have resolved their traumatic experiences in the Yom Kippur War and were entirely free of symptoms between the wars. The vast majority showed some degree of heightened vulnerability to stress in the interwar period. From their symptoms, it was clear that their combat in the Yom Kippur War had left residuals rendering them sensitive to subsequent stress. About half were sensitized only to military stimuli and were apparently unaffected in other areas of their daily lives. More than a quarter of our subjects, however, developed a deeper, more generalized sensitivity to stress and were either debilitated or severely incapacitated by PTSD in the interwar years. For the subjects with such post-Yom Kippur War stress residuals, their CSR in the Lebanon war constituted not so much a reactivation of a dormant stress disorder as the exacerbation of a trauma that had remained very much alive throughout the preceding years.

What our subjects do have in common with the classical reactivation cases usually cited in the literature is that most of them continued to carry out their day-to-day tasks fairly adequately in the interval between the reactions. By definition, all of our subjects had some stress-related symptoms after the Yom Kippur War: the classical reactivation cases only during or immediately after combat, the remainder either sporadically or consistently throughout the interwar period. In contrast, their daily functioning was less impaired. The subjects with classical reactivations and with exacerbation of sensitivity to military stimuli, constituting around three-quarters of the sample, reported no impairment in either civilian or military functioning. Only the casualties in the third and fourth subgroups, the 26% with full-blown PTSD between the wars, showed an impairment of functioning concomitant with their symptomatology. In other words, the retraumatization of most of our subjects in the Lebanon war was preceded by a long period of ostensibly normal functioning in which the outward conduct of their lives did not give warning of their inner vulnerability.

As for the particular stressor that precipitated the recurrence, this was as varied in type and intensity as the sensitivities of our soldiers following their initial traumatization. Though for the veterans who sustained classical reactivations it took major combat exposure to trigger the eruption of a full-blown disorder, veterans whose first traumatization left PTSD residuals broke down under minimum fire or even the simple threat of fire.

Moreover, although we did not study recurrences of our combatants' stress disorders outside the context of war, the generalized sensitivity that many of them exhibited after their traumatization in the Yom Kippur War suggests that nonmilitary stimuli might also trigger reactivation or exacerbation of stress disorders. That is, potentially any event, from a major life crisis through a trivial incident, that stirs up memories of the original traumatization (however remote it might be or seem from war) could provoke the reemergence of the earlier stress disorder. This implication is in keeping with the case presented by Christenson et al. (1981) of an American World War II veteran who broke down when an incident at work reminded him of a wartime shooting, and also with Archibald and Tuddenham's (1965) observations of recurrence of stress disorders brought on by stresses associated with aging.

Notwithstanding the variability of the residuals left by the initial traumatization or of the precipitating factors, however, the reactivations and exacerbations we found of Yom Kippur War traumas in the Lebanon war 9 years later is clear proof of the enduring vulnerability of trauma victims. This holds whether or not their initial trauma had been identified or even surfaced at the time it occurred, and whether or not it left PTSD symptoms or impaired functioning between the wars.

Our findings of reactivation and exacerbation of combat-induced stress disorders show that once traumatized, a soldier is more vulnerable than others to subsequent stress. The reader may recall Titchener and Ross's comparison (discussed in Chapter 10) of the mind of the traumatized individual to a piece of land that has been flooded. As Titchener and Ross (1974) describe it, the full extent of the damage is not always immediately visible. When the flood waters recede, the land may in some cases remain visibly disorganized; in others it soon regains its preflood form, only to harbor invisible structural damage that makes it susceptible to pressure in the future. The same concept applies to our reactivation casualties. All of them had been permanently weakened by their original trauma. Most of our casualties showed visible stress residuals of their Yom Kippur War experience. In the classical reactivation casualties, there was no sign of the "crack" beneath the surface; in all of the reactivation casualties, however, reexposure to combat activated memories of their original trauma and opened up unhealed wounds.

THE CLINICAL PICTURE OF REACTIVATION

But what is the reactivated stress reaction like? Is it similar to the first? Or does the previous trauma affect the shape of the second, causing it to be either more or less severe? The literature has even less to say about the clinical picture of reactivated trauma than about the events preceding and leading up to its reactivation.

To answer these questions, we compared the psychiatric and social status and the cognitive perception of two groups of soldiers that had fought in both the Yom Kippur and Lebanon wars. The reactivation group consisted of 24 veterans who had incurred a CSR in both these wars. The second group consisted of 39 veterans of the two wars who sustained a CSR only in the latter one; this group is referred to here as the "Lebanon group."

The posttraumatic stress residues in the two groups were measured by the Impact of Event Scale (IES), their general psychiatric symptomatology by the Symptom Checklist-90 (SCL-90), and their social functioning by the Social Functioning Problems Scale (SFPS). The findings reveal significant differences in the psychiatric and social status of the two groups, with soldiers who sustained two CSR episodes faring worse on all the measures than soldiers who sustained only one (see Solomon, Oppenheimer, Elizur, & Waysman, 1990b). The two-time casualties reported significantly more intrusion and general distress on the IES, indicating that repeated trauma deepens and intensifies posttraumatic symptomatology. Their endorsement of more intense symptomatology on the SCL-90, which assesses a large range of symptoms not unique to posttrauma, indicates their greater general psychological distress. Their endorsement of more problems in social functioning suggests how much the symptoms of second-time casualties interfere with their day-to-day lives. Together, these measures indicate how much deeper and more intense reactivated trauma is than a one-time occurrence—which, as the previous chapters have shown, already brings its victims a very ample dose of suffering.

It has been repeatedly pointed out that the experience of trauma can color the victim's perceptions of both himself and the world (Janoff-Bulman, 1985; Lifton, 1968; Shaw, 1987). To assess whether the tint (to continue the metaphor) is affected by whether the trauma occurs once or twice, we compared the Lebanon and reactivation groups on two cognitive outcome measures testing their causal attributions of CSR, their opinions as to how enduring a CSR is and how the army should handle it, and their expectations of their own feelings and conduct in the event of a possible war in the future.

In addition to comparing symptomatology and adjustment, we also compared our subjects on two sets of cognitive measures: their attitudes toward CSR and their expectations of how they would feel and cope in a hypothetical future war. Both measures were specially constructed by our research team (see Box 12.1).

BOX 12.1

Cognitive Measures

1. *Attitudes toward CSR* were assessed by a questionnaire consisting of eight pairs of opposing statements, each reflecting the two poles of a particular issue. The issues involved the causes of CSR, the appro-

(*continued*)

BOX 12.1 (*Continued*)

priate administrative response (e.g., evacuation from the front, punishment, the veteran's entitlement to injury compensation), and the long-term forecast. The two statements in each pair were separated by a six-point scale, and respondents were asked to indicate their position on the continuum.

2. *Self-expectations in future wars* were measured by a questionnaire constructed on the basis of a model developed by Lazarus and Laumier that highlights the role of cognitive appraisal and coping mechanisms in determining a person's behavior under stress. The questionnaire consisted of 26 items reflecting thoughts, feelings, and behavior upon receiving a combat mobilization order in some future war. Subjects were required to indicate on a five-point scale ranging from "not at all applicable" to "extremely applicable" the degree to which each statement applied to them.

The items were divided into three scales: (a) *Anticipatory anxiety* (14 items), which assessed respondents' expectations of both threat severity and their own reactions. Items included such beliefs as "I think I'll be killed," and "I'll get very tense." (b) *Positive coping* (6 items), which assessed respondents' expectations of taking positive coping measures, such as seeking information and thinking up ways of dealing with the stresses. (c) *Negative coping* (4 items), which assessed respondents' expectations of using negative strategies such as drinking, taking drugs, or trying to obtain release from combat duty. The assumption is that negative coping strategies are used by people who believe that they cannot cope otherwise with a situation.

Results show that veterans who broke down in the two wars differed significantly from those who broke down in Lebanon alone in both their attitudes toward CSR and their self-expectations in a future war (see Solomon, Oppenheimer, Elizur, & Waysman, 1990b). The soldiers in the reactivation group were more prone than those in the Lebanon group to attribute their CSRs to situational factors and saw their distress as lasting longer. With respect to a future war, they expected to feel more anticipatory anxiety and to employ fewer problem-focused coping strategies. To put it somewhat differently, the reactivation casualties saw themselves as having been more damaged by their CSRs and as more vulnerable to future military stress than the others; they were more anxious about future military encounters and less confident of their ability to cope with them.

The tendency of our reactivated casualties to attribute CSR to situational factors is consistent with Milgram's (1986) contention that external attribution provides trauma casualties with a rationalization for their embarrassing conduct and emotional state, which in turn aids in the recovery process. The entire set of cognitions of the reactivated casualties, however, is better accounted for by the "learned helplessness" theory, propounded by Seligman (1968, 1975) and developed by many others. Loosely speaking, learned helplessness occurs when an individual is exposed to adverse conditions that he cannot escape or control. It entails the conviction derived from that experience that, however one may try, one has little influence over the environment. The Lebanon reactivation casualties were put not once, but twice, in a situation that they found themselves utterly helpless to affect. They had not one, but two, chances to "learn" how little mastery they possessed. Is it any wonder, then, that they viewed themselves as helpless victims of past circumstances and feared being victims of circumstances again in the future?

The measurements discussed earlier show that the psychiatric, social, and cognitive components of the posttrauma following reactivated CSR are all worse than those that attend a single incident. This pattern was confirmed by interviewer assessments of the reactivation casualties made in the summer of 1985. These interviews queried the soldiers' symptomatology and readjustment after both the Yom Kippur and Lebanon wars. At the end of each interview, the interviewing clinician filled out a series of questionnaires (see Box 12.2) detailing his or her impressions of the subject's postwar stress and adjustment. The assessments enabled us to compare not only the two CSR groups, but also the same subjects after one and two wars.

BOX 12.2

Assessments Made by Interviewers

1. *Postwar adjustment* was assessed in work, family, social life, and the military. Assessments were made on the basis of both factual information (e.g., had the subject gotten divorced?) and feelings (e.g., was he satisfied at work?). An overall adjustment score was derived from the weighted averages of the ratings in the four areas.

2. *General symptom severity* was assessed for eight general psychiatric symptoms such as anxiety, depression, hostility and alienation. The score was the average of the severity of all the symptoms.

3. *Posttrauma symptom severity* was assessed for five symptoms specifically associated with PTSD, among them sleep disturbances, re-

(continued)

BOX 12.2 (*Continued*)

current thoughts of the war, and augmentation of symptoms following reminders of the war. The score was the average of the severity of all the symptoms.

4. *Level of disturbance* represents the interviewer's judgment as to the severity of the subject's distress and the degree to which it interfered with his day-to-day functioning. Ratings were made on a seven-point scale ranging from no notable disturbance up to serious disturbance such that the person was a danger to himself and others.

Like the self-report measures, the clinicians' ratings show that the postwar condition of the casualties was significantly worse after a second CSR than a first (see Solomon et al., 1990b). According to the clinicians' assessments, the reactivation casualties suffered from more severe general symptomatology; more severe PTSD symptomatology; poorer family, work, social, and military adjustment; and a higher level of disturbance after their reactivations than after their original CSRs. In short, retraumatization left a deeper imprint on all areas of the casualties' lives—from their psychiatric and social status to their perception of themselves and the world—than one-time trauma.

Some of the ramifications of reactivation can be seen concretely in the lives of the two-time casualties presented in the first part of this chapter. After their first CSRs, they all took up their lives and went forward, however distressed they may have been. Some married and fathered children; all went back to work or school. All continued to serve in the combat reserves. None sought treatment. After their reactivations, none of them could handle combat services, and most could not cope with reserve duty at all. All of them sought treatment, and some of them persisted in it for a considerable span of time.

Whatever their distress following their first reaction, it was palpably worse after their second. Reuven, our classical reactivation case who had virtually no stress symptoms after his Yom Kippur War crisis, suffered from terrible nightmares, sleep problems, sexual problems, and concentration difficulties after his Lebanon CSR. Zohar, who after the Yom Kippur War experienced combat-induced stress symptoms only in connection with reserve duty, could no longer seal off his distress after Lebanon. Yossi, who had lived with PTSD symptoms in the years between the wars, said that after his reactivation in Lebanon, "I didn't function at all, in the family or anywhere." Eitan, who scanned the streets for hidden terrorists after his Yom Kippur War breakdown, became so phobic after his Lebanon CSR that he hardly left his house at all other than to go to work and the grocery store; at home, he sat behind locked doors and drawn shades. Such painful signs of deterioration can be seen, too, in our other reactivation casualties. One especially graphic example is that of a carpenter who was able to build up a lucrative business after his Yom Kippur War crisis, but became so nervous and unfocused after his reactivation that he could no longer take the pressure and settled into a low-paying job.

In this context, it is worth restating the point made in the last chapter that 75% of the Yom Kippur CSR casualties did not serve in Lebanon at all. Our reactivation casualties, among the mere 25% who did fight in Lebanon, were a select group of men, highly motivated and committed. The fact that these soldiers were so seriously injured by their second stress reactions shows the damage of retraumatization.

Why is retraumatization so terrible? What makes the reactivated trauma so much worse than the original? One obvious explanation is that the impact of the second traumatization is compounded by the residues of the first, which apparently lingered on even in men who had superficially recovered. Not only did their stress reaction in the Yom Kippur War make these men vulnerable to a second breakdown, it also made their second reaction more severe. Far from having evaporated, the imprint of the Yom Kippur War reactions was embedded in the Lebanon breakdowns. The second CSR thus is like a wound atop an earlier wound that had never fully healed. The reactivated casualty has to contend with not one failure but two—with two sets of appalling memories, guilt stacked upon guilt, rage upon rage, and stress upon stress.

Moreover, the casualty who has a second reaction has already been weakened by the first. Reuben Hill (1949), in his exploration of adjustment to family crises, proposes a roller-coaster model that seems applicable to CSR as well. The basic pattern, as Hill sees it, is: "crisis–disorganization–recovery–reorganization." Surveying the evidence of earlier studies, Hill observes that although the family may emerge from certain types of crises with increased solidarity and strength, other types of crises are more devastating, and reorganization occurs on a lower level than that on which the family had originally functioned. The same would hold true of individuals.

CSR may be regarded as the latter type of crisis. The men who had combat stress reactions in the Yom Kippur War emerged, as we have seen, with enduring scars and lasting vulnerability. Their continuous struggle to function, even in the reserves, further taxed their coping resources. When they entered the Lebanon war, they went in at a lower level of strength than men who had not had a stress reaction. This not only made them more prone to the second reaction, it also made the recovery from that reaction harder. So much effort had already been invested by the soldier and his family in maintaining an adequate level of coping between the wars that little seems to have been left for overcoming the devastating impact of the second reaction.

In the spring of 1985, the Israel Association of Psychotherapists met to discuss the subject of war-related trauma in Israel. Dr. Emanuel Berman, who had served as a clinical psychologist with the IDF in his annual reserve duty, read a paper entitled "From War to War: Accumulated Trauma." He ended his paper with a barbed political observation that is equally apt here. The comment referred specifically to Israeli politicians who had argued that fighting the Lebanon war would wipe out Israel's humiliation in the surprise attack of the 1973 Yom Kippur War. It could refer equally well to the German leaders who started World War II to eradicate the debacle of World War I, or to the Egyptian leaders who attacked Israel in 1973 to undo their shame at losing the Six-Day War of 1967: "I would like to make one last comment regarding . . . the belief that the Lebanon war would repair the trauma of the Yom Kippur War. Trauma does not heal trauma. Trauma only adds to trauma. Trauma deepens trauma."

13

Is Delayed PTSD Real?

Many of the veterans who sought professional help for war-related emotional injuries approached the IDF psychiatric clinics months or years after their first tours of duty in Lebanon in the summer of 1982. Some came following a life crisis, most in connection with a subsequent call-up to reserves. As time elapsed from that summer of heavy fighting, more and more men who had not had diagnosed breakdowns in Lebanon filed into our offices with all of the characteristic symptoms of PTSD. By 1985, the third year of this study, they constituted about half of all our cases.

This phenomenon was quite new in the short but stormy history of the IDF, no doubt in large measure as a result of technical reasons. In all previous Israeli wars, the IDF and the Ministry of Defense had shared responsibility for war-induced injuries, the IDF taking care of breakdowns on the battlefield and the Ministry of Defense handling subsequent claims for damages. With the Lebanon war, total responsibility was transferred to the IDF, with treatment and records centralized. The abolition of the administrative split provided a fuller range and a more unified picture of psychiatric war injuries than had ever been available in Israel.

It also gave rise to a good deal of concern. We seemed to be witnessing a snowballing of war-induced injuries with delayed onset. According to DSM-III, delayed-onset PTSD is defined by the onset of the disorder at least 6 months after the traumatic event; the outbreak of psychopathology ends a latency period during which the individual appears to have responded adaptively to the stress.

211

Delayed onset has been described among World War II veterans (Archibald & Tuddenham, 1965; Nefzger, 1970), survivors of concentration camps (Eitinger, 1964; Niederland, 1968), and Vietnam veterans. Ever since Vietnam, it has been a major issue in the literature dealing with PTSD. Though American military psychiatrists in Vietnam (e.g., Bourne, 1970) consistently found lower rates of acute CSR than the rates observed in World War II (Grinker & Spiegel, 1945), an alarmingly large number of Vietnam veterans were discovered with a wide range of PTSD symptoms after they came home. Most of the combat stress reactions of Vietnam seemed to have had their onset delayed. Polner (1971) and Van Putten and Emery (1973) noted that many Vietnam soldiers who functioned well in intense combat later developed PTSD symptoms in response to minor pressures in civilian life that they had previously handled well. Boulanger (1985) found that about 10% of the veterans who participated in their study developed posttraumatic symptoms 1 year or more after their return. Laufer, Gallops, and Frey-Wouters (1984) found that more than half of the PTSD soldiers in their sample experienced onset more than a year after they had been discharged.

Was the same thing happening to the veterans of the Lebanon war? How many of them conducted themselves bravely on the battlefield and resumed their studies, work, and family lives when they came home, all the while harboring a latent pathology that would erupt, unexpectedly but inevitably, later on? Such a prospect, certainly never welcome, is particularly alarming in Israel, because the minuscule size of our population forces us to employ the same soldiers repeatedly both in actual wars and in active reserves, thereby subjecting them to precisely the kind of stress most likely to bring a latent combat-induced disorder to the fore.

Along with these concerns, however, some of the clinicians who treated the late arrivals at our clinics expressed doubts as to whether most of them were in fact delayed-onset cases. Doubts had already been raised as to the validity of the diagnoses of delayed PTSD in Vietnam veterans. A number of clinicians pointed out instances where malingering in pursuit of disability compensation, factitious symptoms, drug abuse, and precombat psychopathology were mistakenly diagnosed as delayed PTSD (e.g., Atkinson, Henderson, & Sparr, 1982; Sparr & Pankratz, 1983). Other clinicians (Pary, Turns, & Tobias, 1986) argued that the time lapse is not always a true latency period, because there are usually unacknowledged and untreated residual symptoms. Only the identification—not the onset—was delayed, they claim. Our clinicians had similar reservations about some of the cases they saw.

The many difficulties of carrying out retrospective research with a large and emotionally vulnerable population have led to there being few empirical studies of delayed-onset PTSD. In the United States, the problem is compounded by the relative mobility and wide dispersion of the population (which make subjects extremely difficult to locate) and by the tendency noted among Vietnam veterans to be suspicious and reluctant to cooperate with research activities conducted by governmental and other "establishment" agencies.

Israel's 1982 Lebanon war provided a unique opportunity to carry out such an empirical study free of many of the methodological limitations of earlier investigations. Israel's small size in both area and population, the fact that most Israeli men serve in active reserves up through their 40s and 50s, and the psychiatric registrar established at the end of the Lebanon war containing clinical information on all CSR casualties treated in IDF mental health outpatient clinics greatly facilitated locating subjects and obtaining their cooperation.

Thus, in 1987, my colleagues and I decided to look into the issue more thoroughly. By that time, about half of all our cases had arrived after the DSM-III 6-month interval designating delayed PTSD. Out of several hundred files of veterans who had sought help at any of the numerous IDF clinics dispersed throughout Israel between 6 months and 5 years after their active combat in the summer of 1982, we selected 150 at random for closer assessment (Solomon, Kotler, Shalev, & Lin, 1989). Our aims were (a) to determine which of them were truly cases of delayed-onset PTSD, (b) to try to learn more about the "latency period," and (c) to assess the rate of delayed PTSD among the Lebanon war psychiatric casualties.

Each of the files was separately reviewed by each member of our research team (consisting of four experienced IDF clinicians) to confirm the diagnosis of PTSD and to establish the time of onset. The confirmed diagnoses of PTSD were validated against computerized military records containing the combat history and a somatic and psychiatric medical history of every soldier in the IDF. The availability of this information minimized mistaken and factitious self-reports.

Assessment of the files revealed that genuinely delayed onset was quite rare in our sample. In the vast majority of the cases, there was no true latency period: The veterans had approached the mental health services following protracted, often unremitted suffering. Eighty-six percent of our sample had developed PTSD symptoms shortly after, during, or even before Lebanon (this last group having fought in earlier wars): 33% sought help following the exacerbation of subclinical PTSD, 40% after their chronic PTSD became unbearable, and 13% upon the reactivation of an earlier combat stress reaction. Four percent sought help for problems that turned out to have their roots in prewar psycho-pathology. Only 10% were judged to be bona fide delayed onset. All in all, our research team found five distinct types of cases, only one being delayed onset (defined by DSM-III as beginning no earlier than 6 months after the traumatic event); the others reflected either prewar problems or delayed help seeking.

The five categories and a case representative of each are detailed below.

EXACERBATION OF SUBCLINICAL PTSD

Perhaps the cases most readily confused with delayed onset were those of veterans who sought professional help following the exacerbation of subclinical PTSD. These individuals were traumatized in the 1982 Lebanon war and suffered uninterruptedly from mild residual PTSD symptoms until accumulated tensions or exposure to a subsequent adversity (either military or civilian) resulted in their developing a full-blown posttraumatic syndrome. A summons to reserve duty was the major military trigger. Civilian triggers included life events such as marriage and the birth of a child—which, despite their being happy events, require adjustment, may produce stress, and have been associated in the literature with the development of illness. The veterans in this group sought professional help when their subclinical symptoms were exacerbated by one of these triggers; they constituted 33% of the sample.

Moshe, a good-looking man in his mid-20s with silvering hair, first approached the mental health officer in his unit a year and a half after his service in the Lebanon war as a medic. His symptoms included difficulties falling and staying asleep, nightmares of dead soldiers trying to kill him, trouble concentrating, guilt about mistakes he had made in administering first aid, and a "fear of the army" that was manifested in somatic problems such as nausea and loss of appetite. PTSD was diagnosed.

Although this was the first time that Moshe reported his symptoms, they were not new. At the very beginning of the war, on the second night, he experienced a moment of extreme panic after his unit had come under heavy Katyusha rocket bombardment. Though most of the other men fell asleep when the attack was over, Moshe remained tense and alert. He cocked his weapon and, without orders, began shooting indiscriminately in every direction, all the time aware of how anxious, frightened, and out of control he was. Because the outburst was short-lived, however, and because Moshe acquitted himself well for the remainder of his 30-day tour of duty, the lapse received no more attention.

Moshe had mild posttraumatic symptoms from the time he came home. He had occasional war dreams and pangs of guilt. He was short-tempered and impatient. He tired of his girlfriends more rapidly than he might have done in a calmer frame of mind. Call-ups to reserve duty exacerbated his distress. He became nauseous and lost his appetite every time a summons arrived in the mail. On base, he kept to himself and made efforts to get assigned to guard duty so that he would not have to go out on patrol, which was more dangerous. None of these symptoms, however, was severe enough to seriously interfere with his functioning. Despite his discomfort, Moshe got through two more tours of reserve duty in Lebanon in the year and a half following his first entry; in civilian life he worked in his profession as a hairdresser, running his own business. So long as he maintained an adequate level of functioning, his symptoms could be passed over, just as his moment of panic after the Katyusha attack had been.

Two things seem to have induced the exacerbation of his subclinical PTSD into a full-blown syndrome. One was the accumulated pressure of repeated reserve duty. Moshe's initially mild symptoms became increasingly severe with each call-up until he finally asked for help during his third period of reserve duty following the war.

The second cause was the refresher course in frontline first aid that he was required to take during this last tour of duty. Though superficially innocuous, the course seems to have stirred up feelings he had experienced ever since he was first posted in Lebanon. As a medic, he had been assigned to the battalion aid station on the front during the heaviest fighting of the war. The concentrated exposure to death and injury that medical workers endure during wartime is known to precipitate stress reactions. Moshe had an additional burden of having to take care of his cousin, who was brought in wounded in the spine and stomach, with half a leg missing, and screaming that he was done for. Moshe had grown up with this cousin, and although he kept sufficient hold on himself to do his job and tend to him and the other casualties, the painful encounter would become a major theme in his PTSD. When he finally approached the mental health officer in his unit, he did not ask for therapy, but rather for a transfer to a unit where he would not bear so much responsibility for other people's lives.

What distinguishes Moshe's response from delayed onset is that even though this was the first time that Moshe reported his symptoms, his distress had been mounting since his first days on the front. The eruption of full-blown PTSD during his third and final stint of reserve duty simply pointed up the significance of the milder interim symptoms that Moshe had ignored until then, compelling—or enabling—him to give voice to the unbroken link of distress harking back to his panic on his second night in Lebanon and his cousin's injury.

DELAYED HELP SEEKING FOR CHRONIC PTSD

The veterans in this group were already suffering from chronic PTSD (defined by DSM-III as having a duration of 6 or more months) when they sought psychiatric help. These cases made up the largest proportion (40%) of our subjects. Unlike the soldiers in the previous group, who had mild subclinical symptoms throughout the so-called latency period, these subjects suffered from the full-blown syndrome right from around the time they fought in Lebanon. They sought help not when some external trigger exacerbated their symptoms, but when they could no longer bear their distress. As in the previous group, treatment was often sought during reserve duty, but here the military call-up served as not so much a trigger for the eruption of the syndrome as the setting in which the casualty's ongoing distress became unbearable to him. Whereas the veterans in the subclinical group sought help more or less contiguous to the onset of their full-blown stress disorder, those in the chronic group put a great deal of effort into containing a disturbance that had been relatively severe and disruptive right from the start, until they finally gave up trying to cope with it on their own. Not infrequently, treatment was initiated by a family member who could no longer endure the pressure that the casualty's symptoms created.

Dov, an electrician in his late 20s, was first diagnosed with acute CSR during the Lebanon war following a nighttime ambush in which he got caught up in a roll of barbed wire from which he was unable to extricate himself. In what he interprets as an act of emotional self-preservation, he blacked out, detaching himself mentally from the flying bullets, the screams of the wounded, and his own all too palpable danger. In the morning, he was rescued and sent to the battalion aid station for frontline psychiatric care.

Although the treatment was deemed successful and, after several days, Dov and his therapists both felt that he was ready to return to his unit, Dov never really recovered from his breakdown. As soon as fighting broke out again, he began to shake inside. He felt paralyzed, hardly able to think or move his hands. The next day, he was sent home for a weekend leave and spent all of his time in bed. On his way back to

Lebanon, he began to shake again. This time, when he went to the battalion aid station, the therapist on duty recommended a temporary discharge and referred Dov to the central IDF mental health clinic in Israel for therapy. In the heat of the war, though, Dov's initial breakdown and frontline care were not recorded.

Once at home, Dov had trouble sleeping and was plagued by terrifying nightmares from which his wife had to awaken him. Every mention of the war brought back all of its terrors. He ignored the referral to therapy because, as he put it, "I was afraid that I'd slide into some kind of state that I'd never be able to get out of." There was no period when he was symptom free, and he felt no gradual improvement or relief over time.

Dov sought treatment only when he could no longer function. This happened when his temporary discharge expired and he had to leave his pregnant wife for yet another stint of reserve duty. His nightmares became more frequent and intense, he began to hyperventilate at night, and he woke up exhausted in the morning. He often stayed home from work, and when he did show up, he accomplished very little. He became apathetic, stopped going out for entertainment, and would ask himself whether life was worth living. This went on for a month, up until he reported at his base. There, in front of the headquarters, he saw tanks and ammunition and began to tremble uncontrollably. Once again, he was sent to the battalion aid station, and his condition was finally diagnosed and put on record a year and a half after his initial breakdown.

REACTIVATION

Thirteen percent of the sample showed reactivation of an earlier combat stress reaction—most dating back to the 1973 Yom Kippur War, some even earlier. By the time the Lebanon war broke out, the residuals of the previous CSR had significantly abated, and the soldiers participated in the Lebanon war without a diagnosed CSR. Afterward, some were asymptomatic, whereas others suffered a range of symptoms from mild to more severe but continued to function. They differ from the reactivation cases discussed in Chapter 12 in that they were either well enough or motivated enough to more or less cope with the immediate pressures of Lebanon, and so they were not included in that initial sample of 35. Most of them experienced a reawakening of their earlier trauma in connection with threatening military stimuli. In some cases, the reactivation was triggered by a call-up to the reserves or a change in military unit. In other cases there was no single trigger, but rather the accumulated stress of repeated military exposure in both actual warfare and periodic reserve duty.

Joseph, the idealistic physician discussed in earlier chapters who had persisted in military service despite considerable psychiatric distress (see Chapters 8 and 10), served in four wars and had two CSRs before his PTSD was diagnosed about a year after his first tour of duty in Lebanon.

In his first war, the Six-Day War of 1967, Joseph served as a doctor behind lines without event. In his second conflict, the undeclared war of attrition with Egypt that dragged on after the Six-Day War cease-fire, he had an experience that left him vulnerable ever after. An Israeli stronghold in the Sinai was bombed when he happened to be doing his rounds there. There were many casualties, including the commanding officer. As the highest-ranking soldier still alive, Joseph had to take charge. Feeling not up to the job, he radioed for help. Reinforcements arrived, but when they saw he was managing, they departed, leaving him feeling terrifyingly alone and abandoned. From that time on, Joseph's mental health deteriorated progressively with every stint of military duty he served.

During the next war, the 1973 Yom Kippur War, he was stationed in a medical battalion on the heavily bombarded Golan Heights. Joseph was so frightened by the shelling that at times he wished a bomb would strike him and put an end to his terror. After his discharge, he suffered from nightmares, insomnia, and feelings of alienation, and he virtually ignored the infant daughter to whom his wife had given birth while he was away. When he went back 2 months later, rumors of an impending incident so overwhelmed him with anxiety that he asked his commander to release him. He was sent for psychiatric examination in Israel; he was diagnosed as a CSR casualty and transferred behind the lines.

For the next 10 years, Joseph made ceaseless, gallant efforts to live down what he regarded as the ignominy of his breakdown. As described in Chapter 8, he persistently resisted every attempt to discharge him from combat duty despite difficulties in falling asleep and severe anxiety whenever he was in the field. In 1981, on his return from a 3-year stay in the United States, he went so far as to request reinstatement in a combat unit.

During the Lebanon war, Joseph was flown by hospital helicopter right into the middle of a raging battle. Every shell that exploded and every noise made him jump. The other soldiers noticed and asked why he was so jittery. Somewhat later they were entrenched in foxholes in a dangerous spot, and Joseph lay glued to the ground, unable to direct his crew and get them organized. Nonetheless, by the time the wounded began coming in, he had pulled himself together sufficiently to take care of them. The only sign of his resolutely contained fears was the trouble he had sleeping, and this passed when he got home. There were no other signs of distress.

Joseph's anxiety finally got the better of him when he was sent back to East Beirut 3 weeks later. The city was under constant shelling and 2 days after he arrived, he was evacuated with severe chest pains. A comprehensive cardiological examination in Israel revealed no pathology. No one made the connection between his chest pains and his intense anxiety, though as a doctor, Joseph may have been expected to know the meaning of his cardiac pains and also to have recognized his CSR symptoms (as well as his ensuing PTSD). Joseph's chest pains persisted after his discharge, and he was irritable, forgetful, and sensitive to noise. In addition he became extremely tense whenever he heard bad news about Israel's security situation.

Joseph applied for treatment only in May 1983, when he was once again summoned to the reserves. The summons was particularly disturbing because he was called up to a new unit, which made him feel that he had been thrown out of his former place and confirmed, for him, the ultimate failure of all of his efforts to cope. He was also afraid that if he were sent to Lebanon, he would not be able to function as a military doctor and commander. The relatively minor symptoms he had been having burgeoned into a full-blown reactivation. Nine months after he was first flown into Lebanon, he presented with the following symptoms: frequent nightmares and flashbacks dating back to the 1973 Yom Kippur War, severe anxiety, sleeplessness, exhaustion, hypersensitivity to noise, irritability, concentration and memory problems, frequent uncontrollable outbursts of anger, and a marked decline in sexual desire.

OTHER PSYCHIATRIC DISORDERS

The smallest proportion of our cases, 4%, were veterans who had mild, transient prewar psychiatric disturbances. They erroneously sought help in IDF clinics for problems that were either triggered or colored by their war experiences but not originally induced by military events. The war-related content of their disturbance at first masked the real nature of their disorders.

Gidon, born in 1952, was a veteran of the Yom Kippur and Lebanon wars who came for treatment in 1985, 3 years after his participation in the latter conflict. He had been referred for evaluation by his commander, whom he had approached for help even though he was not serving in the reserves at the time. The commander sent him to the mental health officer at the base, who, suspecting a combat-related disorder, referred him to the IDF central mental health clinic for further examination. His presenting problems were frequent fainting spells; tension, agitation, and hyperalertness; stabbing pains in his left side; a drastic loss of appetite; lack of concentration; nightmares of snakes and monsters; flashbacks of an air attack he had experienced in the Yom Kippur War; and suicidal ideation.

Despite the overlap of his presenting problems with typical features of PTSD and the fact that the appeal for help came through military channels, the history that was taken in the course of his evaluation indicated that Gidon had suffered from many problems throughout his life. He had grown up with a very cold and critical mother and was isolated at school and in his neighborhood, where most of the residents were of a different ethnic origin. He was a good student, but very withdrawn. During his compulsory military service, he was highly dissatisfied and manifested his discontent in impatience, depressive moods, apathy, and occasional outbursts of rage. At one point, he deserted when things were not going his way. The problems were severe enough to bring him to treatment with the mental health officer.

Moreover, with the exception of that incident, Gidon functioned adequately in both civilian and military life up until shortly before his appeal for help. When he was 21, the Yom Kippur War broke out, and he served as a medic on the Sinai front. After the war, he married, fathered two children, and obtained an engineering degree from a top Israeli university. In the Lebanon war, he also functioned adequately for the 3 months that he was in charge of organizing the deployment of medical crews into Beirut. In the following years, he served in the reserves on three separate occasions without event.

His difficulties began in 1984, when he was sent by the Israeli company he worked for to head a large road construction project in Cameroon. He threw himself into the work, but his compulsive and self-righteous manner apparently aroused anger and resentment in his subordinates. His colleagues ostracized him, and very much as in his childhood, he found himself isolated and alone. He became depressed and somewhat paranoid and suffered from a variety of psychosomatic manifestations, which he presented to the IDF after he was sent home from Cameroon for health reasons.

After several interviews, the clinicians reached the conclusion that Gidon was not suffering from combat-related PTSD but rather was undergoing a gradual process of decompensation of a compulsive personality with associated features of anxiety, depression, and paranoia.

DELAYED-ONSET PTSD

Of the sample, 10% really had delayed-onset PTSD. These were the relatively few veterans who participated in the Lebanon war with no apparent psychiatric injury, functioned well during and for some time after the war, and were asymptomatic for a latency period of several weeks to several years after their return home. Then, following exposure to stressful stimuli, such as a call-up to reserves or some other life event, their latent disturbance surfaced and they applied for treatment.

Gad, a bachelor in his mid-20s when he fought in the Lebanon war, showed little sign of emotional disturbance until almost a year after combat. Throughout his stay on the front (for the first 3 weeks of the fighting in the summer of 1982), he conducted himself fearlessly in one gruesome incident after the other. Twice he was sent out as a decoy to draw fire at close range. In one of these instances, his commander was killed, and Gad discovered a bullet embedded in his own flak jacket near his neck. The next day, he saw a close friend blown to pieces by a missile that turned out to have been fired by friendly forces. Then, without respite, he was exposed to a similarly shocking encounter with death on the following day, as his regiment was shot at by 10-year-old "RPG kids"—children and young adolescents wielding deadly RPG submachine guns—as it moved through an area strewn with dismembered Syrian bodies.

At no point during 3 weeks did Gad show signs of a breakdown. He fought staunchly throughout and kept his head about him in the most horrible situations. When he went home for leave at the end of this period, he felt well on the whole. He was sad at the waste of human life, but he consoled himself with the thought that someone had to do the unpleasant duty. He felt an awed pride in the power and succor of the Israeli air force, which had come to the rescue on several occasions. He also believed that his own life had been given to him as a gift, and that his having been spared infused his life with new meaning.

When he was called up to Lebanon again a month later, Gad was not involved in any active fighting, and he completed his 25 days of service without incident. Like most veterans, he had nightmares when he came home; because they occurred only about once a week and he was able to fall back to sleep afterward, they did not seem indicative of a serious problem. He carried on calmly with his life. In January of 1983 he married a girl he had known for a year and a half, and their relationship was good.

The first sign of emotional disturbance appeared only with Gad's second call-up, in April 1983, 10 months after his combat on the front.

This time he became incapacitated by severe diarrhea, which was a typical response to stress in his childhood, and he could complete only part of his service.

PTSD was diagnosed when Gad went to a civilian mental health clinic in his neighborhood following yet another call-up in August of 1983, a year after he had fought in Lebanon. With the receipt of this call-up, all the anxieties he had kept under control broke forth. His nightmares increased in frequency to two or three times a week; he would break out in heavy perspiration, his heart would beat wildly, and he could no longer fall asleep afterward. He woke up every morning with diarrhea. He lost his appetite, his sexual interest declined, and he became nervous and would burst out at family and friends. He began to fear terrorist attacks and worried that he was too emotionally drained to be able to function in battle if he had to fight again.

Only 10% of our cases were, like Gad's, genuine instances of delayed onset. Most of the subjects had clinical or subclinical PTSD dating back to their participation in the Lebanon war or immediately afterward but did not seek help until they or a family member could no longer bear the pressure of their symptoms. In retrospect, this should not be surprising. The reluctance of psychiatric casualties of war to seek help has been extensively documented following Vietnam (Kadushin, Boulanger, & Martin, 1981), and as was pointed out in Chapter 5, our own group found relatively high rates of untreated PTSD among Lebanon veterans (Solomon, 1989b). Nonetheless, our negative findings raise the question of why the rate of delayed onset in our sample is so much lower than in others that have been studied. Numerous reasons may be suggested.

In their essay, "A Prediction of Delayed Stress Response Syndromes in Vietnam Veterans," Horowitz and Solomon (1975) propose that the time of onset of psychiatric disorder is associated with the circumstances of the war that induced it.

> The Vietnam situation led to the kinds of events that predispose participants to a delaying-numbing type of stress response while in military service. Discharge may, be associated with relief and ostensible readaptation to civilian life. Unresolved stress will, however, lead to intrusive-repetitive types of responses even months or years after situational exits. (p. 79)

It seems that the Lebanon experience, which differed in crucial respects from Vietnam—and also from the Nazi Holocaust, the other major catastrophe in which high rates of delayed onset of posttrauma were found—may rather have precipitated stress reactions close to the time of combat and tempered the development of delayed responses.

In Vietnam, where the highest rates of delayed onset have been found, the widespread use of drugs and alcohol facilitated emotional withdrawal and self-treatment for fear on the battlefield; it also masked immediate stress reactions. In Lebanon, substance abuse among Israeli troops was rare and did not play a significant masking or delaying role.

The accident of geography may also have had a differential effect on the time of onset of stress disorders in the two wars. Whereas at least an ocean separated U.S. soldiers in Vietnam from their homes on the North American continent, the Israeli soldier had only a few short hours by jeep or bus before he was on home ground. This simple fact meant that Israeli soldiers were allowed frequent home leaves during which they could relax in comfort and security, quite in contrast to their American counterparts, who served on the front for yearlong tours of duty relieved only by R & R abroad. In their article, Horowitz and Solomon contemplate that the onset of a stress reaction might occur only when circumstances allow the individual to sufficiently relax his defenses:

> It might only be with the vision of continued safety, with the permissible relaxation of defensive and coping operations, that the person might then enter a phase in which intrusive recollections of the experience were reemergent. (p. 69)

Such a sequence would explain the reverse salience of immediate and delayed stress reactions in Lebanon and both Vietnam and the Nazi Holocaust. The American soldier had to wait to cross the Pacific before he could let down his guard enough for repressed traumatic contents to surface. The Holocaust victim had to wait for a time when letting down would not mean almost certain death. The Israeli soldier in Lebanon had only to go on home leave; find himself nervous, unable to sleep, disturbed by nightmares, withdrawn, and unbearably anxious; and report to the nearest IDF mental health clinic to ask for treatment or a discharge.

In fact, during the Lebanon war, many cases of CSR were diagnosed when soldiers on home leave applied for mental health assistance. The IDF labeled such cases acute CSR, even though the process—the repression of traumatic contents and their expression only when circumstances made it safe—is similar to the course of the disease in delayed onset. The only difference is that in this variant of "acute" CSR, the period preceding the externalization of the disorder is strongly compressed.

Another relevant difference has to do with the possibilities for ritual mourning in Lebanon, as opposed to those available to both Vietnam veterans and Holocaust survivors. Formal rites, including the burial of the dead and the consolation of the bereaved, bring comfort and relief and enable survivors to complete the process of mourning. In the Holocaust, the Nazis pointedly disallowed these rites as part of their overall attempt to dehumanize their victims. In Vietnam, the rites of mourning were not observed on account of the long tours of duty and the fact that the soldiers were far from home. Krystal (1968) suggests that when survivors are prevented from mourning at the critical time, they mourn continuously for the rest of their lives. It might be that the unresolved grief of both Holocaust survivors and Vietnam veterans contributed to their subsequent vulnerability, wherein reminders of their loss or other stressors would more readily trigger a reaction at a later date.

In Lebanon, on the other hand, as well as in all other wars in which Israel has been engaged, the IDF made a concerted and well-organized effort to encourage the full mourning process. Every possible effort was made to evacuate the dead and bring them to burial in Israel; soldiers knew that neither they nor their friends would be abandoned on the battlefield, and a special rabbinical unit was in charge of seeing to the proper rites. Soldiers were routinely given leaves to attend funerals and pay condolence calls. The ability to mourn and resolve their grief may have made the soldiers in our sample less vulnerable to subsequent triggering stressors.

Yet another significant characteristic of the Lebanon experience was the positive nature of the soldiers' homecoming. For both Vietnam veterans and Holocaust survivors, the postwar periods continued to be traumatic. Vietnam veterans were denied a heroes' welcome and came back to a United States that had disowned them, to massive antiwar demonstrations and cries of "baby killer." Holocaust survivors had no place to come back to. Most of their families and communities had been exterminated, their homes and property had been appropriated, and the communities where they had once lived were hostile and rejecting. When many of them finally immigrated to new countries, they had to overcome substantial adversity in rebuilding their lives. In both these groups, the accumulation of stress may have eventually led to the delayed onset of latent disorders among survivors who had initially been able to contain their traumatization.

For the Israeli veterans of Lebanon, on the other hand, homecoming by and large brought an end to the trauma of the war. Although public opinion on the war was divided, the soldiers who had fought it were welcomed back with respect and affection as brave sons who had risked their lives in defense of the country. Together with the provisions for mourning, this widespread social support may have promoted the assimilation of the trauma and prevented disintegration and pathology.

With all of these explanations for the relative paucity of delayed onset in our subjects, the fact remains that our figures may be premature, and that the low percentage of delayed onset among our troops may be a direct result of the timing of our study: 5 years after the formal cease-fire in Lebanon and only 2 years after Israel pulled out its troops. The studies that report higher rates, conducted among American veterans of World War II (Archibald & Tuddenham, 1965; Christenson et al., 1981) and Vietnam (Figley, 1978b; Horowitz & Solomon, 1975) and among survivors of the Nazi Holocaust (Ben-Shoshan, 1985; Dor-Shav, 1978), were conducted between 10 and 40 years after the traumatic experience. Furthermore, the literature shows that delayed onset following these and other traumatic events was often triggered by stressful life events associated with aging—for example, retirement, children leaving home, debilitating illness, or a death in the family (Ben-Shoshan, 1985; Van Dyke, Zilberg, & McKinnon, 1985).

There is, unfortunately, reason to believe that a longer follow-up of our sample would also reveal a higher rate of delayed onset. Although the DSM-III stipulates a minimum 6-month latency period, incubation time can be longer, especially where circumstances or cultural factors enable the victims of the trauma to cope for an extended period. Because of the relatively asymptomatic nature of the latency period, we have little way of knowing at this stage what proportion of the Lebanon war veterans who have not yet sought help are in fact healthy and what proportion are harboring dormant pathology. When Horowitz and Solomon (1975) wrote their essay, they predicted that with the passage of time, even more Vietnam veterans would seek help for delayed-onset combat-induced disorders, and history has borne them out. I am strongly inclined to believe that their prognosis is no less applicable to the veterans of the Lebanon war.

Most of the veterans who made up the population for our research were still relatively young (largely in their 20s and 30s) at the time of the study. On the whole, they had not yet experienced the age-related stresses that could lead to the surfacing of latent PTSD, and the stronger defenses of youth had not yet been worn down by the years. From the cases presented in this chapter and in the chapter on reactivation, one can understand, too, how strongly motivated many of our population were to continue serving in the army and how zealously they struggled to cope on their own with whatever distress they felt. It is not unlikely that many more such veterans, both men with latent disorders and men with clinical or subclinical PTSD, will eventually experience an eruption of psychiatric illness as the pressures of life mount and their ability to cope with them declines.

Life in Israel is very hard for adult men, especially for those with latent or unidentified PTSD. Annual reserve duty, periodic terrorist attacks (with the due reporting of casualties and funerals on TV and radio), and the absence of peace with most of our neighbors all pose tangible dangers to which men who have been traumatized could be expected to react at some point or another. Neither the veterans of World War II or Vietnam nor the survivors of the Holocaust who settled in Western Europe or the United States had objective cause for fearing that they or their children would be subjected to a repetition or variation of the catastrophe they had weathered, and they were able to relax their defenses and rebuild or resume their lives free of objective threat. The veterans of Lebanon, on the other hand, continue to be exposed to tangible danger. This continuing threat has divergent implications. In light of Horowitz and Solomon's theory that delayed PTSD tends to erupt when the person's defenses are down, it may be yet another reason for the (thus far) low rate of delayed onset in our sample. On the other hand, the stress that the threat creates can be expected to accumulate and to be involved in the eruption of delayed PTSD in later years.

One of the consistent findings in our study is that both the onset and exacerbation of PTSD among Israeli soldiers occur in connection with reserve duty, in contrast to most Vietnam veterans, whose disorders surfaced following personal or family stresses (e.g., marriage, the birth of a child, divorce, or the death of a close relative) or in connection with a purely symbolic threat (e.g., a child playing war games or a hot humid evening reminiscent of the Vietnam jungles; Figley & Sprenkle, 1978). In the vast majority of our subjects, the outbreak or exacerbation of PTSD was triggered by the summons to reserve duty.

Future threats can be expected to have a similarly precipitating effect. Unless genuine peace is achieved, most of the Lebanon veterans will continue to serve in the reserves. Some of them may be unfortunate enough to have to take part in another war, and many will live to see their children and perhaps even grandchildren go into the army. Our prognosis is glum. As these veterans grow older and the continuous military threat is compounded by the stresses of age, we expect that more and more of them will reach our clinics with PTSD.

Whether they arrive with delayed onset following a long incubation period or after years of silent suffering is somewhat academic in the long run. But in the interim, if the responsible agencies are aware of the probability, they may be moved to provide detection and outreach services to the men who had resigned themselves to living with their symptoms.

14

Fathers and Sons
The Transgenerational Impact of the Holocaust

THE LONG SHADOW OF THE HOLOCAUST

When my friends and I were in the youth movement in the late 1960s, one of the things that our leaders suggested we read was a letter by Ofer Fenninger, a parachutist who was killed in the Six-Day War. Ofer wrote the letter to his girlfriend from the front in the lull before the fighting began. This 3-week waiting period in the spring of 1967 was one of the most tense times since the state of Israel was founded. There was a full call-up, and Israeli soldiers were positioned along the border across from the Egyptian, Jordanian, and Syrian armies. Our forces were greatly outnumbered, and there was an acute sense of existential anxiety in the air. The threats voiced in the Arab media repeated variations on one theme: we'll finish you, we'll slaughter you, we'll drown you in the sea. The Israeli public felt under siege, and this awakened collective fears and anxieties from the past. People remembered the Holocaust and stated that we could be led again like lambs to the slaughter. It was felt that this was a struggle for the continued existence of the Jewish people in the land of Israel.

Ofer Fenninger, a kibbutznik from Giv'at Haim, was called up during this waiting period and was partner to this general anxiety. He had just finished reading the novel *House of Dolls* (Zetnik, 1963), which graphically depicts the atrocities of the Nazi Holocaust, and he wrote the following to his girlfriend:

I feel that out of all the atrocities and impotence a tremendous will grows up in me to be strong, strong to the point of tears, strong and sharp as a knife, calm and terrible. That's how I want to be. I want to know that never again will agonized Jewish eyes look out of electrified fences! They won't only if I'm strong! If we're all strong! Strong, proud Jews! Never again to be led to the slaughter! (Spira 1968, p. 196)

The letter was an inspiration to an entire generation of Israelis. It is a testimony of our continued sense of vulnerability and danger as a nation, and the impulse it expresses—to be strong so that Jews can never again be helplessly slaughtered—still informs Israeli thinking and culture. In Chapter 10, I suggested that the extenuated strength, born of national fear, that makes for dedicated, self-motivated soldiers ("strong and sharp as a knife, calm and terrible") may have negative implications for CSR veterans who had fallen short of their idealized image.

THE SECOND GENERATION

These conclusions, of course, were not yet formulated when I was planning the current investigation. It did, however, occur to me and to my colleagues on the research team that the Holocaust, which underpins that fear, might play a role in the combat reactions of second-generation Holocaust survivors, the adult children of men and women who had gone through the Nazi inferno. A considerable body of literature on the psychological impact of the Nazi Holocaust demonstrates its enduring detrimental impact on both the first and second surviving generations (Barocas & Barocas, 1979; Bergman & Jacovy, 1982; Danieli, 1980; Epstein, 1979). These and other studies have shown that Holocaust survivors suffer from what has been termed "the survivor syndrome," whose symptoms include nightmares and flashbacks, depression, anxiety, and psychic numbing—all reminiscent of those that characterize PTSD. Surprisingly, the transgenerational effects were observed in children of survivors who were not themselves exposed to the Nazi atrocities. The offspring experience similar symptoms, only of lesser intensity. "The children of survivors show symptoms which would be expected if they actually lived through the Holocaust" (Barocas & Barocas, 1979, p. 151). Could not the psychological damage left by their parents' Holocaust ordeal play a role in the combat disorders of the second generation, just as other antecedent psychological maladies might?

Indeed, it seemed to us that certain post-Holocaust effects that have been observed in the second generation should intensify for them the already massive stress of combat and, in consequence, its detrimental effects. The effects include a tendency to react with anxiety to a whole range of stressful changes (Danieli, 1980), high narcissistic vulnerability, survival guilt, and conflicts over the expression of aggression.

That combat entails highly stressful situations that would evoke anxiety in almost anyone is too obvious to require elaboration. Yet it may be perceived as much more threatening to individuals, such as children of Holocaust survivors, whose anxiety threshold is much lower.

High narcissistic vulnerability, noted in the second generation by Barocas and Barocas (1979), is an abiding of fear and heightened sense of vulnerability to death. It is an impairment in the salutary illusion of "It won't happen to me" that most people cling to on an unconscious level, and that Shaw (1983) presents as one of several narcissistic defenses that enable soldiers to function in wartime by keeping out awareness of their biological limitations.

As noted earlier, in war and other situations where people are dying, this illusion is assailed and often shattered. Among the second generation, it is most tenuous to begin with. Most of the second generation grew up in families that had been decimated by the Holocaust. Few children of survivors had living grandparents. Most were acutely aware that uncles, aunts, cousins, and in some cases older siblings had been slaughtered. In not a few survivor homes, the parents were the only ones of their families to have emerged from the Holocaust alive. Having had more and earlier experience of powerlessness and death than most other soldiers, sons and daughters of survivors would consequently have a harder time blocking out fearful reality on the battlefield.

> I was drafted in the spring of 1967, when the tension on the borders began. During those weeks of tension and nervousness it seemed that all the armies of the world were gathering into an enormous force to destroy us. . . . The Arabs were preparing a second Holocaust for us. I thought that this was my fate. . . . It seemed so natural and inevitable. (Lieblich, 1983, p. 101)

This is the feeling that "it *can* happen to me." In combat, it would bring to the surface all the helplessness and fear of death inherent to the situation. As Shaw (1983, 1987) has noted, the feelings of overwhelming helplessness and fear of death that arise when the illusion of safety collapses are among the major causes of combat disorders.

Survival guilt is one of the most salient characteristics of both Holocaust survivors and their offspring. Whereas most people take the fact that they are alive for granted, both Holocaust survivors and their children frequently remain incredulous that they are alive. They often feel that they do not quite have the right to live when so many near and dear to them were killed (Bergman & Jacovy, 1982). This point is made explicitly and emphatically in a letter, also quoted by Lieblich (1983), that a

daughter of Holocaust survivors wrote to her mother: "The most important thing that I want to tell you is that I've felt guilt since the day I
discovered what kind of childhood you've had. . . . I felt guilt that I'm
alive while your family were killed in the Holocaust" (p. 100).

It seemed to us that such strong residual guilt would compound for
the second generation the guilt-creating potential of combat, where
friends, acquaintances, and officers are killed in front of one's eyes.
Members of the second generation who feel as this young woman does
would question more than others their right to live when people around
them are dead or dying. They would also wrestle with more than the
usual qualms about killing to secure their own lives. We wondered
whether the force and depth of the conflict in the second generation
between the organism's desire to live and the guilt-ridden approbation
of that desire might not affect their reactions to combat.

Conflicts about the expression of aggression have also been found
to be quite strong in Holocaust families. Henry Krystal (1968), a Holocaust survivor and a pioneer in work with survivors and their children,
has observed that many survivor parents unconsciously encouraged aggressive behavior in their children that they themselves had once had to
suppress to stay alive in the totalitarian environment of the concentration camp. Axelrod, Schnipper, and Rau (1980) noted that survivors
often vented their pent-up aggressions on their children, triggering in
them similar feelings of hostility. At the same time, open aggression is
even more taboo in survivor families than in many others. Hillel Klein
(1973), a noted Israeli psychiatrist who had worked with survivors and
their children, noted that both survivors and their children have a profound fear of being aggressors, and a great need to justify any aggression as temporary and purely defensive. Moreover, in Holocaust families, the normal anger and hostility that children sometimes feel toward
their parents is kept tightly in check by the children's awareness of how
much their parents had suffered, and so it is stored up. In combat, the
tension between the opportunity for the release of aggression and the
internalized prohibition against killing that is common to almost all soldiers would be all that much stronger in the second generation, because
it duplicates (albeit in vastly extenuated form) a tension in their upbring-
ing.

Another young Israeli of Holocaust background described this conflict in terms of a conflict between being either a perpetual victim or a
Nazi himself. He told of a recurrent dream in which he is a small boy in
his parents' house in a ghetto in Poland:

> It is night. I wake up to heavy knocking on the door. It's the most frightening noise I
> know. The noise is like kicks on the door with hobnail boots and rifle butts. I know

how it feels on the outside of a house at moments like these. In hunting for terrorists, we conducted searches of houses in Arab villages. There I was the one who
knocked on doors at midnight. . . . The problem is, I hate the gestapo, but I also
hate being their victim. . . . [For me] there is no middle way. (Lieblich, 1983, p. 87)

This dream and its association show a built-in catch-22. The sense of
perpetual victimization would make aggression in the name of defense
all the more necessary; at the same time, the failure to distinguish on an
emotional level between Nazi genocide and the defensive aggression
involved in doing house-to-house searches for terrorists puts moral and
emotional obstacles in the way of even the most justified combat. For the
men and women of the second generation who share the dilemma depicted in this dream, both winning and losing a battle would be fraught
with psychological peril.

PTSD AMONG SECOND-GENERATION HOLOCAUST SURVIVORS

Taken together, it seemed to us that these transgenerational effects
of the Holocaust would make the second generation of survivors more
vulnerable to the stresses of combat. Our close pairwise matching of CSR
casualties and controls resulted in the two groups having nearly the same
number of second-generation veterans and so prevented us from investigating the possibility that a Holocaust background is a risk factor in the
sustaining of a combat breakdown. To assess the impact of a Holocaust
background on recovery from combat-induced traumatization, we compared the responses on the PTSD inventory of 44 CSR casualties who
had at least one Holocaust-survivor parent and 52 casualties without that
background for each of the first 3 years after the Lebanon war. Our aim
was to investigate whether the Holocaust cast a shadow on the sons of
survivors who fought in Lebanon and sustained combat stress reactions.
In other words, did those CSR casualties who were children of Holocaust
survivors suffer from more severe and more prolonged posttraumatic
residues than those CSR casualties whose parents were not Holocaust
survivors?

The subjects in this study were taken from the population of soldiers who fought in the Lebanon war and were identified by IDF clinicians as CSR casualties (for details, see Chapter 2). Because we wanted to
examine the impact of parents' experiences in Nazi concentration camps
in Europe during World War II, only subjects whose parents were of
European descent were included in the study. Ninety-six such soldiers
participated at all three points of time. The subjects were divided into

two groups according to whether at least one of their parents was a Holocaust survivor: 44 soldiers were offspring of survivors, and 52 were not.

Statistical analyses showed that the two groups did not differ significantly with respect to any sociodemographic, health, or military variable. Yet throughout all three years of the study, the second-generation CSR casualties suffered from higher rates of PTSD than their nonsurvivor counterparts (see Solomon, Kotler, & Mikulincer, 1988). Whereas 60% of the nonsurvivor CSR subjects were diagnosed with PTSD the first year of the study, 52% the second year, and 39% the third year, the PTSD rates in the second-generation group were 70% the first year, 73% the second, and 64% the third. Moreover, as can be seen from these figures, although in both groups PTSD rates declined between the first and third years, the decline was considerably less steep among the children of Holocaust survivors, so that by the third year of the study the gap in the psychopathology rates of the two groups was much wider than it had been at the onset. In short, PTSD was both more prevalent among second-generation CSR casualties and lasted longer.

A similar trend was apparent in the number of PTSD symptoms endorsed by the two groups, though here the significant difference did not appear until the third year after Lebanon. During the first 2 years of the study, both groups endorsed an average of about half the symptoms in the 13-item PTSD inventory. In the third year, however, second-generation casualties reported significantly more symptoms than their nonsurvivor counterparts. Moreover, though the number of symptoms endorsed by the nonsurvivor subjects decreased significantly between the first and third years, only a slight decrease occurred for the second generation. These findings indicate that the wounds of war are particularly deep and enduring for CSR casualties who are also the offspring of Holocaust survivors. It seems that the passage of time did not have the same healing effect on the PTSD of the second generation as on that of other soldiers. Three years after Lebanon, the second generation were still suffering nearly as intensely from their psychological war wounds as they had only 1 year after the war.

To obtain a more detailed and sensitive account of the clinical picture presented by the subjects in the two groups, we adopted the four criteria for PTSD proposed by Laufer et al. (1984)—intrusiveness, emotional numbing, hyperalertness, and cognitive impairment—and added guilt feelings as a fifth index of our own. We found that the two groups also differed in the clinical picture that emerged from their item endorsement on the PTSD inventory. Although the second-generation soldiers suffered from more emotional numbing, cognitive impairment, and guilt feelings, their greater suffering was especially marked with regard to intrusion and hyperalertness.

SECONDARY TRAUMATIZATION

The findings of greater PTSD prevalence, duration, and number of symptoms among the second-generation CSR casualties point to their greater distress and retarded recovery from combat traumatization. These outcomes are strikingly parallel to those found in the children of American combat veterans. In a study of children of Vietnam veterans, Rosenheck and Nathan (1985) defined a process of "secondary traumatization" whereby the sons and daughters of combatants with stress disorders showed traumatic stress symptoms similar to those of their fathers. Then, in another highly instructive article, Rosenheck (1985) reported on an extremely severe and intractable form of posttraumatic disorder in a small but distinct group of Vietnam veterans whose fathers had fought in World War II, tracing its "malignancy" to the combat experience of the parent generation. Like Rosenheck's studies, ours shows devastating effects of growing up with the secondhand experience of a catastrophe that one's parents had experienced directly.

Like the children of traumatized Vietnam and World War II veterans, the children of Holocaust survivors seem to have a heightened vulnerability, not only to general and war-related stress (as was noted above) but also to combat's detrimental aftereffects. As with the other subjects in our study, the second-generation casualties were ostensibly healthy before the war, in that they had all passed the physical and psychological tests for IDF recruitment as frontline soldiers. Their combat exposure seems to have unmasked and/or exacerbated a latent vulnerability that had not been activated by more run-of-the-mill life events.

Indeed, the PTSD of the second generation may be in effect a reactivation of a latent posttraumatic syndrome deriving from their parents' Holocaust experience. The second generation's pattern of more symptoms lasting for a longer period of time parallels that found in the cases of reactivation discussed in Chapter 12. We seem to be witnessing a similar phenomenon here, with the antecedent trauma not a prior combat breakdown but the secondhand experience of the Holocaust.

Support for this view may be found in the distinct clinical picture of second-generation PTSD casualties. Their relative proneness to intrusive imagery and their greater hyperalertness than other PTSD casualties are both highly reminiscent of the symptoms of their survivor parents. To some extent, the similarity in the symptomatology of the two generations may reflect learned behavior. For example, the second-generation PTSD casualty who grew up with parents who had Holocaust nightmares may have learned to vent his pent-up emotions in dreams; where his survivor parents bristled at the sounds of trains and barking dogs (which the Nazis had used to transport and hunt Jews), he also tends to jump at the sounds of planes, explosions, and associated noises, which are his danger signals.

On the other hand, as occurs in the eruption of reactivated PTSD (see Chapter 12), the symptoms that emerge as augmented in the PTSD of second-generation Holocaust survivors had existed previously. Well before the Lebanon war, therapists to whom children of survivors in both the United States and Israel had flocked in inordinate numbers reported on dreams and nightmares in their young patients with Nazi-era content (Bergman & Jacovy, 1982). They also noted that as a group, children of survivors showed a high level of trait anxiety (Dor-Shav, 1978). Helen Epstein (1979), a journalist and a child of survivors, confesses in her book *Children of the Holocaust: Conversations with Sons and Daughters of Survivors* to feeling perpetually suspicious and observes that many of the young men and women she interviewed felt similarly wary. The road from pervasive diffuse anxiety and suspiciousness to the hyperalertness of the second-generation PTSD casualty is not very long.

Pressures in the Holocaust family may also have contributed to the intensity and duration of the distress of our second-generation PTSD casualties. Broadly speaking, there are two relevant pressures that may continue to exert an influence even on adult children who have left their parental homes, married, and had children of their own.

One pressure, derived from the survivor generation's abiding fear of loss, is the pressure against separation and individuation. Having lost so many in the Holocaust, survivor parents cling to their children and generally have greater difficulty than other parents with the very real hardship of parting from them. In a book-length study based on in-depth interviews with second-generation survivors, Robert M. Prince (1985) emphatically states that the outstanding feature of Holocaust families is the inhibition of separation from parents: "The central demand of survivor parents is that their children never leave them" (p. 71). Implicit in this demand is the pressure on the second generation not to grow up and take off on their own.

Among the ways in which this demand is conveyed is through a well-documented overprotectiveness on the part of people whose history had made them hyperalert to peril and inordinately anxious for their children's safety (Bergman & Jacovy, 1982). The natural care and concern that are aroused when a son or daughter is ill may be considerably exaggerated in survivor families. A father who brought his CSR son to our interviews provides a somewhat extreme, but nonetheless apt illustration. The father, over 60, led his oversized 24-year-old son by the hand, found him a place to sit, brought him coffee and cake, sat down next to him when the questionnaires were distributed, and was about to help him fill them out when he was finally asked to leave the room.

It may be suggested that in his slow recovery, the second-generation PTSD veteran is unconsciously acquiescing to lifelong parental demands that he remain infantile and dependent, while perhaps also enjoying the secondary gains of being pampered and catered to that his disorder affords—even if he may also find them smothering.

Moreover, if (as was earlier suggested of other PTSD casualties) the afflicted son of survivors was unconsciously tempted to prolong his stress disorder to avoid returning to the front, he might well have found very supportive allies in his survivor parents. At the time the first two waves of interviews were being conducted, Israel was still sending reservists to Lebanon, and there was real danger that anyone serving there could be killed. Obviously, no parents relish the thought of losing a son in battle. But for the Holocaust survivor, for whom every death is a replay of earlier deaths, the threat might be all that much more terrifying, and the urge to ward it off so much greater. It is not impossible that some survivor parents may have unconsciously discouraged the recovery of their CSR sons so as to avert the danger of the latter having to return to the front and perhaps being killed.

The other pressure works in the opposite direction to similarly devastating effect. In contrast to the pressures that discourage the PTSD casualty from taking responsibility for his recovery, this is the pressure on children of survivors to be their parents' "guardians" and "saviors" (Epstein, 1979). According to Bergman and Jacovy (1982), "The children feel that they have a mission to live in the past and to change it so that their parents' humiliation, disgrace and guilt can be converted into victory over the oppressors, and the threat of genocide undone with a restitution of life and worth" (p. 101).

In the state of Israel, which was founded to undo the effects of persecution, the generational roles are often reversed, with the children-soldiers ensuring the safety and survival of immigrant and refugee parents. We have seen something of this reversal in Ofer Fenninger's "never again," quoted at the opening of this chapter. But second-generation survivors have been brought up to take that responsibility very literally and very personally.

Serving in the army in a Jewish state that was founded to put an end to the persecution of Jews would provide a prime opportunity to meet this well-ingrained expectation. "There was the desire to win," wrote a daughter of Holocaust survivors at the outbreak of the Six-Day War, "to pull together all my powers, to the maximum of my ability, so that there wouldn't be a second Holocaust! Never again! And so that you, mother, will be able to feel secure and not suffer any more" (Lieblich, 1983).

Thus, although soldiers classically fight for home and country, the second generation's messianic obligation gives this time-honored raison d'être for war a special force for them. It probably weighs heavily on the battlefield. It would also color the meaning of any CSR and magnify its psychological consequences. As I already have pointed out, almost all CSR casualties feel that they have failed and suffer agonies of shame and reduced self-esteem. Among the second generation, however, the meaning of their failure is more profound. Not only did they fail to protect their country, but they clearly failed to live up to the expectation to undo the damage that the Holocaust had brought to their parents' lives. The magnitude of this expectation probably cuts deeply and intensifies both the stress on the battlefield and, in particular, the failure implicit in a combat stress reaction.

15

Why Don't They Seek Treatment?

My colleagues and I were fortunate in our research to have been able to reach most of the treated psychiatric casualties of the Lebanon war. In the course of our work, however, it has become increasingly clear that there are many untreated casualties: distressed veterans whose disorders went unidentified and who never reached IDF mental health services.

My first inkling of undiagnosed and untreated PTSD following the Lebanon war came during the first wave of measurements in 1983. The casualties were seated in small groups, with the CSR and non-CSR control subjects sitting together. Naturally, the examiners and I were blind as to which soldiers were controls and which ones were CSR subjects. After completing the tests, numerous soldiers came up to me and began to talk. They talked about their war experiences and subsequent distress. Many went into considerable detail about their war dreams, fears, sleeplessness, tenseness, and other problems that originated with their combat. Not a few, though we had been complete strangers only a few hours earlier, asked me whether I thought they should see a psychologist and how to go about doing it.

Their confessions were moving and totally unexpected. In the excitement of getting the research under way, I told the men where they could obtain help, but I did not record these encounters or fully register that they might represent a considerable number of untreated casualties. Then the figures came in: 16% of the control group, the "untreated" group, met DSM-III criteria for PTSD the first year of the study, 19% the second year, and 10% the third year. Furthermore, our analyses of the delayed-onset cases (see Chapter 13), who still knock on IDF clinic doors as I write this chapter, showed that the vast majority of these veterans apparently suffering from delayed PTSD were actually cases of chronic PTSD with delayed help seeking. All of these men suffered from diagnosable PTSD. In some cases, their symptoms were severe. Yet they all met the challenge of combat and carried on their lives without having had their disorder identified, diagnosed, or treated.

Neither I nor my colleagues had anticipated the rates of untreated PTSD that we found, much less that the second-year rate would be higher than the first. The control subjects, it should be recalled, were drawn from the same combat units as the psychiatric casualties and had fought in the same battles, but were not identified as CSR casualties. They were chosen as controls precisely because their files contained no indication whatsoever of any war-induced psychiatric disorder. Because they were chosen on the basis of their similarity to the CSR soldiers and not at random, however, we cannot say for certain whether the rates of unidentified PTSD in this group apply to all IDF veterans of the Lebanon war. Even so, it seems safe to extrapolate from these rates and to conclude that the untreated veterans that we found are but a portion of a much larger group, and that on the whole the untreated PTSD veterans of the Lebanon war far outnumber the identified casualties.

The relatively large number of untreated PTSD veterans is especially surprising when one considers that they all could have received treatment free of charge at any one of the many IDF mental health clinics dispersed throughout Israel. Moreover, in addition to a possible alleviation of their distress, a request for treatment is likely to have brought them at least temporary release from combat duty at a time when Israel still had its forces in Lebanon and they could have been sent back to the front.

This finding of substantial numbers of unidentified and untreated PTSD veterans led us to examine the issue of help seeking in more depth. This chapter will discuss the phenomenon of untreated illness in general, and untreated PTSD in particular: the complex process that people undergo prior to seeking help, and the individual characteristics that differentiate between those who seek help and those who choose to endure their suffering unaided by professionals.

Untreated illness is a well-known phenomenon. Literature dealing with help seeking has shown that there is no direct relationship between the need for help and readiness to seek and receive it (DePaulo, 1982; Rosen, 1983). Among other reasons, people in need may refrain from seeking help out of a desire not to reveal personal limitations (DePaulo, 1982), embarrassment at admitting their need (Shapiro, 1983), fear of rejection (DePaulo, 1983), and the desire to solve their problems by themselves (Ames, 1983).

The disinclination to seek psychological or psychiatric help is especially widespread (Fischer, Nadler, & Witcher, 1982). Help seeking has been found to be more prevalent when symptoms are severe (Fink et al., 1970; Greenley & Mechanic, 1976; McMichael & Hetzel, 1974; Reed, 1976). Yet epidemiological surveys of the general population have shown that even when symptomatology is severe, some people do not make contact with help-giving agencies (Langer et al., 1974; Ryan, 1969). Nontreated populations have been shown to include more men (Brown, 1978), more people of lower socioeconomic status as measured by education and income (Gurin et al., 1960; Veroff, 1981), and more people with poor self-esteem and poor self-acceptance (Theoreson, 1970).

The reluctance to seek help despite serious psychological problems has also been found among veterans suffering from PTSD. Kadushin, Boulanger, and Martin (1981) reported that more than a third of the Vietnam veterans in their sample who were still suffering from PTSD fifteen years after the end of the war had never sought help.

THE PROCESS OF HELP SEEKING

The literature on the subject points out numerous components in the help-seeking process, whether for physical or psychological ailments. From the knowledge to date, we can construct a five-stage process: (a) the perception of severe distress, (b) the identification of the distress as requiring professional assistance, (c) the weighing of the possible benefits and costs of that help, (d) the decision to seek help, and (e) the selection of the type of help. Although these steps are overlapping and interrelated, the model is useful for unfolding the complexities of the issue.

1. The first condition for seeking help is *the perception of severe distress* (Brickman, Rabinowitz, Karuza, Coates, & Kidder, 1982; Fischer et al., 1983). Most soldiers experience some distress symptoms at homecoming. Nightmares, depressive mood, alienation, and other PTSD symptoms are natural residuals of the inhumanity of combat. Returning soldiers are generally occupied with resuming their lives. They are usually fairly young, with families and responsibilities. Generally, they want to put the war behind them. Even where their symptoms are relatively severe,

many soldiers prefer to ignore them or shove them aside—to leave the nightmares to the night. The symptoms that are most noted, then, are those that force themselves on the veteran because they interfere with his functioning. Such symptoms include impotence, inability to concentrate, and uncontrollable outbursts of temper. Even if the afflicted veteran would rather dismiss these symptoms, his wife, his boss, and the victims of his rage are likely to bring them to his attention. The intrusive symptoms of PTSD, the nightmares and recurrent thoughts and images of the war, are easier to repress or discount. Many soldiers do so "successfully," employing a slew of avoidance tactics from throwing themselves into their work to refusing to go to war memorials or to open war albums. A number of men who subsequently sought treatment had initially tried to run away from their distress by going abroad.

2. The second condition, the *identification of the symptoms as requiring professional help,* is a difficult task in the case of PTSD. Identifying symptoms as PTSD is not the natural thing to do once the veteran is back home. PTSD is not a well-known disorder, and with the exception of dreams, nightmares, and recurrent thoughts and images, the connection between many (if not most) PTSD symptoms and the trauma that gave them birth is indirect and remote. Symptoms such as memory and concentration problems, for example, do not seem on their face to be related to war. And as we mentioned in Chapter 9, many casualties (and some of their doctors) mistake the somatic manifestations of PTSD for purely physical problems.

Then, too, even where the wartime origin of the symptoms is apparent, there is the dilemma of determining when symptoms are normal transient responses to the abnormality of war and when they signify an emotional breakdown for which help is needed. Some symptoms, such as recurrent nightmares, are suffered by nearly all soldiers to one degree or another. In order for the veteran to identify symptoms as requiring treatment, the symptoms must occur with a relatively high frequency and at a high level of intensity. If several times a week he has nightmares that make it difficult for him to fall asleep and that cause him to wake up anxious and exhausted in the morning, he is likely to recognize the need for treatment. If, however, the nightmares occur relatively infrequently and do not significantly disrupt his functioning, he is less likely to apply for help.

Although the literature has shown that symptom severity is the variable that most strongly determines the decision to seek help, the soldier's assessment that he needs help depends a good deal not only on his symptoms, but also on what may be termed his *identification threshold.* The identification threshold refers to the level of psychopathology that is tolerated before it is labeled and treated as such. The threshold is not identical with symptom severity; it depends rather on the view of what is a normal or acceptable response to the stress of combat, and it indicates the level of symptoms that can be absorbed and dealt with without turning to professional help.

The soldier's interpretation of his predicament undoubtedly influences his assessment of whether or not he requires help. The soldier who sees his flashbacks and nightmares as sick or crazy may say to himself, "I cannot cope with this on my own. I need help." The soldier who sees his condition as a normal response to an abnormal situation may think, "It'll pass; I'll get a hold on myself. I don't need help."

Help seeking for PTSD thus is often blocked at this early stage of identification. "I didn't see a doctor all that time," said one badly afflicted PTSD casualty, "because I didn't think it was all that serious." "I thought it would pass," told another PTSD veteran who shook with terror every time a plane flew past overhead. Ron, who did not know that he had sustained a CSR when his legs locked in battle, also failed to identify his subsequent symptoms (including explosive rage, suicidal ideation, and recurrent nightmares) as a war-related emotional disorder. Not a few of the veterans in our sample who were retrospectively diagnosed with PTSD made erroneous negative assessments of their distress, even when their symptoms seem unequivocal in hindsight.

3. Once the veteran concludes that he needs help, he must *weigh the "costs" of help seeking against its expected benefits.* There are ample secondary gains; the ticket out of the danger zone provided by release from reserve duty procures both physical safety and a certain emotional respite from the military stimuli to which PTSD veterans are inordinately sensitive. It enables traumatized veterans to stay away from a situation that had already overtaxed their coping powers and that even thinking about makes them anxious.

Moreover, Israel's Ministry of Defense provides compensation to injured war veterans, including those with war-induced psychiatric disorders. The lure of monetary gain, sufficient in itself, might also be particularly tempting to men whose ability to work and to support themselves has been undermined by their traumatization. These secondary gains of help seeking are potentially quite significant, in addition to the direct gain of emotional therapy that might reduce or eradicate severe emotional distress.

Yet although many PTSD veterans are heartily relieved when they are spared the emotional strain of regular call-ups, in regular civilian life the benefits of help seeking for PTSD are not so obvious. PTSD symptoms are unpleasant and uncomfortable but not usually dangerous.

PTSD therefore can usually go untreated without jeopardizing the casualty or the people around him. For all that PTSD does to undermine the casualty's capacity to feel and to live fully, most casualties manage to get through their day-to-day responsibilities without major mishap. Nor is there the life-and-death pressure of the battlefield to force a conclusion. Thus, the PTSD veteran who feels alienated and depressed may withdraw into himself, cut himself off from his family, and stop meeting with his friends; but he does not generally put his own life or the lives of his family and friends at risk. He (and they) can therefore suffer his symptoms without having to do something about them.

In a society like Israel's, which of necessity values military service and in which the masculine self-image is closely associated with military prowess, help seeking for a combat-induced disorder can have a very high price. Going to therapy implies, for many people, a confession of weakness, of the inability to do it alone. For the Israeli veteran, the confession is double: It not only tells him that he cannot solve his problems on his own, it forces him to admit that he could not cope "like a man" with the task of defending home and country.

The threat to self-esteem is compounded by the threat, real or imagined, of social rejection. Israel is a less psychologically oriented society than the United States, and as was observed in Chapter 10, Israeli men are not encouraged to be introspective or open about their weaknesses. In many circles, and particularly among men, psychological treatment still carries a stigma. PTSD casualties may thus fear being labeled as crazy and losing their self-respect by seeking help. An even greater stigma is attached to not doing reserve duty, especially where the incapacity is an emotional one.

The stigma of psychiatric treatment and of not doing reserve duty, along with the blow to the help seeker's self-esteem, have probably deterred many distressed veterans, as one may learn from casualties who endured their PTSD or tried to cope with it on their own for a long time before they finally sought help. "I didn't go to the mental health department," reported a casualty who doctored himself with tranquilizers, "because it's shameful. I'm not that crazy. I struggle very hard with myself. I have strength."

That insistence on self-sufficiency and strength is what kept Avraham (whose case was discussed in Chapter 9) from recognizing the psychological origin of the burning sensation in his side and from seeking help in the appropriate quarter, and what drove him to leave therapy before he had recovered:

> I felt I needed support, but I'm usually a person who tries to overcome difficulties on my own. . . . The therapy helped me tremendously. . . . [But] I was in therapy

for 2 years, and that's not very normal. . . . I felt I was becoming more and more dependent, as though I had crutches, and would never be able to cope with it by myself. . . . I actually left the therapist without saying goodbye. I ran. . . . I didn't want to be dependent.

The fear of dependency and the idea that being in therapy is not "normal" are both common among Israeli men.

Another cost of seeking therapy for PTSD is that, like all therapy, it threatens to open up old wounds and bring up unwanted memories. "There are things I like to keep to myself. I prefer not talking about them," said a casualty who had been briefly hospitalized after a battlefield CSR but decided not to pursue treatment for his severe PTSD.

In cases where both the potential costs and benefits are substantial, the weighing process may manifest itself in a kind of ambivalence regarding treatment, where the veteran *almost* applies but not quite, or he begins treatment but then ends abruptly after a brief period. This ambivalence can be seen in the following case:

I didn't have time to begin running around from office to office. The bureaucracy drives you crazy. . . . I went to my G.P., and he sent me to the IDF medical officer, who was sick at the time, and they sent me to the training base, and the officer there was sick, too; and I had to come back at 11 a.m.! Well, I work. So I said, "What do you want from my life? Leave me alone." You give up. . . .

Then I started to see a private psychologist, because I felt something was the matter, that I wasn't quite all right. But I was under a lot of pressure in the business. I was supposed to see him once a week, on Monday at 7. But at that hour, I'm still with clients. It was a lot of money I'd lose if I ran off to a psychiatrist.

Circumstances in Israel thus sharply intensify the dilemma that many people face when they consider embarking on professional psychotherapy. On the one hand, the direct and secondary gains of treatment for combat-induced psychological problems are high. They are higher than those afforded Vietnam veterans, for example, who need not worry about reserve duty. They are higher, too, than the benefits promised in treatment of disorders of civilian origin. On the other hand, the price that Israeli soldiers must pay, or fear they must pay, for that treatment may also be inordinately high.

4. The *decision to seek help* for PTSD follows naturally from the weighing of its costs and benefits. It is the veteran's declaration that he is no longer able to cope. Because PTSD is difficult to identify and because the costs are usually more apparent than the benefits, many veterans may simply prefer to manage on their own for as long as they can. In some cases the decision is postponed, as we found when we investigated the casualties with so-called delayed PTSD (see Chapter 13), until the symptoms become so unbearable that he can no longer tolerate them.

Another factor that may play a role in determining whether or not the veteran decides to seek help is the degree to which his distress affects other members of his family, as well as the degree to which they are able or willing to adapt themselves to this. Even if the PTSD veteran does not complain outright of his distress, wives and children are usually the first ones to notice it, and they can either function as a lay referral system or provide an environment that, for good or for bad, accommodates his symptoms.

A good number of our treated PTSD casualties first sought help on the instigation of their wives. In some cases the wives themselves made the first contact, saying that their husband "is not himself" or "has become impossible." Their husband's withdrawal and outbursts of rage, his aches and pains, sexual disinterest, and nightmare-punctured sleep made them realize that something was terribly wrong with him. Often they tended to accept their husband's PTSD symptoms as a normal response to war and waited for them to pass with time, until his behavior became so bizarre or dangerous that they could no longer tolerate it. One woman, for example, pressured her husband to seek help after he told her that while driving the car, he had bent down for cover when a plane flew overhead. Another woman hurried to get a psychiatric referral when her husband threatened to burn down the printing plant that had been his life's work and made her fear that he would do harm to himself. In many cases, the wife realized well before her husband that he needed help.

In other instances, however, the wife can join her husband in perpetuating his disorder by overadapting to the needs of his illness. There are wives of PTSD veterans who entirely take over the running of the house, take responsibility for the finances, put up with their husband's bad temper, keep the children out of his way, understand his sexual disinterest, make no demands of their own for intimacy, and stop inviting friends and family to visit lest their company irritate him. In such homes, the afflicted veteran is free to withdraw into himself or to act out his distress, and he is not encouraged to seek help. Indeed, findings of an earlier study by our group (Solomon, Mikulincer, Freid, & Wosner, 1987) show that married PTSD veterans reported a significantly higher average number of PTSD symptoms than unmarried PTSD veterans, suggesting that the marital situation may in many cases perpetuate the veteran's PTSD symptoms and foster chronicity.

5. Once the distressed veteran makes up his mind to seek professional help, he has to decide *what type of help* he wants. The first recourse of both the afflicted veteran and his wife is usually their family doctor. The family doctor is often the first person to realize that the veteran's

symptoms are emotionally based and to link them to his army experience, especially if he himself has served in the IDF and is familiar with the stresses of combat. In some instances, however, the physician does not draw the connection and fails to refer the patient for psychological assistance. Numerous casualties who eventually reached mental health facilities were doctored on tranquilizers or went from one general practitioner to another before they finally reached an IDF mental health clinic. Less frequently, the distressed PTSD veteran first approaches a military doctor. This usually happens when the veteran waits till he is called up for the reserves before he seeks help, and his motive is to obtain a transfer or discharge.

Psychiatric help is usually the last recourse for the PTSD veteran, because of the lack of awareness and/or fear of stigma mentioned earlier. The latter caused one PTSD veteran in our sample to persist in treatment with a neurologist even after that doctor referred him for psychological help. Moreover, as documented in previous chapters, many veterans are loathe to have their military fitness ratings lowered. To avoid that, and to maintain secrecy, some go to private rather than army psychologists.

WHO SEEKS HELP?

Although we have some understanding of the complexities involved in the process of seeking help for PTSD, it is still unclear why some PTSD veterans apply for treatment, whereas other men suffering from the same diagnosable disorder refrain from seeking help. Which PTSD veterans apply for treatment, and which ones stay away?

In order to identify factors involved in help seeking for PTSD, we looked at two groups of Lebanon veterans 1 year after the war: (a) the 227 CSR casualties who were diagnosed with PTSD; and (b) the 50 untreated non-CSR casualties that we identified as suffering from PTSD at that point in time. We compared the two groups in a number of different areas: sociodemographic variables, severity of psychiatric symptomatology (the Positive Symptom Distress Index on the SCL-90; see Chapter 5); levels of posttraumatic intrusion and avoidance (IES; see Chapter 5); perceived self-efficacy in combat (PSE; see Chapter 8); social functioning (SFPs; see Chapter 7); and somatic complaints (health inventory; see Chapter 9).

Our findings reveal that the two groups differed significantly on all the five assessed variables, with the untreated PTSD veterans reporting consistently lower levels of impairment and distress (Solomon, 1989b).

The untreated PTSD veterans reported a lower intensity of psychiatric symptoms than the treated veterans; overall levels of posttraumatic intrusion and avoidance were also lower among the untreated veterans. Furthermore, untreated PTSD veterans reported better social functioning than the treated veterans, and they had fewer somatic complaints. The most prominent difference between the two groups was in relation to the strength of their perceived self-efficacy in combat: untreated PTSD veterans felt far more confident in their ability to function effectively in future combat situations than treated PTSD veterans.

The explanation that comes most readily to mind is that a person whose symptoms are not severe and interfere only minimally with his day-to-day functioning may simply not identify them as an illness or disorder (which, as noted earlier, is the first step in seeking help). Indeed, it seems reasonable to conjecture that low-intensity symptoms could easily escape the necessary identification and labeling. Moreover, the scattered symptoms may be relatively easy to deny. We cannot be sure that denial did not in fact contribute to the low report of symptoms in the untreated group.

Another central factor discussed earlier that often plays a role in deciding whether or not to seek psychological help is the stigma that this decision may entail (Fischer et al., 1983). The negative impact of the stigma on help seeking would be stronger, it seems, where symptoms are less severe and interfere less in one's daily life. More severe symptomatology might thus outweigh the discomfort of the stigma as well as whatever shame, embarrassment, or personal effort are involved in the process of seeking psychological assistance.

Our results also showed that the treated and untreated groups differed in perceived self-efficacy. The untreated group reported higher perceived self-efficacy than the treated group. This finding is consistent with the literature that shows that when people believe they have the ability to handle given problems, they are significantly more motivated to deal with them on their own, even when the objective difficulties are considerable (Bandura, Taylor, Williams, Mefford, & Barchas, 1985; Clark, 1983; McIntyre et al., 1983). It may be that the untreated PTSD subjects with high perceived self-efficacy in our sample were convinced that they could cope with their symptoms on their own and were determined to do so.

By the same token, applying for professional help might pose more of a threat to the self-image of people with high perceived self-efficacy than to that of people with low perceived self-efficacy. The fear of losing self-esteem might have made the high perceived self-efficacy soldiers in the untreated group more reluctant to seek treatment than their lower perceived self-efficacy counterparts. This suggestion would be consistent with research by our group that has found that PTSD casualties with high perceived self-efficacy employ more denial in stressful situations than those with low perceived self-efficacy (Solomon, Weisenberg, Schwartzwald, & Mikulincer, 1988). It may be that to counter the potentially corrosive effect of both their PTSD symptoms and seeking help for them on their self-esteem, the high perceived self-efficacy subjects in our untreated sample denied having symptoms or minimized the trouble their symptoms gave them more than their counterparts with low perceived self-efficacy. I have already suggested that denial made possible by low symptom severity might have contributed to the avoidance of help seeking in the untreated group. The facts that the untreated group also evidenced higher perceived self-efficacy than the treated group and that higher perceived self-efficacy has been found to be associated with the denial of stressful situations would seem to strengthen this possibility.

Interestingly, our comparison of sociodemographic variables in the two groups revealed that none of the factors studied (age, marital status, educational level, and income) differentiated between the treated and untreated PTSD veterans. This was contrary to expectations, because several studies (e.g., Gurin et al., 1960; Veroff, 1981) have found these variables to be associated with the tendency to seek (or refrain from seeking) professional help. It seems that symptom severity may have canceled out the potential impact of these variables. Once symptomatology becomes sufficiently severe, seeking professional help apparently becomes more likely, irrespective of sociodemographic factors. Another possibility is that because psychological services are free and available to veterans in clinics all over Israel, the potential role of economic and social (i.e., geographic) factors in the decision to seek psychiatric help may have been reduced.

CLINICAL IMPLICATIONS

Our finding that the treated PTSD veterans were more distressed than the untreated veterans raises an important question regarding treatment: Should PTSD casualties who do not apply for treatment be encouraged to do so? Is the lower severity of their symptoms, along with their higher self-confidence, an indication of their having a greater ability to cope and a consequently lesser need for professional assistance? If so, they may tend to recover without the stigmatization or the blow to their self-esteem that treatment may entail. On the other hand, the findings may reflect the untreated PTSD veterans' tendency to deny their problems, in which case treatment may indeed be crucial for their recovery. As I have stressed throughout this book, the detrimental effect of PTSD is not limited to the casualty, and it may have severe implications for other family members as well in the form of symptom "transmission," outbursts of rage, and sometimes child or wife abuse. Denial of the disorder could therefore be disastrous not just for the casualty himself, but also for the other people in his environment. On the basis of the current data, however, I cannot say for certain whether or not these veterans should be brought to treatment. In order to provide a clear-cut answer to this question, it would be necessary to follow up these veterans for a much longer span of time and to weigh the advantages of treatment against the disadvantages. At this point one can only speculate.

We do, however, know from a previous study (Solomon & Benbenishty, 1986) that prompt treatment following a battlefield CSR increases a soldier's chances of returning to his unit and decreases the probability of his subsequently developing PTSD. Frontline treatment, the prevailing military doctrine for treatment of combat stress reactions, is based on three principles: proximity, immediacy, and expectancy. Afflicted soldiers should be treated in close proximity to the combat zone, as soon as possible after the onset of symptoms, and with the explicitly stated expectation of a quick return to combat. Minimal psychiatric intervention is carried out, focused basically on allowing the soldier to ventilate his recent traumatic experiences.

The study cited above compared CSR casualties who had been treated by this approach with other soldiers who received treatment just a short time after leaving the front. Our findings provided clear evidence for the advantages of the frontline approach. Higher rates of soldiers who were treated according to frontline principles returned to their units, and 1 year after the war, the soldiers who received the frontline treatment had lower rates of PTSD (40%) than soldiers treated behind the lines (71%). In other words, immediate intervention at the critical time (i.e., shortly after exposure to the traumatic event) may reduce the long-term detrimental effects of psychic trauma. On the other hand, clinical experience in Israel and abroad has shown relatively low rates of success. On the whole, chronic PTSD appears to be very resistant to treatment (Bleich, Shalev, Shoham, Solomon, & Kotler, 1992).

Moreover, PTSD that has crystallized and become chronic may also entail additional disability. Clinicians have observed that veterans who suffer from PTSD for long periods of time eventually develop personality disorders. There is a considerable narrowing in many areas of their lives: Some of them do not work and live on compensation payments and/or unemployment benefits; there is often an inability to maintain any kind of social relations, even with family; some become physically abusive with their wives or children; and others "medicate" themselves with drugs and alcohol. A few end up involved in crime. It thus appears that if not treated immediately before the syndrome crystallizes, very little can be done to cure this disorder.

For this reason, it seems that the cost of treatment, in terms of stigma and reduction in self-esteem (at least temporarily), may be considerably lower than the price these veterans pay for not receiving treatment on time. The dilemma over whether or not to refer these veterans for treatment is, therefore, a very real one, but in our current state of knowledge it seems that the most advisable step would be to recommend treatment only in cases where there is a clear need for help.

Along with this, I believe that it would be most helpful to publicize the existence of PTSD as widely as possible. Taking the syndrome out of the closet would make it more difficult to overlook, ignore, or deny symptoms. It could also be a first step toward changing attitudes. Efforts should be made to bring home the fact that PTSD is a natural outcome of a particularly stressful situation and that it does not adversely reflect on the character or manliness of anyone who suffers from it. The message should be similar to that of the frontline treatment: The symptoms reflect a crisis that may pass quickly if treated properly. A clearer understanding of these points would make it easier for the PTSD sufferer to acknowledge both his symptoms and his need for help without losing self-esteem.

This information about PTSD and its treatment should be broadcast widely. Briefings for servicemen are a logical beginning. But information should also be provided to the families of servicemen, as well as to the population at large. Familiarity with the problem might reduce the social stigma of seeking help for PTSD and the fear generally associated with any mental disorder, making it possible to enlist the aid of family and friends in helping the PTSD sufferer to identify his symptoms and in encouraging him to seek help. Some professionals are concerned that providing the general public with information about combat-related psychiatric problems might encourage nondeserving veterans to malinger in search of secondary gains, such as monetary compensation or release from military service. While acknowledging this assertion, I maintain that psychiatric casualties have the right to know about the origins of their distress so as to make informed decisions about treatment. It is *our* responsibility as mental health professionals to find ways of discriminating between true casualties and malingerers. The difficulties that this task may entail cannot serve as an excuse for witholding information from these veterans, especially when we consider that a clear grasp of the facts in and of itself may serve to alleviate some of the PTSD veterans' guilt over having broken down in battle, or their fear and shame regarding mental disorders.

Organizational changes in the provision of psychiatric assistance for PTSD are also advisable. Outreach programs would help those who are too embarrassed or ashamed to seek help on their own. The declared extension of military mental health services to people with nonacute mental health problems might encourage those with relatively low levels of symptomatology to seek professional assistance.

16

The Silver Platter

Soldiers rarely go to war of their own accord. They are sent by their governments, who employ them as instruments in some national goal. Whether that goal is defined as defense, the protection or pursuit of a vital interest, or the maintenance of the nation's values or principles, the soldier fights for purposes larger than his own, for others as well as himself. One would therefore expect those who send men to war, endangering their lives and their physical and mental health, to appreciate their sacrifice and to take responsibility for them on their return. One would expect the people, at least of democratic countries, to stand behind their soldiers, and the leaders to spare no effort in the treatment and rehabilitation of those who come back injured. Is this really the case? In this chapter, we will examine attitudes toward casualties of war, focusing particularly on the case of Israel.

Ever since Israel's inception, our largely civilian army has been understood to be the mainstay of our national sovereignty and of our freedom and safety as individuals. The Israeli soldier has been regarded as the "silver platter" on which the Jewish state was given to us. This metaphor, applied in a poem with that title by the late Natan Alterman, a well-known Israeli poet, expresses the enormous sense of gratitude and obligation that Israelis, still beleaguered, feel toward the men who are killed or wounded so that the rest of us can live our lives as a sovereign people.

This sentiment, about as strong as any in this country of strong feelings, is also embodied in government rehabilitation policy, as set forth in the pamphlet *Thirty-Five Years of Rehabilitation* published by Israel's Ministry of Defense:

> The well-being of IDF soldiers wounded in action is an important component of national security. The services for the wounded are intended not only to meet real needs, but also to express this nation's gratitude to those who have paid a heavy price in its service. For this reason, the level of services and benefits provided is intentionally higher than that given to similarly afflicted civilian populations, such as victims of industrial or automobile accidents. The general aim of the Rehabilitation Branch is to aid in maintaining the morale of the fighting forces and of society as a whole, by way of fostering the best possible functioning and social integration of veterans. (Fink, 1985, p. 1)

Nor does the Ministry of Defense merely proclaim its commitment to the nation's war casualties; it backs it up with enormous dedication and large sums of money, offering injured veterans extensive rehabilitation services and monetary compensation that exceeds by far the amount paid in civilian claims. A civilian disabled through illness or accident is entitled to various tax exemptions, a small national insurance stipend to compensate for lost earning power, and certain ambulatory care. The disabled war veteran receives that and much more. He may have his home, including the outside access, renovated to accommodate a wheelchair. He is treated to convalescence and vacation facilities, including organized trips abroad. If he needs it, he may get a regular attendant to assist with the tasks of daily living and a driver to chauffeur him to and from work (Florian & Catch, 1989; Prokatzia & Miller, 1979). The idea is that we owe him.

The Israel public is as positive toward war casualties as the military establishment, as might be expected of a country whose army is composed largely of civilians. In a study of attitudes, Katz and Shurka (1977) showed high school students' videotaped vignettes of disabled persons, some described as injured in automobile and work accidents and others as wounded war veterans; otherwise, the vignettes were identical. When the students were asked to assess the intelligence, morality, attractiveness, and social, personality, and vocational characteristics of the individuals shown, they rated the disabled veterans significantly higher than the victims of road and work accidents. Furthermore, the more serious the war-caused disability, the higher the respect for the casualty. This is in striking opposition to the usual attitude toward the disabled, where the more severe the handicap is, the less social acceptance is shown. The researchers concluded that the higher assessments obtained by the disabled war veterans are related to the respect for the armed forces in Israel. A war injury apparently has such a high social value that it is able to counterbalance the rejection that people generally feel toward the handicapped. Similarly positive attitudes were obtained in a study of Israeli employers (Florian, 1978), who expressed a clear preference for hiring war-wounded veterans over other physically disabled persons. These and other studies, covering diverse segments of the population, indicate something of the broad esteem in which disabled veterans are held by the Israeli public.

Psychiatric injuries are another matter, though. When the injury is to the mind, the picture is more equivocal. Doubts surface; questions are asked. What is this wound where no blood flows, no bones are broken, skin burnt, or organs torn? Is there really an injury? After all, these same men were deemed psychologically sound enough only a short while before. Maybe they faked a breakdown in combat so as to save their skin or to extort compensation money. Maybe they gave into fear and ran. Maybe they're just plain malingerers who chose the easy way out when others fought and died. Although there are those who realize that the battlefield is a potent source of mental damage and who understand that the psychiatrically wounded soldier is as deserving of the country's continued support as his physically wounded comrades, many do not. All too often, the battle-traumatized soldier is treated to blame and condemnation, to the usually unspoken but potent accusation that if he had done his job as he should have, he would have been injured physically and not mentally, as he claims. In extreme cases, he is regarded as a deserter or as the rotten apple that can spoil the whole barrel.

Today, such judgments of the CSR soldier are rarely expressed officially. Indirectly, they are expressed, for example, in the area of compensation. It is much more difficult for the CSR or PTSD casualty to obtain compensation than for the physically wounded soldier. Most physical injuries are visible and relatively easy to prove and account for. Combat-related psychiatric injuries are much less so. Psychiatric symptoms can be faked; their time of onset is variable, and it is most complicated to prove beyond a doubt that the trauma originated in combat and not in some other event. Veterans with psychiatric claims must obtain authorization of causation from a military psychiatrist to show that their condition is the direct result of activities performed in the line of duty. Many cases have also been asked to bring witnesses to vouch that they were indeed mentally healthy before their trauma and that they really did break down in battle. The whole procedure can be trying and humiliating, and it tends to exacerbate the same traumatic memories that the casualties already have trouble dealing with. Once the injury is acknowledged, the disability rating (which reflects the seriousness of the handicap) awarded these casualties is usually markedly lower than that given the physically injured veteran, and the monetary compensation based on that calculation is lower as well. Physically injured veterans are generously compensated for their loss of earning power; psychiatrically injured soldiers may not be, even though (as has been seen) more than a few of them can no longer do the work they previously did, whereas others find it hard to get and hold down any job at all (Solomon, Benbenishty, & Waysman, 1991).

What accounts for the discrepancy? Why are the physically injured honored as "the silver platter" while the emotionally injured considered somewhat less than honorable? There are doubtless many reasons, but I believe that a central one is the differential attribution of responsibility. In the overwhelming proportion of cases, it is amply clear that a physical injury is beyond the control of the casualty. The wound is visible and the cause plainly identifiable, so the physically injured are understood to be innocent victims. CSR is another matter: It is a bloodless emotional wound, and the intangible nature of the injury is difficult for both professionals and laymen to grasp. In contrast to a physical injury, the line between cause and effect is indirect and often convoluted, broken, and difficult to prove. Two soldiers struck in the same part of the body by identical fire will almost certainly sustain similar physical wounds, but two soldiers exposed to what appear to be the same external stresses will not necessarily suffer similar emotional damage. One may break down sooner, the other later or not at all, and symptoms may vary widely between casualties. Thus it is easy to believe—as more than a few people do—that the psychiatric casualties are themselves consciously or unconsciously responsible for their plight.

This attribution has the advantage of simplicity and of being in the timeless tradition of blaming the victim, which is well entrenched in many of this century's military and scientific conceptions of combat stress reaction. This is vividly depicted in the six models of etiology of psychiatric reactions in combat outlined by Kormos (1978); three of the six models clearly implicate the veterans in their own affliction. The "illness model" refers to the disorder as war neurosis and views CSR and PTSD as a result of unresolved childhood conflicts. The underlying assumption is that people who are disturbed from childhood respond maladaptively to combat stress; that is, they were impaired to start with. This accusatory stance is also evident in the "judgmental model," which views CSR as cowardice, weakness, or some other moral lapse. The most blatant example is the "voluntaristic model," which regards CSR as simply a willful attempt to flee the battlefield.

These views, singly or in combination, have been found at one time or another in most armies, at times giving rise to cruel and punitive reactions. The French in World War I forced soldiers who broke down to choose between returning to the front or submitting to primitive, and sometimes fatal, electric shocks (Salmon, 1919). The Germans in World War II simply shot the casualties, denying that traumatic reactions were caused by the combat experience and attributing them instead to the desire to escape the battlefield and, later, to obtain financial compensation (Schneider, 1987). The Americans in that war were less harsh, but they too found it easier to brand CSR casualties as shirkers or cowards, as in this statement by the stalwart American General Patton (cited in Moran, 1987):

> If soldiers would realize that the large proportion of those allegedly suffering from battle fatigue are really using an easy way out, they would be less sympathetic. Any man who says he has battle fatigue is avoiding danger and forcing on those who have more hardihood than himself the obligation of meeting it. (p. 169)

The negative reactions of the military establishment derive from highly practical considerations. Battlefield psychiatric injuries, if not treated in an effective and organized manner when they occur, can be contagious. CSR can spread to epidemic proportions, and even when it does not, an entire unit can be demoralized by the emotional breakdown of just a few soldiers. Senior commanders are understandably loath to give any kind of legitimacy to a phenomenon that has the potential to undermine the fighting power of the whole army.

Even keeping these considerations in mind, it is still difficult to comprehend the universally antagonistic attitudes toward traumatized war veterans. Moreover, blaming victims for their plight is a common response to victims of many other types of trauma as well (e.g., rape victims). Perhaps the encounter with trauma victims forces us to confront our basic human vulnerability; it unmasks what Jon Shaw (1987) has termed our "illusion of safety," our most basic defense mechanism, in which our sense of the world's continuity and our own security is anchored. In the case of trauma induced by war and other manmade atrocities, we are forced to face yet something else we prefer not to recognize: the tremendous cruelty and suffering that human beings can inflict on one another.

The denial of the trauma victim's suffering and the tendency to avoid taking responsibility for their treatment is manifested also in the fragmentation that exists in the scientific study of the subject. As Mangelsdorff (1985) puts it, the entire history of trauma research is characterized by "lessons learned and forgotten." Though many of this century's bloody wars have given birth to studies of the mental consequences of combat, these have generally gained attention in the period during and immediately following the war, with very little sustained follow-up or continuity in research over the years. For this reason, there was great confusion in treatment of casualties at the start of World War II, for example, even though considerable experience had accumulated during World War I (Copp & McAndrew, 1990).

Combat stress reaction, often followed by a lifetime of posttrauma, is the psychological price that some soldiers pay for the proclivity of the human race for war. The price is high, and it is also inevitable. There is no way that men can kill and maim, see their friends killed and maimed, and fear being killed or maimed themselves without at least some of them breaking down. The best way to prevent combat-induced psychopathology is to stop making war. As we human beings, the most violent of all animal species, have not been able to do this since Cain murdered Abel, all we have left to fall back on is our other great distinction as *Homo sapiens:* our minds, our ability to learn and understand. In undertaking the research that went into this book, my fervent hope was that the findings would form part of a body of knowledge that could help the CSR casualties who have lost so much on behalf of the rest of us. I also hope that the book itself may make some contribution to opening up our hearts and minds to these men and to chipping away at those encrustations of denial that blind us to their sufferings and our own part in them.

Appendixes

A

Sociodemographic Characteristics of the Sample

	CSR group		Non-CSR group	
	N	*%*	*N*	*%*
Age				
18–25	47	22	24	21
26–28	54	25	23	20
29–32	49	23	28	24
33 and over	63	30	41	35
Education				
Elementary	38	18	17	15
Partial high school	58	27	25	22
Completed high school	68	32	48	41
University	49	23	25	22
Place of origin				
Asia/Africa	39	19	29	25
Europe/America	36	17	18	16
Israel	131	64	67	59
Marital status				
Single	56	27	39	34
Married	153	73	75	66
Economic status				
High	104	50	60	52
Average	57	28	39	34
Low	45	22	16	14

B

PTSD Inventory

Below you will find a series of statements describing feelings and difficulties which people experience. We ask that you relate to these feelings from two points of view:

First, indicate whether the statement matches your feeling in the past month.

Second, if you did have such a feeling or difficulty, indicate when you began to feel that way.

To the extent that a particular statement matches your feeling, circle the appropriate time of onset. If you do not understand how to complete the questionnaire, do not hesitate to ask those in charge.

	Did you feel that way during the past month?	If you had such a feeling, when did it begin?		
1. Recurrent scenes or thoughts about the war	Yes/No	1 year ago	3 months ago	10 months ago	Before the Lebanon war

(*continued*)

	Appendix B (*Continued*) Did you feel that way during the past month?	If you had such a feeling, when did it begin?
2. You have recurrent dreams and nightmares about the war	Yes/No	
3. Sometimes when things remind you of the war you feel or act as if reexperiencing battles you fought in	Yes/No	
4. Less interest in activities that were once important to you (for example: work, family life, friends, hobbies)	Yes/No	
5. You feel detached or estranged from others	Yes/No	
6. You get less upset or angry about things that once caused you to be upset or angry	Yes/No	
7. You are overalert or oversensitive to noises	Yes/No	
8. You have sleep difficulties (hard		

	Appendix B (Continued) Did you feel that way during the past month?	If you had such a feeling, when did it begin?
to fall asleep, insomnia, awaken in the middle of the night, sleep too much, don't sleep enough)	Yes/No	
9. You have difficulty remembering or concentrating	Yes/No	
10. You feel guilty about surviving while others died in the war	Yes/No	
11. You avoid activities that recall war experiences (don't want to return to your previous unit or assignment, don't want to hear or see things that recall the war, don't want to talk about the war)	Yes/No	
12. Sleep disturbances or oversensitivity to noise become more severe when you see or		

(continued)

	Appendix B (*Continued*) Did you feel that way during the past month?	If you had such a feeling, when did it begin?
hear things that recall experiences you had in the war	Yes/No	
13. You feel guilty about your behavior during the Lebanon war	Yes/No	

C

Number of PTSD Symptoms

In order to assess the scope of the PTSD syndrome at the three points of time, we computed the number of symptoms endorsed each year. The table presents the average number of symptoms reported in each study group at each time of measurement. A two-way analysis of variance for study group and time of measurement yielded significant main effects for study group [$F(1,318) = 125.86, p < .01$] and time [$F(2,636) = 48.44, p < .01$]. The two-way interaction did not reach significance.

Means and Standard Deviations of Total Number of PTSD Symptoms in Each Study Group at Each Time of Assessment

	CSR		Non-CSR		
	M	SD	M	SD	F ratio
First year	6.86	3.73	2.59	2.72	117.53[a]
Second year	6.44	3.73	2.45	2.97	98.32[a]
Third year	5.01	3.96	1.47	2.70	74.34[a]

[a]$p < .01$.

As can be seen from the above table, CSR veterans endorsed more PTSD symptoms than non-CSR veterans at all three points of time. In both groups, however, the number of endorsed symptoms decreased significantly as the time between measurement and the war increased.

D

Analyses of SFP Scales Data

Pearson Correlations between SFP Scales and Number of PTSD Symptoms in Each Study Group at Each Time of Assessment

	CSR			Non-CSR		
SFP scales	Year 1	Year 2	Year 3	Year 1	Year 2	Year 3
Work	.54	.54	.47	.45	.24	.49
Family	.62	.54	.50	.33	.31	.38
Sexual	.58	.46	.37	.31	.37	.25
Social	.68	.60	.55	.59	.37	.42
Motivation	.66	.56	.47	.41	.36	.33
Satisfaction	.37	.46	.38	.47	.44	.42
Independence	.41	.49	.33	.50	.23	.31

Note: $p < .01$ for all correlations.

Mean Percentage of Endorsement and F Ratios for SFP Scales in Each Study Group at Each Time of Assessment

	Means						F ratios		
	CSR			Non-CSR			Study group	Time	Interaction
SFP scales	1	2	3	1	2	3			
Work	44	42	42	18	24	17	48.94[b]	1.71	2.79[a]
Family	44	40	37	12	19	13	58.42[b]	3.36[a]	3.55[a]
Sexual	39	38	36	8	19	13	34.91[b]	0.60	2.52
Social	45	42	42	17	19	15	71.55[b]	1.94	0.25
Motivation	54	49	50	18	18	17	61.96[b]	0.62	0.50
Satisfaction	54	49	50	18	18	17	39.87[b]	2.47	1.05
Independence	26	25	24	8	14	11	25.70[b]	0.36	1.91

[a] $p < .05$.
[b] $p < .01$.

References

American Psychiatric Association. (1980). Diagnostic and statistical manual of mental disorders (3rd ed.). Washington, DC: Author.

Ames, R. (1983). Help-seeking and achievement orientation: Perspectives from attribution theory. In B. M. Depaulo et al. (Eds.), *New directions in helping* (Vol. 2). New York: Academic Press.

Amikam, Y. (1983, February). *Yediot Aharonot,* p. 10.

Antonovsky, A., Maor, B., & Downy, N. (1971). Twenty-five years later: A limited study of the sequelae of the concentration camps. *Social Psychology, 6,* 186–193.

Archibald, H. C., & Tuddenham, R. D. (1965). Persistent stress reaction after combat. *Archives of General Psychology, 12,* 475–481.

Atkinson, R. M., Henderson, R. G., & Sparr, L. F. (1982). Assessment of Vietnam veterans for post-traumatic stress disorder in Veterans Administration disability claims. *American Journal of Psychiatry, 139,* 1118–1121.

Axelrod, S., Schnipper, O. L., & Rau, J. H. (1980). Hospitalized offspring of Holocaust survivors: Problems and dynamics. *Bulletin of Menninger Clinic, 44,* 1–14.

Bailey, P., Williams, F. E., Komora, P. O., Salmon, T. W., & Fenton, N. (1929). *The medical department of the United States Army in the World War: Vol. X. Neuropsychiatry.* Washington, DC: Government Printing Office.

Bandura, A. (1977). Self efficacy: Toward a unifying theory of behavioral change. *Psychological Review, 84,* 191–215.

Bandura, A. (1982). Self efficacy mechanism in human agency. *American Psychologist, 37,* 122–147.

Bandura, A., Hess, L., & Adams, N. E. (1982). Microanalysis of action and fear arousal as a function of different levels of perceived self-efficacy. *Journal of Personality and Social Psychology, 43,* 5–21.

Bandura, A., Taylor, C. B., Williams, S. L., Mefford, I. N., & Barchas, J. D. (1985). Catecholamine secretion as a function of perceived coping self efficacy. *Journal of Consulting and Clinical Psychology, 53,* 406–415.

Barocas, H., & Barocas, C. (1979). Wounds of the fathers: The next generation of Holocaust victims. *International Review of Psychoanalysis, 5,* 331–341.

Bartemeier, L. H. (1946). Combat exhaustion. *Journal of Nervous and Mental Disease, 104,* 359–425.

Baum, A., Gatchel, R. J., & Schaeffer, M. A. (1983). Emotional, behavioral and physiological effects of chronic stress at Three Mile Island. *Journal of Consulting and Clinical Psychology, 51,* 565–572.

Beebe, G. W., & Apple, J. W. (1951). *Variation in psychological tolerance to ground combat in WWII, final report.* Washington, DC: National Academy of Sciences, National Research Council, Division of Medical Sciences.

Ben Shoshan, D. (1985). *Long-term effects of the Holocaust in survivors after forty years.* Unpublished master's thesis, Tel Aviv University.

Bergman, M. S., & Jacovy, M. E. (1982). *Generations of the Holocaust.* New York: Basic Books.

Bleich, A., Barb, R., & Kotler, M. (1986). Combat stress reaction and the military physician. *Journal of Royal Army Medical Corps, 132,* 54–57.

Bleich, A., Shalev, A., Shoham, S., Solomon, Z., & Kotler, M. (1992). PTSD: Theoretical and practical considerations as reflected through Koach—an innovative treatment project. *Journal of Traumatic Stress, 5*(2), 265–272.

Block, M., & Zautra, A. (1981). Satisfaction and distress in a community: A test of the effects of life events. *American Journal of Community Psychology, 9,* 165–180.

Bornstein, P. E., & Clayton, P. J. (1972). The anniversary reaction. *Diseases of the Nervous System, 33,* 470–472.

Borus, J. F. (1973). Re-entry II: "Making it" back to the states. *American Journal of Psychiatry, 130,* 850–854.

Boulanger, G. (1985). An old problem with a new name. In S. M. Sonnenberg, A. S. Blank, & T. A. Talbott (Eds.), *The trauma of war: Stress and recovery in Vietnam veterans.* Washington, DC: American Psychiatric Press.

Bourne, P. G. (1969). *The psychology and physiology of stress.* New York: Academic Press.

Bourne, P. G. (1970). *Men, stress, and Vietnam.* Boston: Little, Brown.

Brickman, P., Rabinowitz, V. C., Karuza, J., Coates, D., & Kidder, L. (1982). Models of helping. *American Psychologist, 37,* 368–389.

Brown, B. B. (1978). Social and psychological correlates of help seeking behavior among urban adults. *American Journal of Community Psychology, 6,* 425–439.

Brown, G. W., & Harris, K. T. (1978). *Social origins of depression: A study of psychiatric disorders in women.* New York: Free Press.

Burgess, A. W., & Holmstrom, C. C. (1974). Rape trauma syndrome. *American Journal of Psychiatry, 131,* 981–986.

Cannon, W. B. (1953). *Bodily changes in pain, hunger, fear, and rage.* Boston: Branford.

Card, J. J. (1983). *Lives after Vietnam.* Lexington, MA: D. C. Heath.

Card, J. J. (1987). Epidemiology of PTSD in a national cohort of Vietnam veterans. *Journal of Clinical Psychology, 43,* 6–17.

Cavenar, J. O., & Nash, J. L. (1976). The effects of combat on the normal personality: War neurosis in Vietnam returnees. *Comprehensive Psychiatry, 17,* 647–653.

Center for Policy Research. (1979). *The adjustment of Vietnam veterans to civilian life.* New York: Author.

Chodoff, P. (1962). Late effects of the concentration camp syndrome. *Archives of General Psychiatry, 8,* 323–333.

Christenson, R. M., Walker, J. I., Ross, D. R., & Maltbie, A. (1981). Reactivation of traumatic conflicts. *American Journal of Psychiatry, 138,* 984–985.

Clark, M. S. (1983). Some implications of close social bonds for help seeking. In B. M. DePaulo et al. (Eds.), *New directions in helping* (Vol. 2). New York: Academic Press.

Coleman, J. C., Butcher, J. N., & Carson, R. C. (1980). *Abnormal Psychology and Modern Life*. Glenview, IL: Scott, Foresman.

Condiott, M. M., & Lichtenstein, E. (1981). Self efficacy and relapse in smoking cessation programs. *Journal of Consulting and Clinical Psychology, 49*, 648–658.

Copp, T., & McAndrew, B. (1990). *Battle exhaustion: Soldiers and psychiatrists in the Canadian army 1939–1945*. Montreal: McGill-Queen's University Press.

Danieli, Y. (1980). Families of survivors of the Nazi Holocaust: Some long and some short term effects. In N. Milgram (Ed.), *Psychological stress and adjustment in time of war and peace*. Washington, DC: Hemisphere.

Danieli, Y. (1984). Psychotherapists' participation in the conspiracy of silence about the Holocaust. *Psychoanalytic Psychology, 1*, 23–42.

Davidson, L. A., & Baum, A. (1986). Chronic stress and post-traumatic stress disorder. *Journal of Consulting and Clinical Psychology, 54*, 303–308.

Davidson, S. (1979). Massive psychic traumatization and social support. *Journal of Psychosomatic Research, 23*, 395–402.

Delay, R. S., & Ishaki, D. M. (1981). Secondary depression in anxiety disorders. *Comparative Psychology, 22*, 612–617.

DePaulo, B. M. (1982). Social psychological processes in informal help seeking. In T. A. Wills (Ed.), *Basic processes in helping relationships*. New York: Academic Press.

DePaulo, B. M. (1983). Perspective on help seeking. In B. M. DePaulo et al. (Eds.), *New directions in helping* (Vol. 2). New York: Academic Press.

Derogatis, L. R. (1977). *The SCL-90-R manual I: Scoring, administration, and procedures for the SCL-90*. Baltimore: Johns Hopkins University, School of Medicine.

Dohrenwend, B. P., & Shrout, P. E. (1985). "Hassles" in the conceptualization and measurement of life stress variables. *American Psychologist, 40*, 740–785.

Dor-Shav, N. K. (1978). On the long range effects of concentration camp internment on Nazi victims: 25 years later. *Journal of Consulting and Clinical Psychology, 46*, 1–11.

Eaton, W. W., Sigal, J. J., & Weinfeld, M. (1982). Impairment in Holocaust survivors after 33 years: Data from unbiased community sample. *American Journal of Psychiatry, 139*, 773–777.

Egendorf, A., Kadushin, C., Laufer, R. S., Rotbarth, G., & Sloan, L. (1981). *Legacies of Vietnam: Comparative adjustment of veterans and their peers*. New York: Center for Policy Research.

Eitinger, L. (1964). *Concentration camp survivors in Norway and Israel*. London: Allen and Unwin.

Eitinger, L. (1969). Psychosomatic problems in concentration camp survivors. *Journal of Psychosomatic Research, 13*, 183–189.

Endicott, N. A., & Endicott, J. (1963). Improvement in untreated psychiatric patients. *Archives of General Psychiatry, 9*, 575–585.

Engel, G. H. (1968). A life setting conducive to illness: The giving up complex. *Annual International Review of Medicine, 69*, 293–300.

Epstein, H. (1979). *Children of the Holocaust: Conversations with sons and daughters of survivors*. New York: Putman.

Epstein, S. (1983). Natural healing processes of the mind: Graded stress inoculation as an inherent coping mechanism. In D. Meichenbaum & M. E. Yarenko (Eds.), *Stress reduction and prevention* (pp. 39–66). New York: Plenum.

Erikson, K. (1976). Loss of community at Buffalo Creek. *American Journal of Psychiatry, 133,* 302–305.

Faltus, F. J., Sirota, A. D., Parsons, J., Daamen, M., & Schare, M. L. (1986). Exacerbations of post-traumatic stress disorder symptomatology in Vietnam veterans. *Military Medicine, 151*(12), 648–649.

Figley, C. R. (1976, October). *Combat related stress disorder: Family therapy implications.* Paper presented at the annual meeting of Marriage and Family Counselors, Philadelphia.

Figley, C. R. (1978a). Psychosocial adjustment among Vietnam veterans: An overview of the research. In C. R. Figley (Ed.), *Stress disorders among Vietnam veterans: Theory, research, and treatment* (pp. 57–70). New York: Brunner/Mazel.

Figley, C. R. (1978b). Symptoms of delayed combat stress among a college sample of Vietnam veterans. *Military Medicine, 143,* 107–110.

Figley, C. R., & Sprenkle, D. H. (1978). Delayed stress response syndrome: Family therapy indications. *Journal of Marriage and Family Counseling, 4,* 53–60.

Fink, A. (1985). *Thirty-five years of rehabilitation* [Hebrew]. Jerusalem: Ministry of Defense.

Fink, R., Shapiro, S., & Goldensohn, S. S. (1970). Family physician referrals for psychiatric consultation and patient initiative in seeking care. *Social Science and Medicine, 4,* 273–291.

Fischer, E. H., Winer, D., & Abramowitz, S. I. (1983). Seeking professional help for psychological problems. In B. M. DePaulo, A. Nadler, & J. D. Fischer (Eds.), *New directions in helping.* New York: Academic Press.

Fischer, J. D., Nadler, A., & Witcher, A. S. (1982). Recipient reactions to aid: A conceptual review. *Psychological Bulletin, 91,* 27–54.

Florian, V. (1978). Employers' opinions of the disabled person as a worker. *Rehabilitation Counseling Bulletin, 22,* 38–43.

Florian, V., & Catch, S. (1989). Support symptoms for families who have a child with a disability: An Israeli perspective. In A. Gartner (Ed.), *Family support systems: An international perspective.* New York: City University of New York.

Freud, S. (1920). Beyond the pleasure principle. In J. Strachey (Ed. and Trans.), *Complete psychological works of Sigmund Freud* (Vol. 18). London: Hogarth.

Gal, R. (1986). *A portrait of the Israeli soldier.* Westport, CT: Greenwood.

Gleser, G. C., Green, B , & Winget, C. (1981). *Prolonged psychosocial effects of a disaster. A study of the Buffalo Creek.* New York: Academic Press.

Glover, H. (1984). Survivor guilt and the Vietnam veteran. *Journal of Nervous and Mental Diseases, 172,* 393–397.

Glover, H. (1988). Four syndromes of post-traumatic stress disorder: Stressors and conflicts of the traumatized with special focus on the Vietnam combat veteran. *Journal of Traumatic Stress, 1*(1), 57–78.

Golomb, D. (1985). Symbolic expressions in post-traumatic stress disorder: Vietnam combat veterans in art therapy. *Arts in Psychotherapy, 12,* 1–12.

Greenley, J. R., & Mechanic, D. (1976). Social selection in seeking help for psychological problems. *Journal of Health and Social Behavior, 17,* 249.

Grinker, R. P. (1945). Psychiatric disorders in combat crews overseas and in returnees. *Medical Clinics of North America, 29,* 729–739.

Grinker, R. P., & Spiegel, J. P. (1945). *Men under stress.* Philadelphia: Blakistan.

Gurin, G. (1960). *Americans' view of their mental health: A nationwide interview survey.* New York: Basic Books.

Haley, S. A. (1974). When the patient reports atrocities. *Archives of General Psychiatry, 30,* 191–196.

Haley, S. A. (1975). *The Vietnam veteran and his preschool child: Child rearing as a delayed stress in combat veterans.* Washington, DC: American Orthopsychiatric Association.

Haley, S. A. (1978). Treatment implications of post-combat stress response syndromes for medical health professionals. In C. R. Figley (Ed.), *Stress disorders among Vietnam veterans: Theory, research, and treatment* (pp. 254–267). New York: Brunner/Mazel.

Helzer, J. E., Robins, L. N., Wish, K. E., & Hesselbrock, M. (1979). Depression in Vietnam veterans and civilian controls. *American Journal of Psychiatry, 136,* 526–529.

Helzer, J. E., Robins, L. N., & McEvoy, L. (1987). Post-traumatic stress disorder in the general population. *New England Journal of Medicine, 317,* 1630–1634.

Hendin, H., & Pollinger-Haas, A. (1984). *Wounds of war: A psychological aftermath of combat in Vietnam.* New York: Basic Books.

Hill, R. (1949). *Families under stress: Adjustment to the crisis of separation and reunion.* New York: Harper.

Hockings, F. (1970). Extreme environmental stress and its significance for psychopathology. *American Journal of Psychotherapy, 24,* 4–26.

Hogancamp, V. E., & Figley, C. R. (1983). War: Bringing the battle home. In C. R. Figley & H. I. McCubbin (Eds.), *Stress and the family, vol. II: Coping with catastrophes* (pp. 149–165). New York: Brunner/Mazel.

Horowitz, M. J. (1976). *Stress response syndromes.* New York: Jason Aronson.

Horowitz, M. J. (1982). Psychological processes induced by illness, injury, and loss. In T. Milton, C. Green, & R. Meagher (Eds.), *Handbook of clinical health psychology* (pp. 53–68). New York: Plenum.

Horowitz, M. J., & Solomon, G. F. (1975). A prediction of delayed stress response syndromes in Vietnam veterans. *Journal of Social Issues, 31,* 67–80.

Horowitz, M. J., & Solomon, G. F. (1978). Delayed stress response syndromes in Vietnam veterans. In C. R. Figley (Ed.), *Stress disorders among Vietnam veterans.* New York: Brunner/Mazel.

Horowitz, M. J., Weiss, D. S., & Kaltreider, N. (1984). Reactions to the death of a parent: Results from patients and field subjects. *Journal of Nervous and Mental Diseases, 172,* 383–392.

Horowitz, M. J., Wilner, N., & Alvarez, W. (1979). Impact of Event Scale: A measure of subjective stress. *Psychosomatic Medicine, 41,* 209–218.

Ingham, J. G., & Miller, P. M. (1982). Consulting with mild symptoms in general practice. *Social Psychiatry, 17,* 77–88.

Janis, I. L. (1971). *Stress and frustration.* New York: Harcourt Brace Jovanovich.

Janoff-Bulman, R. (1985). The aftermath of victimization: Rebuilding shattered assumptions. In C. R. Figley (Ed.), *Trauma and its wake: The study and treatment of post-traumatic stress disorder* (pp. 15–35). New York: Brunner/Mazel.

Kadushin, C., Boulanger, G., & Martin, J. (1981). *Legacies of Vietnam: Comparative adjustment of veterans and their peers* (Vol. 4). Washington, DC: Veterans Administration.

Kahan, Y., Barak, A., & Efrat, Y. (1983). *Final report of the commission inquiry into the events of the refugee camps in Beirut* [Hebrew]. Jerusalem: Government Publication Office.

Kalmus, A. (1949). On war neurosis [Hebrew]. *HaRefuah, 36,* 43–44.

Kardiner, A. (1947). *War stress and neurotic illness.* New York: Hoeber.

Katz, S., & Shurka, E. (1977). The influence of contextual variables on evaluation of the physically disabled by the nondisabled. *Rehabilitation Literature, 38,* 369–373.

Keinan, G. (1979). *The effects of personality and training variables on the experienced stress and quality of performance in situations where physical integrity is threatened.* Unpublished Ph.D. thesis, Tel Aviv University.

Kettner, B. (1972). Combat strain and subsequent mental health: A follow-up report of Swedish soldiers serving in the United Nations forces, 1961–1962. *Acta Psychiatrica Scandinavica* (Suppl. 230).

Klein, H. (1973). Children of the Holocaust: Mourning and bereavement. In E. J. Anthony & C. Koupernik (Eds.), *The child in his family, vol. 2: The impact of disease and death.* New York: Wiley.

Klinger, E. (1975). *Meaning and word: Inner experience and the incentives in people's life.* Minneapolis: University of Minnesota Press.

Kormos, H. R. (1978). The nature of combat stress. In C. R. Figley (Ed.), *Stress disorders among Vietnam veterans* (pp. 3–22). New York: Brunner/Mazel.

Krell, R. (1979). Holocaust families: The survivors and their children. *Comprehensive Psychiatry, 20,* 560.

Krystal, H. (1968). *Massive psychic trauma.* New York: International Universities Press.

Kutz, I. (1987, May). *When the front is the home front.* Paper presented at a conference on Traumatization and Retraumatization, Van Leer Institute, Jerusalem.

Langer, T. S., Gersten, J. G., Greene, E. L., Eisenberg, J. G., Herson, J. H., & McCarthy, F. D. (1974). Treatment of psychological disorders among urban children. *Journal of Consulting and Clinical Psychology, 42,* 170–179.

Laufer, R. S., Gallops, M. S., & Frey-Wouters, E. (1984). War stress and post-war trauma. *Journal of Health and Social Behavior, 25,* 65–85.

Levav, I., & Abramson, J. H. (1984). Emotional distress among concentration camp survivors: A community study in Jerusalem. *Psychological Medicine, 14,* 215–216.

Lidz, T. (1946). Psychiatric casualties from Guadalcanal. *Psychiatry, 9,* 193.

Lieblich, A. (1978). *Tin soldiers on Jerusalem Beach.* New York: Pantheon.

Lieblich. A. (1983). Between strength and toughness. In S. Breznitz (Ed.), *Stress in Israel* (p. 102). New York: Van Nostrand Reinhold.

Lifton, R. J. (1968). *Death in life: The survivors of Hiroshima.* New York: Random House.

Lifton, R. J. (1973). *Home from the war.* New York: Simon & Schuster.

Lifton, R. J. (1976). *The life of the self.* New York: Simon & Schuster.

Lifton, R. J., & Olson, E. (1976). The human meaning of total disaster: The Buffalo Creek experience. *Psychiatry, 39,* 1–18.

Lindeman, E. (1944). Symptomatology and management of acute grief. *American Journal of Psychiatry, 101,* 141–148.

Lumry, G. K., Cedarleaf, C. B., Wright, M. S., & Braatz, G. A. (1970, April). *A further look at Vietnam.* Paper presented at the fifth annual conference of the Veterans Administration Cooperative Studies in Psychiatry, Houston.

Maier, S. F., & Seligman, M. E. P. (1976). Learned helplessness: theory and evidence. *Journal of Experimental Psychology, 105,* 3–46.

Mangelsdorff, A. D. (1985). Lessons learned and forgotten: The need for prevention and mental health interventions in disaster preparedness. *Journal of Community Psychology, 13,* 239–257.

Manning, M. M., & Wright, T. L. (1983). Self efficacy expectations, outcome expectations and the persistence of pain control in childbirth. *Journal of Personality and Social Psychology, 45,* 421–431.

Margalit, A. (1987, May). *Stress trauma and retraumatization in the Israeli context.* Presented at a conference on Traumatization and Retraumatization, Van Leer Institute, Jerusalem.

Maslow, A. (1971). *The further reaches of human nature.* New York: Viking.

McCubbin, H. I., Dahl, B. B., Lester, G., Banoon, O., & Robertson, M. (1976). Coping repertoires of families adopting to prolonged war-induced separation. *Journal of Marriage and the Family, 38*(3), 461–471.

McFarlane, A. C. (1988). The phenomenology of post-traumatic stress disorder following a natural disaster. *Journal of Nervous and Mental Diseases, 176,* 22–29.

McGarth, T. R., & Brooker, A. E. (1985). Combat stress reaction: A concept in evolution. *Military Medicine, 150,* 186–190.

McGrath, J. E. (1970). Setting measures and theses: An integrative review of some research of social and psychological factors in stress. In J. E. McGrath (Ed.), *Social and psychological factors in stress* (pp. 58–96). New York: Holt, Rinehart & Winston.

McIntyre, K., Lichtenstein, E., & Mermelstein, R. J. (1983). Self-efficacy and relapse in smoking cessation: A replication and extension. *Journal of Consulting and Clinical Psychology, 51,* 632–633.

McMichael, A. J., & Hetzel, B. S. (1974). Patterns of help seeking for mental illness among Australian university students: An epidemiological study. *Social Science & Medicine, 8,* 197–206.

Meichenbaum, D., & Fitzpatrick, D. (in press). A constructivist narrative perspective of stress and coping: Stress inoculation applications. In L. Goldberger & S. Breznitz (Eds.), *Handbook of stress.* New York: Free Press.

Menninger, K. (1938). *Man against himself.* New York: Harcourt, Brace and World.

Mikulincer, M. (1986). Motivational involvement and learned helplessness: The behavioral effects of the importance of uncontrollable events. *Journal of Social and Clinical Psychology, 4,* 402–422.

Milgram, N. (1986). An attributional analysis of war-related stress: Modes of coping and helping. In N. Milgram (Ed.), *Stress and coping in time of war: Generalizations from the Israeli experience.* New York: Brunner/Mazel.

Moran, L. (1987). *The anatomy of courage.* London: Avery.

Muhlbauer, V., & Zemach, M. (1991). *Onesies twosies* [Hebrew]. Tel Aviv: Am Oved.

Mullins, W. S., & Glass, A. J. (Ed.), (1973), *Neuropsychiatry in World War II, vol. 2: Overseas theaters.* Washington, DC: Army Medical Department.

Murrel, S. A., & Norris, F. H. (1984). Resources, life events, and changes in positive affect and depression in older adults. *American Journal of Community Psychology, 12,* 445–464.

Nace, E., Meyers, A., & O'Brien, C. (1977). Depression in veterans two years after Vietnam. *American Journal of Psychiatry, 134,* 167–170.

Nefzger, M. D. (1970). Follow-up studies of World War II and Korean War prisoners: II. Morbidity, disability, and maladjustment. *American Journal of Epidemiology, 91,* 123–138.

Neuman, M. (1981). Principles of treatment in combat-stress reactions [Hebrew]. *Family Practitioner, 6,* 403–421.

Neuman, M., & Phenig, S. (1986). Fear and avoidance of reserve duty [Hebrew]. *HaRefuah, 110,* 203–205.

Niederland, W. G. (1968). The problem of the survivor. In H. Krystal (Ed.), *Massive psychic trauma* (pp. 8–23). New York: International University Press.

Notman, M. T., & Nadelson, C. C. (1976). The rape victim: Psychodynamic considerations. *American Journal of Psychiatry, 133,* 408–413.

Omer, H., & Alon, N. (1983). *Treatment of the chronic post-traumatic syndrome,* Unpublished manuscript.

Pa'il, M. (1970). Combat discipline or purity of arms [Hebrew]. *Ma'arachot, 209,* 1–11.

Pary, R., Turns, D., & Tobias, C. R. (1986). A case of delayed recognition of post-traumatic stress disorder. *American Journal of Psychiatry, 143,* 941.

Penk, W. E., Robinowitz, R., & Roberts, W. R. (1981). Adjustment differences among male substance abusers varying in degree of combat experience in Vietnam. *Journal of Consulting and Clinical Psychology, 49,* 426–437.

Polner, M. (1971). *No victory parades.* New York: Holt, Rinehart & Winston.

President's Commission on Mental Health. (1978). *Report to the president, vol. 3: Mental health problems of Vietnam-era veterans* (pp. 1321–1328). Washington, DC: Government Printing Office.

Prince, R. M. (1985). *The legacy of the Holocaust: Psychohistorical themes in the second generation.* Ann Arbor, MI: UMI Research Press.

Prokatzia, A., & Miller, A. (1979). *The rights of the handicapped in Israel* [Hebrew]. Jerusalem: Hebrew University Press.

Rahe, R. H., Gunderson, E., & Arthur, C. R. (1970). Demographic and psycho-social factors in acute illness reporting. *Journal of Chronic Disease, 23,* 245–255.

Rangell, R. (1976). Discussion of the Buffalo Creek disaster: The cause of psychic trauma. *American Journal of Psychiatry, 33,* 313–316.

Reed, U. L. (1976). *Family medical care-seeking behavior.* Unpublished doctoral dissertation, Boston University.

Rolbant, S. (1971). *The Israeli soldier: Profile of an army.* New York: Thomas Yoseloff.

Rosen, S. (1983). Perceived inadequacy and help seeking. In B. M. DePaulo et al. (Eds.), *New directions in helping* (Vol. 2). New York: Academic Press.

Rosenheck, R. (1985). Father-son relationships in malignant post-Vietnam stress syndrome. *Journal of Social Psychiatry, 5,* 19–23.

Rosenheck, R., & Nathan, P. (1985). Secondary traumatization in the children of Vietnam veterans with posttraumatic stress disorder. *Hospital and Community Psychiatry, 36,* 538–539.

Rubin, R. T., Gunderson, E., & Arthur, C. R. (1972). Life stress and illness patterns in the U.S. Navy: Environmental, demographic, and prior life change variables in reaction to illness onset in naval aviators during combat cruise. *Psychosomatic Medicine, 34,* 445–452.

Rubin, R. T., Gunderson, E., & Doll, R. E. (1969). Life stress and illness patterns in the U.S. Navy. *Archives of Environmental Health, 19,* 740–757.

Ruch, L. O., Chandler, S. M., & Harter, R. A. (1980). Life change and rape impact. *Journal of Health and Social Behavior, 21,* 248–260.

Ryan, W. (Ed.). (1969). *Distress in the city: Essays in the design and administration of urban mental health services.* Cleveland: Case Western Reserve University Press.

Salmon, T. W. (1919). The war neuroses and their lesson. *New York State Journal of Medicine, 51,* 993–994.

Schneider, R. J. (1987). Stress breakdown in the Wehrmacht: Implications for today's army. In G. Belenky (Ed.), *Contemporary studies in combat psychiatry: Contributions in military studies.* Westport, CT: Greenwood.

Seligman, M. E. P. (1968). Chronic fear produced by unpredictable electric shock. *Journal of Comparative and Physiological Psychology, 66,* 402–411.

Seligman, M. E. P. (1975). *Helplessness: On depression, development, and death.* San Francisco: Freeman.

Selye, H. (1956). *The stress of life.* New York: McGraw-Hill.

Shalev, A., Bleich, A., & Ursano, R. J. (1990). Posttraumatic stress disorder: Somatic comorbidity and effort tolerance. *Psychosomatics, 31,* 197–203.

Shapiro, E. G. (1983). Embarrassment and help-seeking. In B. M. DePaulo et al. (Eds.), *New directions in helping* (Vol. 2). New York: Academic Press.

Shaw, J. A. (1983). Comments on the individual psychology of combat exhaustion. *Military Medicine, 148,* 223–231.

Shaw, J. A. (1987). Unmasking the illusion of safety. *Bulletin of the Menninger Clinic, 51,* 56–58.

Shontz, F. C. (1975). *The psychological aspects of physical illness and disability*. New York: Macmillan.

Sigal, J. J., Silver, D., Rakoff, V., & Ellin, B. (1973). Some second-generation effects of survival of the Nazi persecution. *American Journal of Orthopsychiatry, 43*(3), 320–327.

Silver, R. L., & Wortman, C. B. (1980). Coping with undesirable events. In J. Garber & M. E. Seligman (Eds.), *Human helplessness: Theory and application* (pp. 279–340). New York: Academic Press.

Smith, J. R. (1981). *Veterans and combat: Towards a model of the stress recovery process*. Paper presented for the VA Operation Outreach training program.

Solomon, Z. (1988). Somatic complaints, stress reaction and post-traumatic stress disorder: A 3-year follow-up study. *Behavioral Medicine, 14*, 179–186.

Solomon, Z. (1989a). A three year prospective study of post-traumatic stress disorder in Israeli combat veterans. *Journal of Traumatic Stress, 2*, 59–73.

Solomon, Z. (1989b). Untreated combat-related PTSD: Why some Israeli veterans do not seek help. *Israel Journal of Psychiatry and Related Sciences, 26*, 111–123.

Solomon, Z. (1989c). Characteristic psychiatric symptomatology in PTSD veterans: A three year follow-up. *Psychological Medicine, 19*, 927–936.

Solomon, Z., & Benbenishty, R. (1986). The role of proximity, immediacy and expectancy in frontline treatment of combat stress reaction among Israelis in the Lebanon war. *American Journal of Psychiatry, 143*, 613–617.

Solomon, Z., Benbenishty, R., & Waysman, M. (1991). *A study of compensation procedures for war veterans with psychiatric injuries*. Unpublished manuscript.

Solomon, Z., Garb, R., Bleich, A., & Grupper, D. (1987). Reactivation of combat-related post-traumatic stress disorder. *American Journal of Psychiatry, 144*, 51–55.

Solomon, Z., Kotler, M., & Mikulincer, M. (1988). Combat related post-traumatic stress disorder among the second generation of Holocaust survivors: Preliminary findings. *American Journal of Psychiatry, 145*, 865–868.

Solomon, Z., Kotler, M., Shalev, A., & Lin, R. (1989). Delayed onset PTSD among Israeli veterans of the 1982 Lebanon war. *Psychiatry, 52*, 428–436.

Solomon, Z., & Mikulincer, M. (1987a). Combat stress reaction, PTSD and social adjustment: A study of Israeli veterans. *Journal of Nervous and Mental Disease, 175*, 277–285.

Solomon, Z., & Mikulincer, M. (1987b). Combat stress reactions, post-traumatic stress disorders and somatic complaints among Israeli soldiers. *Journal of Psychosomatic Research, 31*, 131–137.

Solomon, Z., Mikulincer, M., & Benbenishty, R. (1989). Combat stress reaction: Clinical manifestations and correlates. *Military Psychology, 1*, 35–47.

Solomon, Z., Mikulincer, M., Fried, B., & Wosner, Y. (1987). Family characteristics and posttraumatic stress disorder: A follow-up of Israeli combat stress reaction casualties. *Family Process, 26*, 383–394.

Solomon, Z., Mikulincer, M., & Jacob, B. R. (1987). Exposure to recurrent combat stress: Combat stress reactions among Israeli soldiers in the Lebanon war. *Psychological Medicine, 17*, 433–440.

Solomon, Z., Mikulincer, M., & Kotler, M. (1987). A two-year follow-up of somatic complaints among Israeli combat stress reaction casualties. *Psychosomatic Research, 31*, 463–469.

Solomon, Z., Oppenheimer, B., Elizur, Y., & Waysman, M. (1990a). Exposure to recurrent combat stress: Can successful coping in a second war heal combat-related PTSD from the past? *Journal of Anxiety Disorders, 4*, 141–145.

Solomon, Z., Oppenheimer, B., Elizur, Y., & Waysman, M. (1990b). Trauma deepens trauma: The consequences of recurrent combat stress reaction. *Israel Journal of Psychiatry and Related Sciences, 27,* 233–241.

Solomon, Z., Oppenheimer, B., & Noy, S. (1986). Subsequent military adjustment of combat stress reaction casualties: A nine year follow-up study. *Military Medicine, 151,* 8–11.

Solomon, Z., Weisenberg, M., Schwartzwald, J., & Mikulincer, M. (1988). CSR and PTSD as determinants of perceived self-efficacy in battle. *Journal of Social and Clinical Psychology, 6,* 356–370.

Sparr, L., & Pankratz, L. D. (1983). Factitious post-traumatic stress disorder. *American Journal of Psychiatry, 140,* 1016–1019.

Spira, A. (Ed.). (1968). *Siach Lochamim* [Hebrew]. Tel-Aviv: The Kibbutz Movement Publishers.

Stauffer, S., Lumsdaine, A. A., Lumsdaine, M. H., Williams, R. N., Smoth, J. L. K., Star, S. A., & Cottrel, L. S. (1949). *The American soldier, vol. III: Combat and its aftermath.* Princeton, NJ: Princeton University Press.

Strayer, R., & Ellenhorn, L. (1975). Vietnam veterans: A study exploring adjustment patterns and attitudes. *Journal of Social Issues, 31,* 81–94.

Stretch, R. H. (1986). Post-traumatic stress disorder among Vietnam-era veterans. In C. R. Figley (Ed.), *Trauma and its wake, vol. II: Traumatic stress theory, research, and intervention.* New York: Brunner/Mazel.

Stuen, M. R., & Solberg, K. B. (1972). The Vietnam veteran: Characteristics and needs. In L. J. Sherman & E. M. Caffey (Eds.), *The Vietnam veteran in contemporary society* (pp. 106–112). Washington, DC: Veterans Administration.

Theoreson, P. W. (1970). The use of self description in identifying and predicting students who seek help with their emotional problems. *Dissertation Abstracts International, 31,* 1552–1557.

Titchener, J. L. (1986). Post-traumatic decline: A consequence of unresolved destructive drives. In C. R. Figley (Ed.), *Trauma and its wake, vol. II: Traumatic stress theory, research, and intervention.* New York: Brunner/Mazel.

Titchener, J. L., & Kapp, F. (1976). Family and character change at Buffalo Creek. *American Journal of Psychiatry, 133,* 295–299.

Titchener, J. L., & Ross, W. O. (1974). Acute and chronic stress as determinants of behavior, character, and neurosis. In S. Ariety & E. B. Brody (Eds.), *Adult clinical psychiatry: American handbook of psychiatry* (pp. 47–70). New York: Basic Books.

Van der Kolk, B. A. (1986). The psychological consequences of overwhelming life experiences. In B. A. Van der Kolk (Ed.), *Psychological trauma* (pp. 1–23). Washington, DC: American Psychiatric Press.

Van Dyke, C., Zilberg, N. J., & McKinnon, J. A. (1985). Post-traumatic stress disorder: A thirty-year delay in World War II veterans. *American Journal of Psychiatry, 142,* 1070–1073.

Van Putten, T., & Emery, W. H. (1973). Traumatic neuroses in Vietnam returnees: A forgotten diagnosis? *Archives of General Psychiatry, 29,* 695–698.

Veroff, J. B. (1981). The dynamics of help-seeking in men and women: A national survey study. *Psychiatry, 44,* 189–200.

Vinokur, A., & Selzer, M. (1975). Desirable versus undesirable life events: Their relationship to stress and mental distress. *Journal of Personality and Social Psychology, 32,* 329–337.

Walker, J. F. (1981). Vietnam combat veterans with legal difficulties and psychiatric problems. *American Journal of Psychiatry, 138,* 976–982.

Walker, J. I., & Cavenar, D. (1982). Vietnam veterans: Their problems continue. *Journal of Nervous and Mental Diseases, 170,* 174–180.

Walker, J. I., & Nash, J. L. (1981). Group therapy and the treatment of Vietnam combat veterans. *International Journal of Group Psychotherapy, 31*(3), 379–389.

Weiner, A., Gerber, I., Batlin, D., & Ark, A. M. (1975). The process and phenomenology of bereavement. In B. Schoenberg, I. Gerber, A. Wiener, A. M. Kutscher, D. Peretz, & A. C. Carr (Eds.), *Bereavement: Its psychological aspects.* New York: Columbia University Press.

Weisenberg, M., Schwarzwald, J., & Solomon, Z. (1991). Effects of combat stress reaction and posttraumatic stress reaction on perceived self-efficacy in battle. *Military Psychology, 3,* 61–71.

Williams, C. M. (1980). The veteran system with a focus on women partners: Theoretical considerations, problems, and treatment strategies. In T. Williams (Ed.), *Post-traumatic stress disorders of Vietnam veterans* (pp. 71–124). Cincinnati, OH: Disabled American Veterans.

Wilson, J. P. (1978). *Identity, ideology, and crisis: The Vietnam veteran in transition.* Cincinnati, OH: Disabled American Veterans.

Wolf, S., & Ripley, H. (1947). Reactions among Allied prisoners of war subjected to three years of imprisonment and torture by the Japanese. *American Journal of Psychiatry, 104,* 180.

Wolff, H. G. (1953). *Stress and disease.* Springfield, IL: Thomas.

Worthington, E. R. (1977). The Vietnam-era veteran, anomia and adjustment. *Military Medicine, 142,* 123–134.

Yitzhaki, T., Solomon Z., & Kotler, M. (1991). The clinical picture of the immediate combat stress reaction (CSR) in the Lebanon war. *Military Medicine, 156,* 193–197.

Zetnik, K. (1963). *House of dolls* [Hebrew]. Tel Aviv: Dvir.

Zilberg, N. J., Weiss, D. S., & Horowitz, M. J. (1982). Impact of Event Scale: A cross-validation study and some empirical evidence supporting a conceptual model of stress response syndromes. *Journal of Consulting and Clinical Psychology, 50,* 407–414.

Index